Local Governance
in Africa

Local Governance in Africa

The Challenges of Democratic Decentralization

Dele Olowu
James S. Wunsch

with contributions by
Joseph Ayee
Gerrit M. Desloovere
Simon Fass
Dan Ottemoeller
Paul Smoke

LYNNE
RIENNER
PUBLISHERS

BOULDER
LONDON

Published in the United States of America in 2004 by
Lynne Rienner Publishers, Inc.
1800 30th Street, Boulder, Colorado 80301
www.rienner.com

and in the United Kingdom by
Lynne Rienner Publishers, Inc.
3 Henrietta Street, Covent Garden, London WC2E 8LU

Library of Congress Cataloging-in-Publication Data
Olowu, Dele.
    Local governance in Africa : the challenges of democratic decentralization / Dele Olowu
and James S. Wunsch ; with contributions by Joseph Ayee . . . [et al.].
      p.   cm.
    Includes bibliographical references and index.
    ISBN 1-58826-173-5 (alk. paper)
    1. Local government—Africa.   2. Decentralization in government—Africa.   I. Wunsch,
James S. (James Stevenson), 1946–   II. Title.
JS7525.O46   2003
320.8'096—dc21

                           2003046724

British Cataloguing in Publication Data
A Cataloguing in Publication record for this book
is available from the British Library.

Contents

Tables and Figures

Tables

Figure

Preface

I n 1990 we published *The Failure of the Centralized State: Institutions and Self-Governance in Africa*. That book explored the centralizing patterns and dynamics of African states since independence. It argued that these led to ineffective, corrupt, and sometimes abusive governance. It also argued that decentralization in a number of forms was required to move beyond these ineffective and at times collapsed states. This would include decentralizing political power to the grassroots through democratic reform at the center, through the privatization of state-owned enterprises, through reestablishment (or establishment) of effective local governance, and through the empowerment of the people and local civic organizations.

Many African countries, under prodding from their own people and international organizations, have initiated new programs and policies of decentralization since the publication of that earlier book. These efforts have coincided with the wave of liberal political and economic governance reforms that have swept through the continent since the late 1980s. Much has been written on democracy and privatization in Africa in the last fifteen years, but little has been published taking an overview of the evolution of local governance during this time. This book is an attempt to fill that gap. It offers information regarding several important and theoretically provocative country cases, as well as two frameworks to try to make sense of what has happened. One framework explores what seems necessary for self-governance to emerge at localities (local-level prerequisites for local governance). The second explores the contextual and prior factors (intervening variables) that affect the presence of the prerequisite variables. While these are preliminary models, we believe they are helpful in integrating and interpreting what is occurring in Africa regarding local governance.

Many people deserve our thanks for their contributions to this book. They include of course our five contributors for their diligence and wisdom, as well as for their patience with us as we developed and revised the book's agenda. John Harbeson of the City University of New York, Terry Clark of Creighton University, Simon Fass of the University of Texas–Arlington, as well as several anonymous reviewers, contributed to the book's merit through their insightful criticism and suggestions. Lynne Rienner and Sally Glover of Lynne Rienner Publishers have been helpful and patient with us as we trudged through key decisions and the final preparation of the manuscript. Hannah Wunsch assisted with final proofreading. Our mentors, Elinor and Vincent Ostrom and Ladipo Adamolekun, continue to sustain our work with the power of their ideas and their continued intellectual support.

Financial assistance during the development of this project was provided by the American Philosophical Society and the dean of the College of Arts and Sciences at Creighton, who helped fund Dr. Wunsch's sabbatical and research activities overseas. The dean of the graduate school at Creighton also provided financial assistance for the preparation of the manuscript. We also want to thank faculty and students at the Institute of Social Studies in The Hague, Netherlands, who have discussed and critiqued Dr. Olowu's evolving ideas on the subject of decentralization in developing-country contexts.

It is hard to imagine how this book could have been completed without the care, diligence, and patience of Joleen Richwine, Dr. Wunsch's administrative assistant at Creighton. Joleen patiently and quickly typed, retyped, and then typed again our many drafts, as well as helped us catch the many errors that inevitably creep into these enterprises. Her humor and constantly pleasant demeanor throughout the relatively long period of producing the manuscript constituted encouragement to us. Indeed, to all intents and purposes she became the third member of our team.

Finally, we must acknowledge the patience and support of our wives, Mary and Bukky, who were always there for us as we worked through this task. Through many late nights, missed weekends, and delayed holidays, they encouraged us and sustained our commitment to the book. This book is dedicated to them.

Many deserve credit for whatever is meritorious in this book. We alone are responsible for its errors.

1

Introduction:
Local Governance and Democratic
Decentralization in Africa

U nder what circumstances do decentralization reforms bring about viable systems of local governance in Africa? For nearly thirty years, Western analysts and African scholars have advocated decentralization to reach such goals as enhanced participation, greater control over programs by beneficiaries, and increased resource mobilization for development projects as a foundation for democracy, and as a tool to achieve better governance (Owens and Shaw 1972; Chambers 1974; Mawhood 1983; Adamolekun, Roberts, and Laleye 1990). Unfortunately, in most cases where African governments announced "decentralization," these results did not occur (Wunsch and Olowu 1990a). However, since the late 1980s, decentralization reforms in several African states became more substantial to the point where they were of a fundamentally different order, and could be considered as what we call "democratic" decentralization. By this we mean that significant elements of authority, responsibility for services, and fiscal and human resources were transferred to local governments. Furthermore, major revisions in accountability were made so that the local public had a significant role in its own "local governance." By local governance we mean there exist working local systems of collective action that manage a locality's public affairs and are accountable to local residents.

Our goal is to understand the factors that explain why some decentralizing states made more progress toward local governance than others. We begin by reviewing Africa's history of decentralization. Next we explore the factors that have led to the expansion of "democratic decentralization" since the late 1980s, recurring problems of decentralization, and recent institutional initiatives affecting decentralization. Then we focus on seven cases of decentralization and the outcomes of each for local governance (Tilly 1984).

Implicit in our analysis is the conviction that decentralization reforms only make sense if they lead to a working political outcome: effective local governance. The first, decentralization, is a lengthy and complex process of reform that, beginning with constitutional and/or statutory changes at the center, ideally progressively distributes responsibilities, resources, authority, and autonomy from center to periphery. The second, local governance, is the situation that obtains when localities are able effectively to manage their public affairs in a way that is accountable to local residents.

Decentralization and local governance are not new issues in developing countries generally nor in Africa in particular (World Bank 1989a). However, since the early 1990s, there has been a renewed interest in the potential of decentralization associated with the process of democratization occurring in many developing countries.[1] A joint study by the World Bank and two United Nations organizations in the early 1990s found that only twelve out of seventy-five developing countries with a population of over 5 million had not embarked on a program of transferring political power to their local governments (Dillinger 1993:1). Certainly, the process of establishing local governance and implementing decentralization is circuitous and lengthy, as the experiences of many industrialized countries demonstrate. Indeed there are still ongoing debates on the nature and extent of decentralization in these countries (Calvert 1975; Batley and Stoker 1991). In Asia, several Indian states (Karnataka, Kerala, and West Bengal) have pursued decentralization, as have the Philippines. Similarly, decentralization reforms in Latin America have led to substantial transfer of responsibilities, public-sector employees, and fiscal resources from central to local governments. There is evidence from Asian and Latin American countries that decentralization reforms have led to significant gains in terms of the transfer of authority, responsibility, resources, and accountability to localities. In each case, successive reforms—political, administrative, and fiscal—have helped to strengthen fledgling local governance institutions (World Bank 1997; OECD 1997; Crook and Manor 1998; Schiavo-Campo 1998; Fukusaku and Hausmann 1998; ILO 2001).

In contrast to the experience of other developing countries, very little is known about the decentralization experiences in Africa that followed the democratic upsurge of the 1980s. An analysis of the World Bank's decentralization projects noted that Africa's decentralization experiences were the least studied even though they constituted the largest proportion of the Bank's decentralization projects (Litvack, Ahmad, and Bird 1998:35). While there are studies of specific national decentralization programs—Ghana, Côte d'Ivoire, Ethiopia, South

Africa, Uganda, and Nigeria—there are few systematic and focused studies of these countries' experiences (Barkan 1998). Some observers have also argued that earlier decentralization initiatives were not faithfully executed and that the political context was not right in those earlier years (Mawhood 1983; Wunsch 2001a; Crook and Manor 1998). It is important to find out whether the democratic environment of the 1990s has indeed made decentralization more feasible, and if current reforms have had a greater impact on local governance. Thus, a particular goal of this volume is to review decentralization in the context of the democratization of the 1990s. In this period, many reformed governments in the region included more effective and democratic systems of local governance in their commitment to democracy.

The case studies in this book cover states whose rhetoric and legal reforms suggest that serious democratic decentralization has begun. They offer valuable insights for understanding effective and successful decentralization efforts through both the successes and failures they highlight. However, this is not intended to be a series of comprehensive and descriptive reports on the seven states explored in Chapters 4 through 9. The studies and their varying foci were included, instead, because they provide informative analyses that have theoretical implications for understanding the success and failure of decentralization reform. While each chapter can stand alone as an insightful case study, the authors attempt in Chapter 10 to extract generalizations from the chapters that help to explain how these "democratic" decentralization reforms do—and do not—achieve what the authors call "local governance."

The volume has several emphases. One is on the critical context set by national institutions, policies, and practices. Another has to do with different relationships among levels of governance that affect decentralization. A third is on issues of design, operation, and effectiveness of the local institutions established by decentralization reforms and local governance. The fourth is on the social capital and structure of demand for goods by the local community. It is well accepted in the literature that national commitment—"political will"—is necessary for decentralization to be real and to succeed. We surely grant that. However, it is not our goal to try to explain why that "will" does or does not come about. Nor do we focus on the politics of the center as they affect that will. That is certainly an important topic, but not ours. Instead, we focus on what is occurring in the usually neglected "periphery" and what that tells us regarding decentralization reforms and local governance. These may appear to be "technical" issues to some, but in fact they go to the heart of key collective action problems that determine how and why local governance does or does not occur. Failure to address these problems increases the likelihood that decentralization will fail regardless of the political commitment the center may or may not make to it.

Local Governance in Africa

Definition of Terms and
Approaches to the Study of Local Governance

Governance has been defined in many ways and with diverse emphases. One approach emphasizes the exercise of authority by state leaders (World Bank 1992b; UNDP 1997). Another approach emphasizes sharing authority for public policy management and delivery of services between state and nonstate institutional actors (Kooimans 1993). This book subscribes to a third, more comprehensive approach that views governance as developing and operating the "regimes" or the fundamental (constitutive) rules that structure and regulate the relationships among the populace in the management of their public affairs (Ostrom 1997; E. Ostrom 1990; Hyden 1992; Hyden, Olowu, and Okoth-Ogendo 2000). These rules may be formal or informal, and are in fact usually both. Each level at which "governance" is intended to occur must be understood as a set of rules that do, or do not, sustain the behaviors and relationships necessary for it to be effective and sustained. When they are looked at comprehensively, they create a structure of permissible and forbidden actions, and a set of incentives and disincentives that structure the pattern of governance that occurs among people at the grassroots.

By *local governance*, therefore, we mean a rule-governed process through which residents of a defined area participate in their own governance in limited but locally important matters; are the key decisionmakers in determining what their priority concerns are, how they will respond to them, and what and how resources will be raised to deal with those concerns; and are the key decisionmakers in managing and learning from those responses. Representatives of these local residents may and frequently will perform these functions as agents of those people, but they remain accountable to (and removable by) the people included in the local regime through procedures specified by law. Their choices and limits are structured through rules determined by the larger political systems of which they are a part. Thus intergovernmental relations are a key factor affecting the nature of any governance regime.

By *decentralization reforms* we mean those legal acts and administrative measures that initiate a transfer of responsibility (authority), resources (human and financial), accountability, and rules (institutions) from central government to local entities. This involves a long political, fiscal, and administrative process. According to conventional definitions, when only responsibility or authority is transferred, but not resources or local accountability, one has deconcentration. When responsibility, authority, and resources are transferred, but accountability still resides in the center, there is delegation. When there is transfer, by law and other formal actions, of responsibility, resources, and accountability, one has devolution (Smith 1985; Adamolekun 1999). As this chapter and the remainder of the book will make clear, our interest is only in the devolutionary forms of decentralization. By these definitions, only devolution can bring about local governance: each of the others lack any local political accountability. This is reflected in our analytical framework.

It is very important to understand what has, and has not, developed from these reforms in Africa. Legal acts providing for decentralization are among the prerequisites to local governance, but do not in themselves achieve it. In the first place, many such programs, on closer examination, are flawed and limited in key but subtle ways. Second, even transferring responsibilities to local governments does not ensure that effective local governance will be sustained, or even begun! Local public life can be fragmented by local conflict, captured by local elites, or stillborn in poorly designed local governance institutions. Local public affairs can remain the preserve of local civil servants, be starved by lack of resources, or come under continued indirect and stubborn control from the center. Although each case study provides only a few aspects of the overall picture, if regarded inclusively they can begin to provide worthwhile insights.

There are two ways of evaluating local governance. The first is to focus on process: whether the transfer of authority, resources, and accountability, and the development of an open local political process and local political and administrative institutions, are working in ways that suggest local priorities and needs are driving local decisionmaking. Table 1.1 provides a contrast between intentions and actual policy paths of decentralization programs in many countries. The other way is to focus on outputs and outcomes: whether local governance is bringing expected tangible benefits in terms of better schools, health systems, water supply, or roads, or intangible "empowerment" and social service delivery that enhance peoples' welfare (intangible outcomes) (Steinich 2000). Because it is difficult to obtain data on intangibles, and in view of the long process involved in building local governance and the rela-

Table 1.1   Ideal Versus Actual Life Cycle of Decentralization Policies

Idealized Process by Which Local Governance Emerges from Decentralization Reforms	Frequent Actual Experience of Decentralization Reforms
1. Elite chooses to devolve authority, resources, and accountability to localities. ↓	1. Elite announces reforms to devolve authority, resources, and accountability to localities. ↓
2. Decentralization reforms are defined and promulgated. ↓	2. Some decentralization reforms are defined and promulgated. ↓
3. Redistribution of authority, resources, and accountability to localities occurs. ↓	3. Redistribution of authority, resources, and accountability to localities is announced. ↓
4. Decisionmaking institutions, broadened participation by the public, and greater accountability to localities emerge. ↓	4. Several patterns emerge: • Incomplete statutory reform blocks effective control by local authority; • Resources are retained or recaptured by central actors via "conditional" grants, continued control of civil service posted to localities, ignoring local authority's decisions, etc.; • Resources of localities are consumed paying for salaries of officials they do not control, or for basic administrative overhead; • Local councils are ineffective because of low levels of education, poor organization, infrequent meetings, internal division, and executive dominance; • Local institutions are designed to maintain central control; and/or, • Local elites dominate local governance from behind the scenes. ↓
5. Improved performance and accountability of local governance institutions reinforce local support for reformed system. ↓	5. Poor performance and nonaccountability of local governance institutions discourages local support for them. ↓
6. "Local governance" is a going concern.	6. Local governance remains weak and ineffective. ↓
	7. Recentralization occurs.

tively recent appearance of serious decentralization reforms in Africa, we focus mainly (but not exclusively) on process indicators and the extent to which they indicate that effective local governance is emerging out of decentralization reforms.

A Theory of Local Governance

Political science is relatively clear that local governments must meet certain basic requirements if they are to be able to solve problems effectively. They must be able to identify problems, set priorities, mobilize resources, implement programs, evaluate results, learn from those results, and maintain popular legitimacy. At the very least, they must have a defined area and population, be of reasonable size (balancing scale of problem and resource adequacy with the need for some sense of community among the population), have authority and resources proportionate to the problems they face, and be working institutions that make decisions and enforce accountability to their population. Additionally, the political process must provide accountability and be open to widespread political participation, and have a stable set of rules to organize local affairs (Ostrom 1990). Achieving these is essential if local governance is to be considered operational.

Area and population must be delimited in order to break problems into manageable size and encourage individuals to work with one another over time to resolve those problems. This is also necessary if "social capital" is to begin to develop in a specific population (Putnam 1993). Authority is needed to permit and legitimize the initiation of policies and programs. Resources are needed to sustain the policies and programs, reward participants, and pay the overhead costs of local governance (buildings, supplies, vehicles, etc.). Accountability, through an open and broadly based political process, is needed to steer decisions and actions as well as to legitimize local governance institutions. These are reflected in conventional definitions of local governance. In addition, effective institutions are needed to organize and structure the official and public actions needed, and to assure that decisionmaking processes are effective, reliable, and legitimate. Finally, there must be an effective and supportive set of rules that regulate local affairs in general in order to rule out actions destructive to local governance (fraud, corruption, intimidation, violence) by partisans and others, and to settle disputes that might otherwise paralyze or disrupt it (Wunsch 1999).

Basic Simonian assumptions about human nature help to confirm this set of prerequisites and to explain the importance of these preconditions for effective local governance. Assume human beings are rational, goal-oriented actors, who have limited resources and therefore seek to make careful choices about those resources, even if they seek only goal satisfaction rather than maximization. They will seek to make decisions that, over time, emerge as successful strategies to reach their goals. If they are not successful, rational actors will seek alternate strategies and perhaps other venues to achieve their goals. Over time, individual and collective learning will tend to converge on personally rational strategies, given local conditions (Ostrom 1980). Such rational strategies, under some circumstances, could include opting out, corruption, and violence. Other circumstances could lead to the cooperation and collective action needed if effective local problem solving is to occur. The key question students of local governance must pursue is which structures lead to the latter results under a given set of circumstances.

As noted above, governance is the process by which humans make collective choices and implement them. It requires that people expend some finite personal resources to sustain it: time, energy, money, influence, opportunities foregone, attention to detail, developing skills of persuasion, organization, and management, and the like. It would not be rational to invest those resources in governance processes and institutions that lack authority in making decisions in key areas of citizens' concern, or in ones that lack the fiscal and human resources to implement their own decisions. Nor would it be rational to invest resources in institutions accountable to others rather than to the prospective actors (absent effective local accountability), nor ones that exclude the populace (a closed political process), or are prone to ineffective or perverse outcomes (absent effective institutions). Thus, Herbert Simon's work on rational behavior and complex organizations brings us to much the same conclusion as the general literature on local governance: one needs all of these features in order to have sustained, viable local governance. Research in the case-study countries helps confirm this working model of the prerequisites of local governance. Tocqueville (1966) came to much the same conclusions, in less formal language, regarding local government in the United States in 1831.

Many of these requirements can be addressed, or at least initiated, by central reforms: resources and policy may be redistributed by the center through changes in policy and practice. Local institutions may be granted legal status and guided into workable designs by national laws and policies. In some cases (see Chapter 7 on Chad) those authoritative rules can be found in accepted local practices, experiences, and customs, and national political weakness means formal, legal status is essentially irrelevant. Nonetheless, these will generally require national constitutional changes, and almost always require changes in statutes and procedural regulations in areas such as finance and personnel (Ayee 1994, 1997b). Many times these reforms will be found to be incomplete, whether in formal law or in actual implementation. Indeed, the ways to neutralize seemingly substantial reforms are myriad, as the case studies in this book make plain.

Designing Effective Local Governance Institutions

Even when the above conditions and actions seem to have been met, local governance has encountered serious problems in many parts of the world. Local councils are unable to agree on policies to resolve key problems, the public remains seemingly inattentive to local affairs, local administrative personnel seem disconnected from public leadership, or local institutions are unable—or unwilling—to raise funds locally. As Vicki Clarke recently noted, even when many elements of decentralization are present, improved governance does not always emerge (Clarke 2001).

The frequency of these problems suggests that they grow from more than cultural or system-specific problems. Indeed, "collective" or "rational" choice theory, as developed over the last several decades, provides great insights into the reasons why these problems are so frequent and so stubborn. Briefly, it shows how outcomes that might be reasonably agreed to as rational or "good" for a group are often not achieved because the actions necessary to reach them are irrational—in some cases even highly costly—for individuals key to those outcomes. For example, many key goods produced by local governments are "public goods": the benefits produced are available to all if available to any. However, such benefits tend to stimulate the temptation to "ride free" and collect the good, and avoid paying one's share of it. If a large portion of the population rides free, there will be insufficient resources to pay for the good. If even a noticeable proportion choose to contribute and are able to do so, the rest may refuse to provide the resources to provide the good. Furthermore, the reality that most "communities" are anything but homogenous, and are divided by wealth, political power, political factions, occupations, and frequently ethnic and religious diversity, means that agreeing on which public good to provide, often from many options, is rarely easy.

Another example of this dynamic lies in designing effective local legislative bodies. Weak authority and defective institutional and operational rules can make it difficult to reach decisions, and thereby lead to policy failure and weakened local governance. Specific examples of the problems the rules must resolve include the need to organize legislative bodies so members have incentives to reach agreement and avoid paralysis, are able and willing to bear unavoidable and necessary organization and operation costs, avoid internal "free-rider" problems, and assure that asymmetries in wealth and power among populations do not allow a few to siphon off benefits that should flow to the general populations.

Coordination issues among members can also impede the activities of legislative bodies, such as local councils. These are generally conceptualized as having two variations. In the easier of the two, there are common general preferences among the members of the legislative body, but no system to establish who is responsible for shaping the agreement into a specific proposal or budget, or for following through to hold the coalition together when building consensus on those specifics. Since these can be tedious and time-consuming tasks, and can make those who take them visible to potential opponents outside the body, no one may step forward to do it. In this case, nothing will get done or the executive might take over the task. In the second and more difficult of the two scenarios, oblique preferences among members require logrolling or other means of trading preferences if anything is to be accomplished. Kenneth Arrow's theorem shows how this condition can paralyze legislative bodies, absent effective rules that structure business among legislators so they can reach a compromise position (Arrow 1951).

Typical ways of dealing with these are assigning and specifying responsibilities to committees and subcommittee systems, and establishing strong leadership roles to apply rules agreed to move legislation along. Additional problems can arise, however, when procedural requirements or decision-rules are unrealistic given the nature of the body: e.g., when extraordinary majorities of the total membership are required to pass measures; when travel and attendance are difficult; when there are requirements that executives review and approve initiatives before they can be voted; or when there are such infrequent meetings that legislators never develop the expertise or knowledge to deal with their agenda, etc. As Rick Wilson (1999) noted in his article on governance in transitional bodies, there are no "ideal" rules or systems to resolve these dilemmas, which are often called ones of "collective choice." What is fairly clear, however, is that failing to resolve them will lead to ineffective legislative bodies and hence to paralysis or executive dominance. Either result will intensify management (principal-agent problems) and public-accountability issues, damage the effectiveness of local institutions to resolve local problems, and will likely eventually weaken public involvement in the local political process, in effect dissipating what authority local institutions have been granted. Thus, they seriously compromise the prospects for local governance. Avoiding these problems hinges in large part on the effectiveness of the legislative body's organization and its rules of procedure, the relationship between the executive and legislative branches, and the resources the latter has. A number of chapters in this volume explore these problems and their impact on local governance. While these problems by no means exhaust the obstacles that stand between the reforms of decentralization and the achievement of effective local governance, they are serious ones, particularly as they affect executive and administrative accountability to the public through its representative and legislative body.

The collective action problems of legislative bodies are often mirrored by the difficulty in developing and sustaining broad political organizations to hold local governments accountable. There are a number of reasons for this, including the usual diversity of priorities among the public, the existence of social divisions and factions (ethnic, religious, clan) found in most local areas, the fact that political organizations face chronic "free-rider" issues as discussed above, the types of goods and services often provided and demanded at the local level, and the high costs in time, resources, and forgone income to organize and sustain them. Since national political parties are generally organized at the center and largely ignore the countryside and smaller urban areas (except for brief moments during election campaigns), the resources to organize and sustain such organizations must come from localities, and the poverty typical of Africa makes this unlikely. Local governments' histories of ineffectiveness, corruption, and outright collapse make it even more unlikely they will develop. Added to all these issues are the principal-agent problems that make legislative control over executives, and executive control over administrative and service-delivery personnel, challenging at best and frequently simply impossible. Incomplete legal authority by the former over the latter, asymmetries in resources and information, access to power brokers outside the locality, and the like make this a frequent problem. The case studies on Ghana (Chapter 6) and Uganda (Chapter 8) are particularly insightful on this problem, as is the study in Chad (Chapter 7) and the solutions local dwellers found to these issues.

Some of these case studies highlight the role of community-based organizations as units of de facto local government, and the case of Chad is instructive in this respect. But these crucial institutions are also found in the other cases, and it is important that the economic, social, and political impact of these institutions are being rediscovered, especially in developing countries (see Narayan et al. 2001). There is evidence that civil society—i.e., occupational, community-based, and religious organizations—exists at localities all over Africa, and in some circumstances can be an important participant in service delivery and in enforcing accountability (Barkan 1994; Dia 1996; Olowu and Erero 1996; Adedeji 1997; Coulibaly 1999; Ribot 2000). However, within the framework of the modern state, these highly vibrant organs are largely apolitical, and in some cases antipolitical. Both of these patterns are in large measure a reaction to years of antidemocratic environments in most African states (Davidson 1992; Mamdani 1996).

This creates a dilemma for building accountability at all levels. The case studies in this volume show that these, and small village "interest groups," can be the initial public organizations that constitute the nucleus of participation in local governance. Linkages such as these are strongly affected by the way local governance operates, particularly where hitherto there has been little or no local accountability or participation. Factors such as the size of local political units (small enough so such groups can be heard), the frequency of elections, the openness of the planning-budgetary cycle (see Chapter 6), the committee system of local legislative bodies (see Chapter 8), the size of legislative constituency, the relative strengths of the executive vis-à-vis the legislature (see Chapters 5 and 6), the possible use of several levels of local governance to reduce social fragmentation (see Chapter 8), are all important in facilitating their role. If they are able to participate, they can reduce the costs of organization, and of accessing the political process, that individuals otherwise face, and improve thereby the effectiveness of local governance and accountability (Wunsch 1991a). These issues will be discussed more fully in Chapter 10.

Institutions are valuable insofar as they provide organizational infrastructure that helps people to solve these problems, gather the information they need, and make and implement decisions. When institutions are weak or defective in any number of ways, public life will become (or remain) fragmented, conflictual and ineffective, and public action will swing from long periods of passivity even to short outbreaks of violence. What is likely then will be a return to either administrative dominance from the center, or executive dominance at the locality. For local governance to succeed in Africa it must be organized to avoid these problems. The national context, intergovernmental relations, institutional design, and the nature of local demands all affect its success. The challenge of constructing effective local institutions will be a major focus of this volume.

Contextual Factors and Local Governance

The case studies and their findings cannot be understood outside of several micro- and macro-level "contextual" problems. In Africa, five factors are particularly worth noting. Often they will affect the patterns seen in the case studies. Successful cases find ways to surmount or even take advantage of some of these conditions (see Chapters 7 and 8). The salient factors include, first, severe scarcity in money, skilled human resources, political legitimacy, equipment, vehicles, electricity, fuel, and often information and reliable "theory" regarding pressing development problems. Sufficiency is rare in these necessary ingredients, while redundancy in any of them is virtually unheard of, and breakage or exhaustion of supply or actors usually means simply doing without (Wunsch 1986). Scarcity also is characterized by intense competition among people for available resources. Life is often perceived as a zero-sum rather than positive-sum game, particularly in the political realm (Esman 1991). And of course, frequently it is exactly that. A long-term view of building political institutions, for example, is often a luxury for key actors in this environment. One of the most frequent outcomes for civil-society organizations, for example, is to be captured by a small group or individual that effectively turns it into "private property" for one or two persons' benefit.

A second salient factor is a harsh political and institutional environment, where travel and communications are always difficult and sometimes impossible; where vehicles wear out quickly; where staff is stretched thinly dealing with the labor-intensive challenge of managing personal lives in the midst of poverty, underemployment, and family demands; where nearly everything seems to take longer; and where people are nearly defenseless against many natural disasters. This means participation in governance is frequently squeezed out by the simple necessities of personal and familial survival. This particularly affects the poor and women, who are responsible for most of Africa's agricultural output (Chambers 1983). It is also particularly disturbing that Africa's high poverty levels are not simply due to absolute lack of resources, but also to poor distribution of the available resources. Africa's gini coefficient (44 percent) is second only to Latin America's (52 percent) among the world's regions (World Bank 2002c).

The third key contextual factor is economic and social turbulence. Particularly as a result of scarcity and poverty, as well as government ineffectiveness, the economic context can be almost instantaneously turned upside down by a currency crisis, collapse in a commodity price, or a structural-adjustment program, against which there are no local-level defenses. Social turbulence, often in ethnic, religious, or other conflicts, can also be a serious problem, itself accentuated by scarcity and economic turbulence. Particularly as a result of these factors, local governments are chronically and severely short of resources, key personnel, institutional "experience," and the ability to sustain effective programs. Partially as a result of this weakness, any political-institutional arrangement is inevitably looked on skeptically for a very long time (African Development Bank 2001). Prudence recommends anyone "hedge" his or her commitments to the reforms of the moment. Momentum is difficult to build around local formal rule-structures in such circumstances.

There is a fourth contextual factor that must also be kept in mind: severe asymmetries in wealth and power, and the powerful informal political and economic structures of patron-clientage that grow from them. These often exist outside the formal state structure, but nonetheless dominate decisionmaking, effectively closing nominally "open" political processes. It must be assumed that any formal institutional arrangement has an accompanying "shadow" process that strongly affects what it does. Local governance can nonetheless grow out of such situations, but they cannot be assumed away if one wishes to understand what is occurring and why. These often reflect neopatrimonial relationships that strongly affect what institutions at all levels actually do.

These micro-contextual factors must each be taken into account in analyzing decentralization programs and in explaining their impact on local governance. However, they do not exhaust the contextual issues that affect decentralization. We will now turn to the fifth and last contextual issue, the macropolitical context of decentralization and local governance: the African state.

The National Political Context: African States and Their Governance

There is much variance in the performance of sub-Saharan African states. At one extreme, one finds areas of virtual state collapse such as Sierra Leone, Liberia, Democratic Republic of the Congo, and portions of Somalia. There, central governments have little control of the countryside, or in fact no longer even exist. Bureaucracies do not function, if they exist at all, and the "rational-legal" rule of law is absent. National "government" actions are inconsequential, infrastructure decays, lawlessness is frequent, and governments are characterized by chronic instability.

At another extreme are states such as Mauritius, Tanzania, South Africa, and Botswana. There, central governments rule generally without significant challenge, law and order is the norm, bureaucracies generally function, decisions are (generally) made on rational-legal grounds, and economies are stable, if still characterized by frustratingly high levels of poverty and dependency. Not insignificant are the beginnings of democratic elections, which even local opponents have accepted as relatively "free and fair." Indeed, Senegal and Ghana may be considered members of this group of countries as they recently experienced peaceful national turnovers of power consequent to such elections.

However, between these extremes lie the vast majority of Africa's states: not in chaos, but nonetheless performing at levels that offer little promise of economic progress, effective governance for their peoples, or the prospect of long-term social peace. Beneath this poor or even mixed performance lie several stubborn problems that combine to erode the ability of states to make and implement policy effectively, solve problems, and engage the public to build support for the regimes. These will have a powerful impact on any reform effort, whether it be liberal-democratic reforms at the center, or decentralization to the periphery. There is, in the literature, broad agreement on these problems, which can be analyzed at several levels (Herbst 2000; Bayart 1993; Jackson and Rosberg 1982; World Bank 2000).

Visible to most observers are several chronic features of the large majority of African states. These include strongly personalistic political systems, leaders who will do nearly anything to retain power, severe poverty in general, slow economic growth rates, and weak bureaucratic institutions, particularly below the senior levels. Rule of law is formalistic more than real, with regulations and rules invoked more to capture "rents" than in pursuit of public-policy purposes. Formal political institutions (and constitutions) are also far more formalistic than real, with real power lying elsewhere and decision processes obscured and beyond the reach of law. Many observers describe these systems as "neopatrimonial" (Bratton and van de Walle 1997; Hyden, Olowu, and Okoth-Ogendo 2000).

Explaining these patterns are a number of largely socioeconomic features that combine to weaken the power of those whose interests might be served by a stronger and more autonomous state, or who might be able to support such a state. These include vast gaps in wealth between a small, usually politically connected elite, and the mass of impoverished smallholder agriculturists and usually un- or underemployed urban dwellers. A small, dispersed, economically marginal middle class of small traders, teachers, and middle-grade civil servants is far closer to the poor in their vulnerability and insecurity than to the wealthy. Complementary to and reinforcing these patterns are usually very weak civil-society organizations that might aggregate interests, such as unions, agricultural cooperatives or movements, and professional societies. But they as well are fragmented and unable to pursue their group interests. Furthermore, as Robert Bates (1981) has shown us, potential leaders are vulnerable to co-optation through individualized benefits from the state.

These are groups that elsewhere historically have been interested in state action to improve working conditions, establish wage floors, improve marketing systems, enhance farm productivity, and increase public support for the service professions. In short, these are groups that, when strong, have elsewhere supported a lawful and effective state as a critical means to enhance their ability to live securely, to create wealth, to redistribute wealth to themselves, and to increase their ability to practice their professions to their and the public's benefit. Their weakness and fragmentation indirectly contribute to the weakness of the African state, as the voice they would bring to counter the patterns discussed above is absent or stillborn, as is therefore their power.

Civil society, while not absolutely powerless, has generally been vulnerable to the state's coercive force when it directly defied it. In a few cases such as Kaunda's Zambia or Banda's Malawi, widespread economic decline and overreaching abuse of powers pushed the population to the very edge. Then, leaders of key civil-society organizations came together. Led particularly by churches, they were able to push the regime out, only to fragment once again soon after. More typical has been Houphouët's Côte d'Ivoire; or Rawlings' Ghana, where the state largely intimidated civil-society organizations into docility. Alternatively, as Joel Samoff has discussed and Aili Mari Tripp has shown in Uganda, grassroots civil society in Africa has more frequently fled from the state, choosing not to engage it if it could be left alone to pursue basic social and economic reproduction (Tripp 2001). In all of these cases, social forces whose interests might have been served by a more effective state and by better governance were absent from political life. The mass media, most frequently controlled by government, concentrated in the capital cities, and printed in European languages, was another factor that might have otherwise called for and supported less particularistic and corrupt states (Hyden, Olowu, and Okoth-Ogendo 2000).

Along with this weakness at the "base" of the society is the weakness of market-based organizations and interests that would also benefit from a neutral state that predictably and professionally enforced laws. However, as has long been recognized, Africa is extremely weak in the private commercial and industrial sectors. To this might well be added the modern service sector. Instead, African economies have historically, since the preindependence era, been dominated by state-owned enterprises (SOEs). While SOEs had an interest in a powerful state, they did not support an autonomous and publicly governed state. Instead, their interest, like privately owned monopoly enterprises, was in a state they could capture or at least very strongly influence. In fact, who captured whom is rather moot, as most analysts agree a small, closed circle ran both the enterprises and the state. Unfortunately, efforts at privatization have had a mixed record throughout the continent (Grosh and Mukandala 1994; Tangri 1999).

Other social forces that might have been able to demand a more neutral, autonomous, and publicly oriented state, such as competing political parties, civil-society organizations, or a mass media, were also ineffective in the privatization process. Leading political parties decayed soon after independence, becoming at the same time all-inclusive national parties, and "headless" parties as their leadership left for bureaucratic and state posts. In becoming "all things to all men," they became nothing in particular to anyone, except a trough for patronage. In any case, once they were leaderless, they became impotent. Thus was lost an organization with an interest at least in pushing the state to please broad portions of the public. Competing parties were banned or reduced to impotence.

While all these underlying factors worked to weaken the constituency for professional, transparent, accountable, lawful, and publicly oriented governance, several other factors worked to push the African state into the modal patterns already discussed. These included the concentration of wealth, status, and political power in the hands of a very few; an international system that recognized and supported their monopoly of political power (and discouraged challenges to it); regional/religious/ethnic cleavages that were frequently exploited by small ruling groups to keep the public divided; severe language gaps between elites and masses that reinforced the effective political disempowerment of the latter; legal and institutional legacies of colonial rule that facilitated heavy-handed state responses to dissent and to any serious political challenge; and traditions of patron-clientage (reinforced by colonial laws and policies) that created "big-men"–"small-boy" dynamics, which in turn reinforced socially and economically the political asymmetries of power discussed above (Price 1975). Overall, these factors meant that a small elite controlled the key resources of power at the center; was reinforced by international recognition, aid, and support; could legally utilize harsh and intimidating coercive force against any who might threaten them; could manipulate preexisting regional, religious, and ethnic rivalries to distract large groups from governance failures into conflict that did not threaten the regime; and could, through patron-clientage, selectively co-opt or isolate the leadership of potentially challenging groups, leaders who could then selectively use the same strategies to consolidate and maintain their hold over their followers, strengthening the status quo in the process.

The problems, then, of the contemporary African state are not, therefore, simple or easily changed. Establishing free elections, legislatures, and courts, no matter how well intended, will not change these underlying conditions. Indeed, as Linda Kirschke (2000) argues, such reforms when the society is still fragmented and the ruling clique is dead-set against them, will in all likelihood make things worse. Government-sponsored violence has been used against the opposition in such cases, with deadly and widely disruptive results. It would seem the only escape from this dilemma are reforms that would fundamentally redistribute power from these small ruling elites to the grassroots, which would seem to be an uphill struggle. Given all this, what can be the realistic expectations of decentralization? Richard Crook and James Manor suggest that its prospects are not hopeless in their landmark study, *Democracy and Decentralization in South Asia and West Africa* (Crook and Manor 1998). In such disparate areas as Ivory Coast, Ghana, Bangladesh, and Karnataka State (India), areas all characterized by many of the very factors discussed above, serious decentralization reforms achieved varying but notable successes. Thus decentralization can lead to local governance in an imperfect national context.

Supporting the case for decentralization is the likelihood that such efforts, because of their smaller scale, closeness to the people, and other factors, might avoid some of the problems of governance at the national level. For example, the problems of distance between rulers and ruled deriving from the need to use English, French, or Portuguese at the center are eased by the greater likelihood that a single vernacular language can be used in local governance. Indeed, such is exactly the case in "subcounty" governance in Uganda (Wunsch 2001b; Chapter 8 of this volume). Similarly, the temptation of rulers to play off regional, religious, and ethnic differences in "divide and rule" strategies is reduced by the greater homogeneity of many local areas, though to be sure not all. Also, the great social distance between political leaders and rank and file is similarly compressed in local politics, though certainly not entirely eliminated.

Furthermore, civil society, as it is most frequently found in Africa, is more likely to match in size and scale of local governments than national ones. Market associations, women's associations, village-improvement unions, churches, and the like are typical of Africa, in contrast to strong and broadly based national-level societies. The fragmentation at the national level of middle-class groups such as teachers, health and agricultural workers, and better-off farmers and traders is less likely to hinder them at the local level, where their literacy and organizational skills will mean they can play a stronger political role. One might also expect the formal coercive arm of the state will reach less into purely local affairs.

On the other hand, several problems typical of national governance are often also present at the local level. Political parties are poorly formed at local levels, a local mass media is virtually nonexistent (even in most urban areas), "external" interference by foreign states and the donors is replaced by interference from the capital or from regional offices, the local civil service generally remains weak both in skills and as an institution, and patron-clientage and "big men" are present at the local level of politics just as they are at the national level. If the scale of the resources they control is smaller than at the national level, so is the number of people they need to co-opt, while the poverty of the rank and file they face is often even greater. Added to all these problems is the fiscal weakness usually found in local governments, the inexperience of their elected leaders, the reluctance of civil servants formerly employed by and responsible to national bureaucracies to accept local direction, the newness of most local institutions (with the usual "bugs" they need to work through), and the steep learning curve they all must travel. Thus there are many problems local governments must solve if they are to function well. Nonetheless, at least as one considers the case from this perspective, they are no worse off, and indeed in some ways more than a bit better off than national governance institutions have been. However, they still have to deal with the problematic impact of national politics and governance on them. One question to be probed in this book is whether local governance institutions can reasonably be expected to succeed in adverse national contexts.

Indigenous Systems of Governance and Contemporary Africa

In view of the foregoing, it is not surprising that the record of African local governments to date has not been a glowing one. This has led to the search for alternative structures of governance at the local levels. In this search, institutions referred to as "indigenous," "traditional," alternative, informal, parallel, endogenous, communal, primordial, etc., have been highlighted (Smock 1971; Ekeh 1975; Ake 1990; Ayittey 1991; Dia 1996).

Research into these institutions has suggested several insights into their nature and attributes. First, they are nearly ubiquitous throughout African states. They are frequently found in countries that have experienced two impulses of institutional development: the indigenous organs of precolonial Africa, and the second "exotic" structures associated with colonialism. Next is their variety. Some have become highly formalized while others have remained largely informal and governed by consensus. There are indigenous governance systems found in the economy (e.g., markets, often governed by women), ones reflecting local communities (self-help and community improvement organizations), ones organized around age (youth organizations), and others around general interest groups (e.g., farmers' unions). Perhaps the most important distinction among them is between institutions of traditional rulership on the one hand, and community organization on the other.

Third, in most countries, traditional institutions were part and parcel of the colonial administrative system. Colonialism severely modified these institutions by making them much more powerful, but also more dependent on the colonial state and less accountable to their subjects (Firmin-Sellers 2001). In many countries, all the powers of governance, frequently formerly separated when ruled by indigenous peoples (legislative, administrative, judicial), were concentrated in selected, unaccountable, traditional officers. Inevitably, such powers were abused, and often represent the early beginnings of neopatrimonialism in African politics and government (Mamdani 1996). These rulers were thus frequently corrupted. In the postindependence period, therefore, traditional institutions confronted a serious dilemma: they were regarded as a part of the colonial apparatus of oppression against which the anticolonial struggle was directed. At the same time, nonetheless, they were accepted and sometimes venerated in many circles as the key institutions of indigenous governance. Thus, a fourth common feature of indigenous governance systems is that reconciling these disparate viewpoints often becomes one of the most contentious issues that new states had to face in designing systems of local governance.

Tanzania and a host of other socialist-inclined African countries "abolished" the traditional institutions altogether in the 1970s. On the other hand, in countries such as Swaziland or Lesotho, traditional institutions still muster considerable political clout and provide rulership at the national level, a fact that gives these countries monarchical systems of governance. Other countries lie between these extremes. In the Republic of South Africa, as in Mozambique and other southern African countries such as Zimbabwe and Namibia, the roles to be assigned to traditional chieftaincy institutions have become major policy and constitutional issues (Ndiyepa 2001; Ntebeseza 1999).

Several countries, such as Uganda and Nigeria, both discussed in this book, have displaced traditional institutions from their position of power. Some have replaced them by secular/modern ones (Uganda), while others have allowed them to continue, but largely subordinated to formally elected local governments (Nigeria and Botswana) (Egwurube 1988; Olowu and Erero 1996; Wynne 1989). Other countries have tried to modernize traditional institutions by making them elective and open (Zimbabwe). One reason why the issue of traditional institutions is important is because they have been frequently assigned responsibilities for managing critical rural resources, such as land, forests, and, in some countries, water. In some states, even when they nominally have lost this power to the central government, they still exercise many of these functions (Nigeria). As custodians of tradition, they have at times succeeded in articulating and defending such values as sharing the use of these resources across local communities. Also, in times of severe economic stress, they have resolved conflicts such as those dealing with witchcraft accusations that secular/modern institutions were unable and ill-suited to deal with (Cameroon). Also, the issue of land rights has become particularly important in post-settler states, as well as in communities of other African states characterized by substantial internal migration. These have given new impetus to a reconsideration of the roles of traditional institutions, as well as other local institutions, in the management of land and other crucial rural resources (Turner and Ibsen 2000; Ribot 2000). On the other hand, such authority has also led to such abuses as the neglect of ethnic minorities and women, and concentration of wealth and often of political power in the hands of the traditional leaders.

Local governance, in this context, must deal with the continued power and status of traditional leaders in many African states at the same time that it broadens participation, accountability, and modernity. Traditional leaders may ignore, co-opt, or try to erode local governance regimes, as the latter are potential threats to their power in zero-sum situations. However, traditional leaders can greatly enhance the success of local governance if they appreciate that their communities are evolving dynamically, e.g., through improvements in economic production, availability of social and infrastructure services, access to modern information technologies, or direct-donor activities in local communities, and try to facilitate these processes. All of these are bringing radical changes to the relationships between traditional leaders and their subjects.

Importantly, traditional leaders can also enhance their legitimate power and possible wealth if they perceive decentralization as constituting an opportunity to change the static, zero-sum politics typical of centralization and local economic stagnation into a positive-sum process for themselves and their communities. This can occur as the local community gains greater control over important local spheres of activity and begins to respond more effectively to local needs. Here both traditional leader and community can grow in power as the communities' capacity to act and its economy grow. Indeed, traditional leaders can use their status and networks to help in resolving many of the collective-action problems discussed above, and in doing that can enhance their status and community prosperity simultaneously (Chapter 3).

Along with traditional leaders, other forms of local governance (associations, unions, etc.) can contribute greatly to converting decentralization reforms into effective local governance. They can fulfill the critical role of a civil-society partner for local governance, extend the legitimacy and reach of local governments, mobilize individuals into political affairs, and themselves model participatory decisionmaking processes. Insofar as they have operated effectively in taking and implementing collective choices, they can also help model institutional forms for local governments that might be successfully used in local public affairs, both formally and informally. The challenge, then, is not overpowering indigenous institutions, but learning how to build on and with them. Two case studies in this book (Chapters 7 and 8) particularly demonstrate the difficulties and possibilities of doing this.

Conclusion

"Democratic" decentralization, as currently conceptualized and pursued by several African governments, focuses on the promulgation and implementation of revised rules and responsibilities for administrative and political personnel, and on establishing the framework for some sort of local, accountable political institutions. It is a necessary prerequisite for local governance, but in itself it is incomplete, as it must be sustained and refined over time, deal with the many problems discussed above, and develop a locally sustainable political process if local governance is to be effective.

This chapter has observed that a substantial though fragmented literature has developed around decentralization in Africa. It points out several issues that seem repeatedly to cause operational problems. These include the politics of decentralization; ineffective local participation; ineffective decisionmaking by local legislative bodies; inadequate resources for local services and projects; inadequate local authority over policy implementation and personnel; an unstable and unsupportive macropolicy context; shortfalls in national legislative and policy changes needed for decentralization to operate; and informal and neopatrimonial political and economic structures among "big men" that are more powerful than formal political institutions and impede accountability while they close nominally open political processes. While there are other issues that might be raised, these and the factors that resolve or make them worse are the focus of this book.

As one tries to analyze the challenges of decentralization as a means to achieve local governance in Africa, one must keep in mind the political context. To oversimplify a bit (but not much), the juxtaposition of severe scarcity with persistent patron-clientage politics throughout Africa means that the very resources localities need (funds, skilled personnel, authority over resources and programs, the ability to mobilize new actors into politics) are in high demand at the center and by powerful actors throughout the society. Genuine and successful decentralization would reduce the resources and leverage held by key players, particularly at the center, who are already influential. Thus it is possible to identify a diversity of interests at the national government level with respect to decentralization, some working for it and others against it, depending on how the policy affects those concerned. At times those opposed appear to have at least implicit consent of that same leadership at the very top that initiated the reforms. This is not peculiar to Africa (Eaton 2001). Chapters 5, 6, 8, and 9 all demonstrate these problems.

Having said that, there are nonetheless many grounds for hope. Politics is never simple, and seeds planted by a regime interested in local governance as part of a limited nonparty "national movement" democracy (Ghana or Uganda) may grow into something quite different nearly two decades after that motivation became politically obsolete. The absence of the central state in peripheral regions and at the grassroots (Chad) may encourage the emergence of self-organization skills that localities had not shown for decades, and which grow into something the center dare not quash, even if it could and wanted to. Or, the vast size of such federal entities as Nigeria may encourage genuine local governance in spite of the political-economic battles it brings, if only because it cannot manage governance in any other way. Similarly, governance patterns at any level are not fixed, particularly in an era of democratic elections, structural-adjustment program (SAP) pressures, growing activity by internationally linked nongovernmental organizations (NGOs), donor activities, globalization of information, and the ways that interests of leaders at the center may begin to shift so they begin strengthening local governments (see Chapter 9). Also, as Tripp shows us in the Democratic Republic of the Congo (Zaire), as the state recedes, local initiatives develop in diverse areas (Tripp 2001; McGaffey 1992). Weak states leave space for communities with social capital to "take back" activities earlier lost to national governments, as seen in Chapter 7 on Chad. Similarly, as Kathryn Firmin-Sellers shows us in Côte d'Ivoire, Ghana, and Cameroon, national institutional frameworks have deep, unintended long-term impacts on the structure of local politics, in some instances reinforcing the interest local elites have in working in and through local political institutions, and in others doing the opposite (Firmin-Sellers 2000). Several chapters in this book will illustrate these dynamics.

The book is organized into ten chapters. In Chapter 2 the authors present a historical overview of decentralization in Africa. It is both descriptive in presenting this history, and analytical in assessing the consequences of Africa's several phases of historical experience with decentralization. It focuses in some detail on how SAP-driven decentralization of the late 1970s and early 1980s had serious flaws.

Growing from this, Chapter 3 discusses the multiple and differing pressures toward decentralization in Africa in the mid-1980s and since. These include the ongoing economic crises, but also strong pressure from domestic civil society in Africa, pressure from the donors for democratic reforms, and the difficult administrative and managerial issues raised by recent urban and metropolitan growth. Furthermore, ethnic-conflict management strategies led to decentralization in several states. In this regard, it argues that the momentum for decentralization is much stronger recently than in earlier "waves."

Chapter 3 also explores ongoing challenges to serious decentralization reforms that grow from the ideological, institutional, and social legacies of colonialism and the early independence era. This chapter illustrates their deep roots and continued challenge to decentralization and local governance. Finally, the chapter also reviews a serious challenge to decentralization and local governance: local elite capture. It concludes that even though many legal changes and reforms have been promulgated, several factors have frequently meant democratic decentralization and local governance face stubborn resistance.

Chapter 4 applies the model developed in this chapter to local government in South Africa and Botswana. While this is a limited test, it suggests that the book's working model of local governance is a viable one. It also explores the factors that have affected achievement of four aspects of local governance in these cases, and particularly emphasizes the importance of the national government in generally providing a stable and supportive legal and economic framework. Moreover, it also notes the difficulty in developing an effective local political process to provide accountability, and in getting effective local institutions of collective choice to engage issues. While these two cases generally benefited from central-government performance, in Botswana the framework also greatly circumscribed local autonomy, and in South Africa the legacy of apartheid weakened local institutions and local accountability. It also emphasizes the importance of an open and accountable political process in sustaining effective local governance.

Chapter 5 explores management and governance at the local government level in Nigeria, and their impact on primary health care (PHC) there. In Nigeria, PHC is almost entirely a local function. The chapter reports that while local autonomy largely existed in law, ineffective local institutions of collective action, severe shortfalls in local resources, a flawed local political process, and economic and political turbulence rendered performance in local government very weak. It suggests the failure of the national government to establish a stable and supportive legal, political, and economic context, weakness and flaws in the design of local institutions, the tendency of local dwellers to see local governments as primarily a source of private goods, and highly ineffective intergovernmental mechanisms to encourage better local stewardship and personnel management, all played important roles in Nigeria's weak local governance.

Chapter 6 reviews Ghana's experience with decentralization in the last decade. Joseph Ayee finds that Ghanaian decentralization could be characterized as a case of "missed opportunities." The most important problems lay in the national framework, which, while fairly stable, was not particularly supportive. Local autonomy was greatly limited by incomplete statutory reforms, by continued national control over fiscal resources, and the powerful local executive and administrative personnel posted to localities. National interference in elections limited an effective local political process and accountability, and also engineered key flaws in the design of local institutions. Limitations in all these areas meant there were few resources available for local priorities and general disenchantment with local governance by the people.

Chapter 7, on local school committees in Chad by Simon Fass and Gerrit Desloovere, is a fascinating study of an "outlier case" that brings great insight. While Chad's history of civil war and central governmental collapse meant there was essentially no effective national framework at all, in the Muslim north where Fass and Desloovere did much of their research, strong local norms of community cooperation and recent experience with traditional rules of community collective choice provided a de facto stable context. When that was combined with a strong local demand for a public good, local governance developed and thrived. Autonomy was de facto, institutions were simple but "tried and true," and included open and accountable political processes. Out of this social capital, local residents developed a local governance structure that expanded from education into other activities. Patterns similar to Chad can be found in other parts of Africa.

Chapter 8 on Uganda by James Wunsch and Dan Ottemoeller explores a relatively advanced, yet still troubled, decentralized system. The complex, five-level local governance system in Uganda is impressive in many ways, though it suffers from several problems. While this system is well in place, has constitutional status, controls most administrative and service personnel posted to the districts, and is resourced by local tax authority and national grants, it has not become operating "local governance." It suffers from a national framework that limits greatly the planning, programming, and fiscal autonomy of the district level (the largest and best-resourced level of local governance), poor institutional design at both the district (the superior) and "county" (the intermediate) levels. At each level, legislative bodies are ineffective in guiding or holding accountable strong executives. Interestingly, the poorest and smallest level, the villages, may be the most effective in actually delivering services the people want. It emphasizes low cost and public goods such as security and dispute resolution and seems to benefit from the smaller size and possibly greater social capital found at that level. This chapter is particularly interesting, as it reviews a system that has gone a very long distance toward decentralization, but is still rather ineffective in generating operable local governance.

The last case study, the chapter on Kenya by Paul Smoke, is a powerful statement about the impact on local governance of the context set by national government. Smoke traces the decline of local governance in Kenya through the political goals and strategies of both the Kenyatta and Moi governments. While the trappings of local autonomy are still visible, the controls, delays, ambiguities, and erratic decisions of the central government ministries have rendered local governance ineffective. Additional layers of decisionmaking (such as the district development committee) were laid upon local governments, and sucked away more local autonomy. Generally, these patterns worked to serve a powerful patron-client network that helped keep Kenya's neopatrimonial governing elite in power. Recent local governance reforms are incomplete in key ways, and very problematic.

This chapter has emphasized that human beings everywhere face unavoidable problems and challenges in organizing for governance at any level. It has also emphasized that while decentralization is a necessary step in solving those problems, it is only a first step. Decentralization, even "democratic" decentralization, and local governance are not identical: initiating the first does not mean one has achieved the second. Democratic decentralization, if followed through, promises to shift authority, resources, and accountability to local levels. That alone does not solve the institutional, collective action and other problems we have discussed, nor create the local political process that is necessary if local governance is to occur. We will approach these problems using the "model" of local governance presented in this chapter as an analytical framework. This book uses that model, first to see if there is evidence that the four elements it identifies seem associated with effective local governance. It then asks what factors are crucial to achieving those elements. In Chapter 10, using the analytical strategy outlined by Charles Tilly (1984), the authors will suggest that four factors are critical to achieving the four elements of local governance. These are notable in how persistently they appear among the seven states discussed.

Note

1. Huntington (1991) argues that a third wave of global democratization broke out in the mid-1970s. Hyden shows that 1989 represents the watershed in African democratization efforts (see also Bratton and van de Walle 1997).

2

The Historical Context

As we attempt to assess the factors that encourage the development of effective local governance on the continent, it is important to keep in mind the fact that Africa has a long history of experience in and with local self-governance. This molds and shapes its prospects today. This chapter describes the ebbs and flows of the efforts to create local self-governing organs in African countries since colonial times. It reflects the varying emphases and priorities of African local governance over the last half century, how these came about, and with what consequences.[1] It concludes that in the 1990s several African countries adopted policies that have the potential to create viable and effective local self-governing structures. To the extent that this contrasts sharply with the almost universal preference of past policies and programs of decentralization for deconcentrated structures, often mislabeled "local governments," it is possible to speak of a public-policy paradigm shift with respect to decentralization in several countries. The chapter also provides a rationale for the selection of the national cases included in the book.

Any analysis of decentralization policies and local governance in Africa must, of course, be rooted in an appreciation of the political realities that produce such policies. Generally, African states have been formally centralized since their colonial origins. Indeed, in most cases, they became states in the modern sense of the word only as a result of colonial conquest (Mazrui 1983). Their international and internal domestic boundaries reflect the power plays and perceptions of the colonial powers rather than the reality of cultural forms and norms (Asiwaju 1985). Moreover, since colonized peoples were regarded as possessing neither the intellectual nor cultural capacities for local self-governance, administrative systems that were highly elitist and centralized were initially established all over the region (Mawhood and Davey 1980; Olowu 1988a; Wunsch 1990). The fallacy of that position, as well as Africa's rich heritage of local governance, is pointed out by students of African political history, who have noted the sharp contrast between the polycentric systems of governance in the precolonial empire states of West Africa and the monocentric systems that have been nurtured since the colonial period (Davidson 1993). C. Coulibally (1999:3), for instance, shows that the empire states of the Sudanese civilization (Ghana, Mali, Songhai, Dyula) developed thriving long-distance trade and raised professional armies using the principles of subsidiarity and local governance to organize their public affairs (Davidson 1993; Ostrom, Schroeder, and Wynne 1993).

Colonial Beginnings

Beginning in India and later spreading to Africa, the predominant form of colonial government was "indirect rule" (Hicks 1961; Olowu 1988a; Mamdani 1996). As is well known, this meant rule by a few colonial officials with the aid of the most compliant traditional rulers. Where no such rulers existed, they were created—as in eastern Nigeria, most of French-speaking Africa, and several parts of southern Africa. The objective was to provide only the minimal conditions of law and order, taxation, and justice for the colonial order. Local administration comprised a native court system and a local tax and treasury (Wunsch and Olowu 1990a). While a substantial amount of local *rule* developed within the interstices of the colonial structure, and out of the relative ignorance of colonial officials of what true local customs and practices were, in no way could these have been considered local *governance* as the term is used in this book.

This system succeeded in guaranteeing the conquered territories to their new masters, but it could not serve as the springboard for political, economic, or social development. Importantly, it failed to provide avenues for political participation and expression by the growing number of educated elites that the colonial system itself produced, as well as structures of accountability to the public. It also became increasingly difficult to sustain, as opposition developed to rule by traditional rulers. The latter were in many instances illiterate, ultraconservative, and widely regarded as the minions of the white rulers, and often abused their authority to acquire personal wealth at the expense of their subjects (Firmin-Sellars 1999).

Africa's History of Decentralization

Phase One

After World War II, colonial powers began to consider decolonization for a variety of reasons—political, economic, and humanitarian. Politically, independence was thought of as a gesture of gratitude by the victorious European powers to their colonial subjects who had fought on their side. Continuing agitation by the newly educated elites in the colonies against colonial rule, especially against indirect administration, gave the political argument greater weight. The system was perceived, quite correctly, as rule by European officials through traditional rulers. The imperial countries also had new governments that were in favor of decolonization on humanitarian and economic grounds. The humanitarian argument stood on the idea of self-determination for all peoples of the world. The economic argument emanated from the growing view of the European public that colonies were burdens, especially if wars had to be fought to keep them. They were not only costly in terms of money, but also in human lives. One significant outcome of this was the 1947 dispatch of the British secretary of state for the colonies (Lord Creech-Jones) in which he concluded that the key to success in African administration "lies in the development of an efficient and democratic system of local government" (Hicks 1961:4).

In that dispatch, Creech-Jones emphasized three key words: *efficient, democratic,* and *local.* According to him, the new local government system had to be local so that it was closer to the people and their problems. It had to be efficient in that it was capable of managing local services in a way that can increase the people's standard of living. Finally, it had to be democratic, as it had to "not only find a place for the growing class of educated men, but at the same time command the respect and support of the mass of the people" (Hicks 1961:4).

Largely as a result of this policy shift, important changes were made in local government throughout British Africa. Local government councils were democratized fully or partially (to allow for the representation of special interests), independent revenue sources were established for the local governments, and a genuine effort was made to ensure that local government structures were at once "local, democratic, and efficient." In most cases, it meant a multiplicity of councils and tiers.

The Francophone countries were, of course, wedded to the French administrative system, which provided for a system of hierarchical rule from the central government down to the villages. Nevertheless, several cities benefited from the French municipal tradition. The Municipal Act of 1884 gave municipal status to three Senegalese cities: Goree, St. Louis, and Dakar. Another set of cities was granted mixed commune status in 1920. Unlike the full communes, which were self-governing and appointed their topmost official, the mixed communes were headed by a civil servant, the "administrative mayor," who was appointed by the governor of each colonial territory. Outside the major cities or communes, administration was placed in the hands of chiefs who were carefully controlled by centrally appointed civil servants. Excluding the cities, the system of deconcentrated administration of the full prefectorial variety was found everywhere, with of course the inclusion of the local chiefs as a part of the official transmission belt. In 1955, France issued a municipal law granting city status to forty-four cities in French West Africa under the 1884 municipal law (Olowu 1988b; Laleye 1988).

In sum, during the late colonial period, the outline of a system of local government was already fully established in British Africa, and emerging to some extent in the French municipalities. It had the following key attributes:

- A tradition of elected councils.
- A well-defined local tax system (ranging from per capita flat rates in most places to graduated personal rates in East Africa, and the beginning of a property/land tax in the major urban centers).
- Involvement of local governments in a range of minimal infrastructure services: especially in education, health and sanitation, rural roads and water supply, agricultural extension services, and natural resource management—all of these with carefully articulated grant systems from the central government.
- Involvement of municipal governments in major capital investment activities and the rural local governments in cooperatives and community development activities (Mawhood and Davey 1980).

This period has been described as the golden age of local government in Africa (Hicks 1961; Olowu 1989). Its vitality was demonstrated by the base it provided for many of the leaders who rose to challenge the colonial system. This vitality would suggest that local governance might have been a viable option for an emerging, independent Africa. Unfortunately, this system was not allowed to thrive by these same new African leaders (Kasfir 1983). Reform efforts since that time have attempted to re-assert the above-mentioned principles, but have usually fallen short of effective local governance. Why is of some importance.

Phase Two

Instead of building on this period's gains, Africa's postindependence leaders sought to dismantle this legacy. They offered two major rationales. On the economic front, Africa's new indigenous political leadership believed that the only way to demonstrate the reality of political independence was through rapid development. They subscribed to central-planning and, in most countries, to a socialist ideology to promote development. Kwame Nkrumah, for example, argued that political independence was the springboard for economic and social development. Leaders now had to deliver and they saw democratic local governments as irritants at best, if not obstacles, to their ambitions to build powerful states. Leaders of newly independent states such as Julius Nyerere in Tanzania, Kenneth Kaunda in Zambia, and Sekou Touré in Guinea, among others, followed the same pattern.

Second, the consolidation of the state via a single-party mechanism was also high on the agenda. Part of this effort was implementation of a new wave of local government reforms to reinforce the control capabilities of the one-party or military state. Oddly enough, some governments such as Tanzania and Kenya described these reforms as "decentralization." But, these local governments, in reality local administrations, were designed primarily for the maintenance of central control and law and order, and secondarily for the implementation of centrally determined development plans. Leaders also claimed they were pursuing political objectives such as participation, but these led mainly to consultative assemblies that had no real power over the officials actually in charge of the local governments. Thus, this was largely an illusory "decentralization" (Wunsch and Olowu 1990a). Philip Mawhood best captured this state of affairs:

> In the 1960s, (there followed) for most countries a swing away from local autonomy in favor of central planning and greater control over public resources. A deconcentrated administration was left in charge of the locality, similar to, but weaker than the colonial one. It was aided by committees that hardly had a role beyond discussing development plans and giving help in their implementation. (Mawhood 1983:8)

Olowu also reviewed these policies globally and found that most of these decentralization policies (in Africa as well as other less developed

countries) "were merely attempts at window dressing increasing centralization" (Olowu 1988a:40; Wraith 1972). Legislation was passed,
institutions were established, but the authority and power for local
authorities to grapple with real problems was usually denied.
Essentially, these reforms sought to convert the fledgling local government systems into field administrations, even though they were still
referred to as "local governments."

This movement to centralization via nominal "decentralization,"
together with other dimensions of centralization, has been regarded as
an important explanation for the economic and governance crisis that
engulfed African countries in the late 1970s and 1980s (Wunsch and
Olowu 1990a). Indeed, some of the main actors in the process lamented
these actions afterwards. For instance, former president Nyerere recant-
ed:

> There are certain things I would not do if I were to start again. One of
> them is the abolition of local governments and the other was the dis-
> banding of cooperatives. We were impatient and ignorant. . . . We had
> these two useful instruments of participation and we got rid of them. It
> is true that local governments were afraid of taking decisions but
> instead of helping them we abolished them. Those were two major
> mistakes. (Nyerere 1984:828)

The product of these mistakes was the barren shelf of local governance
as Africa plunged into the economic problems and political crises of the
1970s through the 1990s.

Phase Three

When the economic crisis of the 1970s and 1980s emerged, most
African states responded, usually at the prompting of international
finance institutions, by adopting structural-adjustment programs
(SAPs). They saw decentralization to local governments as a possible
mechanism for cutting back central-government expenditures. The
usual pattern they followed was to devolve responsibilities, but not
financial or human resources, to local units. These early experiments
paid little attention to the particular characteristics of the local institutions they created. All subnational structures were regarded as local
administration or local government. In reality, decentralized structures
everywhere were mere extensions of the central government into the
field. They were dependent on the center for budgets, personnel, and
policy initiatives. In many cases, their management committees were
selected by the central governments.

The genesis and nature of the African economic crisis need not be discussed here, nor the general response of African governments and the international community, given the excellent literature that already exists on the subject (World Bank 1981, 1989b; Cornia and Helleiner 1994; Olowu 1990c). Instead, this section concentrates on how structural-adjustment programs related to decentralization. Many African countries adopted decentralization at this time at the urging of the international financial institutions as part of an effective strategy to cope with the economic crisis. Key questions remain: How did the SAPs impact decentralization and what forms of decentralization did they promote? What lessons does this "phase" of Africa's local governance offer?

Even before SAPs, many governments in Africa sought to hive off their responsibilities to other entities, purely as a response to declining resources. Decentralization of responsibilities for services was sought in a number of countries, not only to state-created structures such as local governments/administrations, but also to community groups. The Kenyan government, for instance, relaunched its program of "Harambee." Here communities provided basic resources for building specific social infrastructure, with the central government complementing these efforts (Oyugi 1990; N'gethe 1998). Similar efforts have been noted in other parts of Africa. This can be seen in the hometown associations and *tontines* of West Africa (Barkan, McNulty, and Ayeni 1991; Nchari 1990; Olowu 1999c).

With SAPs, these initiatives were formalized into policies. The World Bank emphasized that its borrowers should utilize parallel or informal economies and institutions as alternative instruments for delivering services. The reasoning for this was that these institutions could help to promote competition within the public sector in the production of services and goods (Silverman 1992; Litvack, Ahmad, and Bird 1998).

More importantly, African governments were also encouraged to decentralize the provision of services to local governments without increasing local governments' personnel size. This idea was premised on the possibility of separating provision from production responsibilities. *Provision* has to do with deciding what public goods and services ought to be provided in what quantity and quality, how to finance the production of such goods and services, and how to monitor and regulate the production of such goods and services (Silverman 1992). However, *production* is the technical transformation of resources into the delivery of these goods and services (Ostrom and Ostrom 1977). Whereas many of the justifications for decentralization relate to provision functions and most of the criticisms of it relate to the production function, i.e., the lack of capacity to perform the production of these services, the separation of these two functions, with production being turned over to the private sector, reduces the need to create large technical capacities in local government (Wunsch 1991a, 1991b). Furthermore, since the state was in most cases in a financial crisis, funding for these decentralized services was sought not from the traditional tax sources or government transfers but from user fees for basic services like health and education (Silverman 1992; Corkery, Land, and Bossuyt 1995; Leighton 1996).

Paradoxically, previous decentralization programs gave local governments the production responsibilities while the central government kept the provision responsibilities. Many analysts at the time believed that moving local governments out of production and encouraging private-sector competition over production contracts would allow local governments to do more with constant or reduced staffing, while competition in the private section reduced costs and enhanced quality. The expectations of this arrangement were: (1) substantial reduction in the functions and size of all governments including local ones; (2) the possibility of improved capacity of local governments to perform the more limited range of economic management activities; (3) reduction of local government expenditures—both on investments and staffing; (4) reduction of local government and public-sector deficits with possible positive results for increasing the finance available to the private sector; and (5) competitive production of public services that would improve the quantity and delivery of services and also enhance competition and the development of the private sector.

This model of decentralization, which was a component of many SAPs and the accompanying economic restructuring programs (ERPs), suggests that local governments should have the power to make the decisions relating to location-specific investments subject to national guidelines. They should have the right to contract for these services with other agents of production, especially private-sector organizations. Besides ensuring a more efficient allocation of responsibilities between the central and local governments, this pattern of allocating responsibilities would assist development of the indigenous, small-scale private sector. J. M. Silverman (1992:11–12) asserts in a document produced for the World Bank that "demand by local governments for private sector production of public goods and services should result, eventually, in the decentralization of much of the private sector itself." James Wunsch (1991a, 1991b) also developed similar arguments. Under such programs, national governments in many countries trained private-sector enterprise managers who engaged in contracts for the delivery of roads and construction activities with many local governments (e.g., Burundi, Central African Republic, Ghana, Zaire, Kenya, Tanzania, Uganda, and Sierra Leone). Madagascar and Tanzania opened their training schools to private-sector contractors as well.

Considerable effort and resources during this era went into implementing this model of decentralization. The central idea was to seek opportunities to reduce central and local government size and expenditures. In many countries it gave new life to earlier decentralization initiatives. Many countries, notably Ghana, Malawi, and Zambia, to mention a few, adopted decentralization policies. In most cases, however, the policies led to the creation of new structures of "local government," referred to as district development funds or agencies (DDFs) that were patterned after the Kenya "district focus."

The assumption that lead to these structures was that they would make plans for their respective communities or districts in conjunction with field agencies of the main line central ministries operating in that district. However, in reality they were frequently dominated by appointed officials of the central government, including only a sprinkling of locally elected people. Moreover, in Zambia, for instance, health and education services were actually *taken away* from local governments and given to separate central organs to administer. This logic was also followed by many Anglophone countries, which tried to adopt the British model of health services delivery. The hallmark of these organs was the attempt to separate them from "political issues" and tie them closely to the reorganization of the central ministries for effective delivery of services (Smith 1997).

The attraction of these models for many national governments in Africa was that while costs and responsibilities were to be spun off to localities, in reality these agencies remained primarily under central control. This is important for governments that were politically insecure. This was the case with decentralization reforms in Cameroon and Côte d'Ivoire until 1987. Similarly, in Ghana local assemblies' executive committees were chaired by centrally appointed officials, while no opportunities were given for effective political representation or control by the councils. Similarly, a review of the Malawi DDFs shows that their organization promoted effective intersectoral coordination of field agencies by the center. Also, the district development committees (DDCs) generally have had neither legal mandate nor financial or human resources of their own. They are "concerned only with development and not governance or the recurrent costs of development'"(Mbeye 1997:10). Furthermore when these organs did receive financial resources from donors who were interested in assisting decentralization, strong donor direction further eroded them as locally accountable bodies. The Malawi DDFs received 80 percent of their funding from donors. Overall, the results were far below hopes. Major breakthroughs in improved delivery of services, economic performance, and participation have not been realized. If anything, these efforts became obstacles to the development of effective local government institutions, at least as articulated in the relevant constitutions or statutes of these countries.

Kenya and Malawi highlight the problems of this approach. On Kenya, W. O. Oyugi (1990:185) concluded that "what the Kenyan experience seems to indicate is that strong deconcentration affects devolution inversely as the district begins to emerge as the new unit of centralization." Similarly, on Malawi, Mary Anderson's (1995:3–4) conclusion on the Malawi DDC—which was well funded by donors—is instructive: "To summarize, the policy of the single-party government was to strengthen the deconcentrated system of DDCs, while marginalizing the decentralized system of autonomous local authorities. Much of this policy was implemented under the misleading name of 'decentralization.'"

The fundamental weakness of the decentralization reforms of the 1980s associated with SAPs was thus their lack of attention to the nature and type of decentralized structures they were promoting. No clear distinction was made between deconcentration and devolution, and in fact everywhere deconcentration was emphasized. No real changes in *governance* at the localities were made. Yet repeated analysis pointed to the fact that the central problem that these countries faced was one of governance: that power was being used arbitrarily and irresponsibly by those who held it, most of whom were located in the center. During this time, there was no real commitment to shifting power from the center to the localities, and thus no opportunity for any genuine local governance to emerge (Wunsch 1991a, 1991b). That had to wait for the 1990s.

Phase Four

The onset of democratization in the 1990s led to a fourth wave of decentralization reforms in Africa, ones that have been linked to political liberalization and democratization. While there are many explanations for the genesis of these new local government reforms (see Chapter 3 for an in-depth exposition), it is important here to note that this fourth wave has aspects that are a continuation of past approaches to decentralization, but includes for the first time since the late colonial period the possibility of local institutions that are genuinely participatory and responsible to the local community.

By the early 1990s it was possible to classify many African countries as those with progressive or democratic policies on decentralization, and those that maintained old forms of deconcentration-decentralization. A sample of the countries in these various groups is:

- Old/deconcentration: Ghana, Cameroon, Kenya, Malawi, Zambia.
- New/devolution: Mauritius, Botswana, Uganda, Nigeria, Mali, Côte d'Ivoire, Tanzania.
- Mixed/partial devolution: (urban areas only) Namibia, Mozambique, Burkina Faso.

Old forms of decentralization were almost always deconcentration—the transfer of responsibilities to other levels of the same administrative system—subject to central government's prerogatives (Smith 1985; Adamolekun 1999; Wunsch 2001a). Some countries have continued with this model—in which power to make rules and effect decisions on local services as well as the resources and accounting for them continue effectively to reside in the central government in spite of elaborate programs of decentralization—involving the transfer of responsibilities and resources to locally elected leaders. A good example of the latter is Ghana (Ayee 1996). Some countries have also hived off critical services into executive agencies—promising them much greater managerial autonomy—as with health and water services in Ghana and health in Zambia (Larbi 1998; Mackintosh and Roy 1999). It is equally important to note the growing convergence in approaches to managing local governing institutions between Francophone and Anglophone Africa (Stren 1989a). Alternatively, the "new" forms of decentralization move toward allocating independent authority and human and fiscal resources to local governance entities that are accountable to local residents.

The remainder of this section will discuss selection of the seven case studies, and two issues crucial to them. However, it begins with two disclaimers. First, democratic decentralization in Africa has not been limited to these seven countries. Second, these seven countries were not selected because they were all exemplary cases of successful democratic decentralization. Their achievement varies, and in that variance lies the opportunity for insight. These countries were selected because they demonstrate a core point in our argument: the mere fact of decentralization does not constitute local governance. Factors affecting the emergence of the latter include the national political context, linkage between local communities and local governments, the design of local institutions, intergovernmental relations, financing arrangements, and the like.

Furthermore, these seven countries illustrate two key issues. The first is the impact of national democratization on democratic decentralization and local governance. Does democratization at the center help or hinder democratic decentralization at the periphery? On the one hand, countries such as South Africa, Uganda, and Botswana decentralized under democratically elected governments. On the other hand, the decentralization programs in Ghana, Nigeria, and Kenya took place mainly under authoritarian regimes. Chad experienced de facto decentralization during a period of near collapse by the Chadian state.

The second issue the choice of countries helps explore is the differences that may exist between community-based, bottom-up initiatives versus national, top-down approaches to democratic decentralization. The Chad case illustrates the former while all other cases illustrate the latter. Uganda's village level of governance also has certain grassroots elements that resemble those of Chad. These issues are important because self-organization in small communities occurs everywhere in Africa: people create institutions to solve problems often ignoring the formal institutions of local governance that are generally regarded by the people as remote and ineffective. The World Bank and other multilateral development organs are beginning to focus on these community-based organs in their programs of assistance in the region. Several of the book's case studies will explore the problems arising from weak linkages between the community and local government institutions established by central governments.

National Democratic Systems and Decentralization

South Africa's first postapartheid governments were determined to keep the best in the system of government they inherited, while at the same time committing the country to reform and redesign of its state for a newly democratic society. One of the most important issues revolved around the nature of local governance, hitherto centralized under the national apartheid regime. Before the final deal was struck, the two main contestants, the African National Congress (ANC) and the ruling National Party, were divided on this issue. The latter canvassed for a strong federal system of government in which each region would be semiautonomous, while the ANC made a strong case for a unitary system of government (Carbone 2001). Ultimately, the South African transitional constitution provided for a compromise solution, a system of governance in which there are three spheres of governance—national, regional, and newly created local governments—but all within a unitary system of government. This formed the basis for the election of 1994 that brought historic victory to the first majority government (Shezi 1995), and the final constitutional document (Levy and Tapscott 2001).

Today, South African provinces spend more than 66 percent of public expenditure and employ more than 70 percent of public-sector workers (Lodge 2002:32). Their level of autonomy is quite appreciable. Local governance in South Africa is real, even though it has been the subject of much turmoil and change since the ANC came to power in 1994. This is further discussed in Chapter 4. This arrangement has made it possible for opposition political parties that are weak at the center to control two regional governments (Western Cape by the National Party and Inkatha Freedom Party in Kwazulu-Natal). Furthermore, serious discussions on regional competence go on between regional premiers of the ANC and the ANC national government as much as between the center and the opposition regions. An assessment of local government in South Africa noted that rather than attempting to reinvent local government in the Republic of South Africa, the apartheid structures have been adapted, developed, and democratized, reflecting an incremental progression to nonracial local governments (Pycroft 1996:236). No wonder also that Richard Sklar (1999:172) referred to this country as one having federalism in substance without formal recognition. The democratic process that led to this system was important in that many parties ended up accepting some measure of "ownership" of it, and in that the lengthy discussion and set of compromises allowed South Africa to benefit from a broad base of experience in its design. While there is much still to resolve in making it effective, a broad consensus of support for it is facilitating this process (Simeon and Murry 2001; Pycroft 1996).

The nature of Uganda's democracy is unique if not controversial—in particular because of the noninvolvement of political-party competition either at the national or local levels. However, what is important is that the system of national governance incorporates a system of local decentralization and devolution considered by internal and external assessors as significant, free, and popular (Langseth 1995; Steffensen and Trollegaard 2000). Uganda's 1995 constitution made decentralization a core aspect of the National Resistance Movement (NRM) institution-building efforts. And one analyst, even though he was not an enthusiast of the NRM's brand of democracy, conceded that Uganda "retains the form of a unitary but highly decentralised state" (Carbone 2001:241). The stability of the government's commitment to decentralization, the general context of lawful and relatively orderly administration, and the elections that have occurred in the countryside have contributed to a favorable context for decentralization in Uganda (Wunsch 2001b; Batkin 2001).

Botswana has one of the longest track records of liberal democracy in the continent. It has witnessed peaceful change of power from one incumbent prime minister to another since it attained independence in 1965. As Chapter 4 explains, even though the country has been governed by one political party, the Botswana Democratic Party (BDP), since independence, opposition political parties are allowed great freedom to organize for elections, a factor that has helped the growing urban and more radical elements in the Botswana electorate control the Gaberone city council through the Botswana National Front, the second largest party in the country. Relatively free and fair elections, tolerance of high levels of free expression, and a generally stable rule of law have created a favorable context for local governance to develop. In addition, major constitutional changes have influenced the manner in which power is shared between traditional and modern institutions, and these have tended to affect local governance positively, e.g., in the areas of land ownership and gender (Otlhogile 1998; Lekorwe 1998; Molutsi 1998).

Nondemocratic Governments and Decentralization

In contrast to these three country experiences, Nigeria, Ghana, and Kenya began their own decentralization programs under authoritarian governments. In Nigeria, it was the federal military government of General Murtala Mohamed that initiated the program of local government reform as a part of his five-point preparation of the country for the restoration of civilian governance in 1976. When General Murtala was assassinated in 1976, his deputy, General Olusegun Obasanjo, continued with this very ambitious global reform of Nigeria's local government system (Gboyega 1983; Adamolekun 1984). As Chapter 5 demonstrates, the commitment to the reform principles have been upheld by practically every administration that came to power amidst the country's alternations between democracy and military rule. Paradoxically, local government has tended to make less legal and structural progress under civilian governments than under the military, which is often able to make substantial changes because of its nondemocratic rule. Nonetheless, the turbulence of military governance, particularly under Ibrahim Babangida and Sani Abacha, created a social, economic, and political context where legal and structural reforms initiated at the center had great difficulty in growing into any viable system of local governance in the periphery.

Similarly in Ghana, decentralization was presented as a way of bringing back democracy under the military rule of Flight Lieutenant Jerry Rawlings (Rothchild 1995; Clarke 2001). As Joseph Ayee explains in Chapter 6, it is not difficult to understand why the reform did not make much more progress under the Rawlings government, both before and after the formal democratization of the state. This was because at heart the central government was more interested in retaining control than encouraging local governance (Ayee 1996). Thus, the quality of governance at the top did indeed compromise democratic governance at the community level in both Ghana and Nigeria.

Finally, the Kenyan experience is one that points to the severe erosion of local government by a patrimonial and authoritarian government, and the efforts made by civil society and the international community to revive its local government. Kenya, a state that once had an enviable system of local government, as Paul Smoke explains in Chapter 9, had eroded its local governance through the patrimonial patterns of power exercised by an increasingly corrupt and authoritarian center. The fact that the Daniel arap Moi government and his party were finally removed in the elections of December 2002 may now pave the way for a new commitment to local democracy, and for the consolidation of efforts to reform and revive local government. It will likely take several years, at least, to undo the damage done, both to local government and to those central ministries that must act effectively as a partner with local government.

Decentralization Under State Collapse: Bottom-Up Decentralization by Default

War, poverty, and misery could have been a trio that made life in Chad, a semidesert country, one of the perfect examples of the Hobbesian state of nature, with the lives of most of its people nasty, brutish, and short. However, as we show in Chapter 7, in such a difficult political environment of instability and internecine war, local people resorted to trusted institutional arrangements. These institutions made the difference between lives of perpetual squalor and progress. They were built with the grassroots self-organization skills and social capital of Chad's people. Chad highlights the large resources of social capital that exist in Africa, and which many rural people (and indeed urban inhabitants as well) use to solve the problems of their daily lives. Research in Nigeria, Cameroon, Congo, and a host of other countries, particularly with weak central governments, also demonstrate these patterns, though perhaps not as dramatically as in Chad (Olowu, Ayo, and Akande 1991; McGaffey 1992; Olowu and Erero 1996). However, in Chad these institutions were not connected to any formal system of governance, either with the central level via field administration, or via local formal governments. This may have affected the scale of activities in which these village-level institutions were able to engage (Ribot 2002).

This brief review suggests that democratic decentralization, even in the 1990s and since, presents many faces, and also suggests that democracy and state capacity make a difference. They can provide an environment for change that encourages the development of effective local governance or erode earlier well-functioning systems of local governance. State collapse may stimulate local governance efforts at the grassroots, but may also limit the scale to which they can develop. These and other factors will be explored in the case studies included in this book.

Conclusion

The objective of this chapter was to provide the reader with an overview of the historical, political, and economic forces that made decentralization a recurring public-policy theme in African countries, both before and after independence. The four "phases" described above have been closely connected throughout with overall state policy. Hence, when Africa's central governments sought to centralize all formal powers in one-party or military states shortly after they became independent, the hitherto semi-independent, local self-governing organs were converted into the field administration of the central state. Both institutions imply decentralization, but this chapter shows how the institutional principles sustaining the structures of local governance and field administration were very different. Indeed, throughout most of the phase two and three eras, there was in fact very little "local governance." As suggested by the analytical framework provided in the first chapter, field administration may have transferred responsibility and some human and financial resources from the central state to local organs, but there was no accountability of these structures to the local population. The objective of the center may have been to decongest the central government, but not to part with substantive authority. These field administrations were therefore accountable almost exclusively to the central state government. Central government officials made all of the crucial decisions. Moreover, the constitutional/legal environment was premised on monocentricity rather than polycentricity. This is why this arrangement should be understood as only *local administration*. We cannot claim originality in calling attention to this point (Mawhood 1983; Ostrom, Schroeder, and Wynne 1993; Adamolekun 1999).

The chapter has discussed the shift from local administration or deconcentrated structures during the mid-1980s and 1990s, toward democratic decentralization and local self-governance in many African countries. These reforms point in the direction of something new: they point toward the principles of local self-governance, and highlight the transfer of responsibility, resources, and accountability directly to ordinary citizens in the local community. To the extent that this locally constituted body of lay citizens is empowered with general competence to mobilize all available institutional resources to transform its locale, we might speak indeed of local government or even better still of local governance.

These seven cases only illustrate what is widespread throughout the continent in varying forms—countries as different as Ethiopia, Côte d'Ivoire, Mozambique, Mali, the Central African Republic, and several others have embarked on serious decentralization reforms as well. In the next chapter we analyze the factors responsible for this paradigm shift in public policy with respect to decentralization. We will also discuss the numerous dilemmas that still confront democratic decentralization on the continent.

Note

1. While it does not subscribe completely to P. Mawhood's (1983:8) proposition of the wide swings in policy between extremes of centralization and decentralization strategies in many African countries, we do see something similar to this.

3

New Dimensions in African Decentralization

I n Chapters 1 and 2 we described "democratic decentralization" reforms as those aimed at the devolution of resources, authority, and accountability to local levels of governance. This chapter discusses the factors responsible for the upsurge in democratic decentralization in Africa since the 1980s and highlights some of the major dilemmas that these countries confront in designing and implementing decentralization policies and programs. An inadequate appreciation of these dilemmas has often hindered some of the best efforts all stakeholders— national policymakers, citizens, and donors—have made to support democratic decentralization in Africa. The focus of this chapter will be on political issues. By "political" we refer to the struggle for power through the state and the conceptual assumptions that frame that struggle as it affects local governance (Gboyega 1983; Balogun 2000; Ribot 2002; Olowu 2003). Political issues must be explored as they are critical exogenous variables in any analysis of decentralization and local governance and have often been neglected or "assumed away" by policymakers and analysts. This neglect has left them unprepared to respond effectively to the deep political dilemmas they face in implementing decentralization policy. In contrast, fiscal, economic, and technical issues have received sustained and substantial attention (Hicks 1961; Litvack, Ahmed, and Bird 1998; Smoke 1994, 1999b; Ostrom, Schroeder, and Wynne 1993; Oyugi 2000).

The chapter is divided into three major sections. The first part discusses the factors responsible for the policy shift toward democratic decentralization through the changes to the political calculus facing leaders in recent years. In the second section, we discuss several key political dilemmas of democratic decentralization. In the final section, we discuss the mechanisms that are being used by African states to manage some of these problems.

The Shift to Democratic Decentralization in Africa Since 1980

The Changing Political Context

Several factors explain the growth of democratic decentralization in Africa since the 1980s. These, however, can have a mixed impact on the likelihood of its success. They include the following.

Economic and political crises. There is consensus that the failure of centralized public-sector management in the 1980s led to economic, fiscal, and political crises. Negative economic growth, growing external indebtedness, systemic fiscal imbalance, and political instability are well discussed in the literature on African governance (Wunsch and Olowu 1990a; Bayart 1993; Cheru 2002). The resulting decline in state resources increased pressure for economic, institutional (public-sector), and political reforms as part of the search for new paradigms of governance by state officials (World Bank 1981, 1989b; Cornia and Helleinner 1994). Nigeria, Côte d'Ivoire, and Tanzania are examples of this. These crises pushed countries toward reforms as their resource base shrank and intensified the scramble for available state resources. In this context states were brought under pressure by severe resource constraints, complemented by internal and external pressures to devolve some of the responsibilities they carried. Some countries developed formal policies of devolution, transferring their assigned responsibilities to lower-level community organs. In other cases, devolution occurred by default, as is discussed in Chapter 7 with respect to Chad. Pressures for change came not only from the internal logic of hard-pressed governments but also from domestic actors outside state institutions. Many civil-society organizations became more politically visible and more sophisticated in their critique and protest of state policies as the economic crisis bit harder in the 1980s (Bratton and van de Walle 1997). They demanded improved state performance. In several cases, state officials sought decentralized institutional arrangements that might bridge the wide gulf between the state and the citizen, and better synchronize local programs with the highly centralized structures and operations of the state (Dia 1996; Hyden 1999).

While some scholars (Gyimah-Boadi 1998; Monga 1999) have

questioned the depth and strength of civil society on the continent, there is substantial agreement that civil society's critique of, and at times violent resistance to, central rule have led to new constitutional arrangements that ensure that local communities and nongovernmental organs have a much stronger voice in governance (Bratton and Rothchild 1992; Mujaju 2000). For instance, in Mali a peasant uprising in the countryside in 1992 led to the promulgation of the ambitious Malian decentralization program. A U.S. Agency for International Development assessment notes that "the single most important political decision emerging from the 1991–1992 revolution was the commitment to a decentralized system of governance that ensures the achievement of the dual objectives of democracy and sustainable development" (USAID 2002:1). And in some cases where there were guerrilla wars of independence or democratization, such as in Mozambique and Uganda, the structure of governance was transformed into new decentralized governance structures (Davidson 1993). Overall, in several instances where governments found their survival threatened, or new regimes developed from grassroots resistance, a new openness to democratic decentralization developed.

Pressure from donors for good governance. The end of the Cold War meant the withdrawal of Soviet as well as Western military and financial "strategic" support for patrimonial and at times corrupt leadership. At the same time, crisis-ridden economies made several African leaders more dependent on donor funds for their development and even for routine expenditures. On the whole, official development assistance funds were declining in terms of the proportion of donor gross domestic product (GDP) assigned to aid, but for many African leaders they still constituted a substantial portion of their development expenditures. For example, average donor proportion of development expenditures for seven Francophone West African states from 1980 to 1993 was 45 percent and reached 63 percent, 64 percent, and 66 percent for Mali, Niger, and Upper Volta, respectively (Doe 1998). By the 1990s, most donors had become convinced that good governance was a necessary precondition for growth and substantial poverty reduction, hence the increasing use of good-governance conditionalities. Democratic decentralization has been seen as one of the key elements of good governance. Other good-governance elements include electoral and legal reforms, human rights, and public-sector and macroeconomic reforms. These too help push decentralization. For example, many poverty-oriented initiatives, such as the primary health care reforms of Nigeria in the 1990s and Uganda's Poverty Action Funds (PAF) expenditures, require substantial

local management to be effective. Once implemented, these subsequently pressure central governments to devolve resources, personnel, and
authority to follow the initiatives, or see them fail (Olowu and Wunsch
1995; Wunsch 2001a, 2001b). Supporting this point, a major study by
the Organization for Economic Cooperation and Development (OECD)
concluded that civil-service reform without democratic decentralization
would be of limited value (OECD 1997:13). Good governance reforms
that do not emphasize participation seem to have the same negative
results.[1] In Mali, for instance, donor support for civil-society organizations paved the way for more effective representation of the member-
ships of these bodies in local government councils as many of the civil-
society leaders who had benefited from such support became local
government leaders (USAID 2002). Nonetheless, there is a caveat, in
that where reforms emerged from only external pressure, a lack of local
ownership will likely lead to erosion once support is removed. Research
in Tanzania, for instance, shows the crosscutting influence of donor
organizations on public-sector reform generally. Local government was
one of the most crucial elements of these reforms (Therkildsen 2001;
Haynes 2001).

Growing urbanization and metropolitanization. Urbanization varies
across Africa, but it is marked everywhere by high rates of growth. A
continent with only one-third of its people in urban areas by 1990 is
projected to have more than one-half its population (54 percent) in
cities by 2020 (UNCHS 1996). This phenomenon is itself also a symp-
tom of fundamental change in the modes of economic production and
the need for social services on the continent. Some African farmers are
moving from cash and arable farming into agro-based industrialization.
Many more are moving to service industries as higher levels of secondary education encourage young people to seek such jobs in towns
(World Bank 1997:227). Conflicts have also stimulated urbanization,
causing many people to amass around major cities in conflict-prone
countries—e.g., Sierra Leone, Liberia, Côte d'Ivoire, the Great Lakes
area, Angola, etc. (Wekwette 1997). This has affected the political calculus behind decentralization. In the past, African governments
financed urban infrastructure by creating central government parastatals, many of which were inefficient and delivered poor-quality services. The advent of economic crisis and structural adjustment has made
these approaches to urban management unsustainable just as urban
areas were growing rapidly (Rakodi 1997). In response, many such
responsibilities were transferred to multipurpose, semiautonomous local

governments, or privatized. Unfortunately, many countries have not developed institutional mechanisms for effective urban management (Mabogunje 1995b). Urban citizens, generally more politically visible and sophisticated than their rural counterparts, have mounted severe pressure on governments for change in favor of greater devolution of powers. The fact that some such cities demonstrated a capacity to manage without central financial support in the past, and continue to do so in different parts of the continent, particularly in southern Africa (Stren 1989a; Olowu and Smoke 1992), have often made such appeals quite strong. When governments have responded by granting devolution, the political space opened at the local level has given opposition parties a chance to capture power at that level. Thus a number of African cities are managed by political parties in opposition to the central government, such as Gaborone and Harare (Rakodi 1997; Olowu 2000c). Thus, growing urbanization has led to devolution and to a political base for the opposition that will likely support sustained devolution to protect this base.[2]

Decentralization as a conflict-resolution strategy. The conscious use of decentralization as a political mechanism by central governments to neutralize and contain conflicts with regional or local elites has increased substantially (Crook and Manor 1998; Boone 1998). Decentralization has proven in the post-1990 period to be a crucial mechanism in national and international efforts at conflict resolution in several parts of the continent. It played a role, for instance, in the resolution of the long conflicts in Ethiopia, South Africa, and Mozambique, and appears likely to be useful for the resolution of conflicts in Sudan, Angola, Senegal, the two Congos, Rwanda, and Nigeria. Unfolding events in these countries suggest that political leaders who currently are ignoring it will be compelled by the international community and the futility of the unending struggle for power to explore its potential to help manage conflict. If one assumes that the primary motivation of political leaders is to continue to hold power, one can explain both the push to centralization in the immediate postindependence era (see Chapter 2), as well as the openness to devolution in some circumstances in the 1990s and 2000s. As the state weakened in the 1980s, and as stubborn regional conflicts grew worse, staying in power could be aided by careful but genuine devolution.

Globalization. As the pressure for globalization compelled many national governments to focus their attention on strategic issues of national economic and political management, detailed management of cities and communities has at times been delegated to other institutional actors (Collins 2000). Some of these, like religious and philanthropic institutions, have demonstrated their capacity to undertake local economic development projects as well as a range of social services: health, education, rural water, roads, and agricultural extension services (Hyden 1983; Olowu 1999a). While this is still in its early stages, as these nongovernmental organizations expand their activities, power necessarily shifts to the local levels. Decentralization of formal governance institutions is, by corollary, necessary to support these processes and is indeed one of the most important elements of the new efforts at decentralization in many developing countries. Mali has been particularly successful at integrating these nonstate structures, and countries such as Tanzania, Uganda, and Kenya have included these as part of their decentralization programs (Helmsing 2001; for non-African examples, Brilliantes 1998 on the Philippines; and Collins 2001 for other Asian and Latin American cases).

Thus there are numerous political factors leading African governments to explore and expand democratic decentralization. The result has been substantial in many countries, shifting important authority and resources from central governments to peripheral institutions. A number of legal mechanisms are being utilized to transfer authority as well as financial and human resources to local governments in most countries. These include constitutional mechanisms in addition to statutes and administrative measures. If these work, it will make it a little more difficult for central governments to encroach on local responsibilities, as happened in the past. Constitutional mandates, however, can be a double-edged sword: they protect subnational governments but also make evolutionary changes difficult to effect as the society and settlement patterns change. This can be seen in South Africa, Namibia, and Nigeria.

A number of "technical" issues with major political implications are still in great flux, as will be discussed in the case studies. For example, financial resources are usually redistributed by fiscal transfers either through tax-sharing arrangements (Ghana, Uganda, South Africa) and/or specific grants (Uganda). However, getting them transferred reliably, without crippling strings attached to them, and without suppressing local revenue raising, is still an issue for most of Africa. Formulas that determine how much each area gets are also a problem: they frequently lack both transparency and legitimacy, and are subject to political tampering by the center (Smoke 1999a). Human resources are shared between central and local governments using either of three arrangements: separate (Uganda, South Africa), integrated (Ghana, most of the French-speaking countries outside the capital cities), or unified personnel systems (Nigeria, Botswana) (Allen 1990). None of these arrangements is perfect. There are continuous tensions over who controls local personnel; "reforms" are effectively eroded by centrally controlled civil-service personnel, or when these reforms are effective and civil servants come under local control, technical support and personnel morale have at times collapsed. To have effective human resource management for local governments, the appointment of personnel and the apportionment of responsibilities between central and local governments require intergovernmental review mechanisms to ensure that the systems put in place are coordinated and that there is no mismatch between responsibilities and resources. These procedures have rarely been fully established in most states. As a result, there are serious intergovernmental fiscal and personnel paradoxes that often paralyze action at the local level. These problems are reinforced by the lack of human-resource management policies that match the objectives of decentralization (Kolehmanen-Aitken 1998). Nonetheless, as the national political context changes, there is more pressure to resolve these issues and learn from the various approaches that have been taken to them.

Emerging Evidence of Democratic Decentralization

There is empirical evidence emerging that the decentralization of the 1990s has been significantly more substantial than that of earlier eras. For example, a study of six sub-Saharan African countries[3] by a consortium of donors (the National Association of Local Authorities of Denmark, Danish International Development Aid [DANIDA], USAID, and the World Bank) found that:

> Decentralization efforts in the African region are shifting much of the burden of infrastructure management and finance to sub-national levels. . . . As part of their decentralization efforts, many African countries have begun to address democratic decentralization *fiscal resource and mobilization*. The countries in the sub-Saharan Africa are all at various stages in the decentralization process. Indeed, taken as a group, these [six] countries comprise a virtual continuum of the steps necessary to build strong municipal governance and infrastructure delivery systems. (Steffensen and Trollegaard 2000:11–12, 14; italics in the original)

Available data shows that local governments in Africa still constitute a relatively small percentage of public expenditure and employee size of the total public-sector size (compared to other regions). But there have been significant increases in countries such as Uganda, Nigeria, Ethiopia, Mali, South Africa, Benin, Zimbabwe, and Botswana. In Uganda, Nigeria, Ethiopia, and Zimbabwe, subnational governments (state/regional and local authorities) are disposing of as much as 21 percent, 40 percent, 30 percent, and 25 percent, respectively, of total public expenditure (Steffensen and Trollegaard 2000; IMF 2001; Smoke 1999a). A recent study by the International Labour Organization (ILO) shows that local government employee size for countries in Africa (for which it has data) were quite high: Botswana, 18.4 percent; South Africa, 16 percent; Uganda, 12.6 percent; Zimbabwe, 11.2 percent; although Gambia had only 4.1 percent (ILO 2001:84). Additionally, for example, a review of postconflict Mozambique shows that wide jurisdiction has been allocated to district and municipal authorities. This includes responsibility for "social welfare, health, education and roads, the promotion of development, protection of the environment, the management of land, public and private markets, civil protection, control of fire and calamities" (Alexander 1997:15). These powers are similar to local government powers in Nigeria, Uganda, Botswana, Ghana, and other sub-Saharan African states. In sum, local governments have been growing in importance in African countries since the 1990s. This growth is also reflected in the size of the public expenditure and GDP contributed by local government in selected countries (see Table 3.1). The first two countries below (Swaziland and Zambia) have not begun any significant decentralization reforms. The latter four, Ghana, Uganda, Nigeria, and Zimbabwe, have significant decentralization

Table 3.1   Subnational/Local Government Expenditure as a Share of GDP and Total Government Expenditure, 1997/1999

Country	LG Share of GDP (%)	Total Government Expenditure (%)
Swaziland	0.6	2.0
Zambia	0.5	3.0
Senegal	1.8	7.0
Zimbabwe	3.0	8.0
Ghana	3.0	8.0
Uganda	4.0	21.0
Nigeria	5.0 (18.0)[a]	12.0 (23.0)[a]
OECD members	11.0	10–30

Source: Steffensen and Trollegaard 2001 and IMF 2001.
Notes: LG = local government.
a. Subnational expenditures, i.e., state and local governments, are shown in parentheses.

plans in place. Senegal has not pursued decentralization recently, but has several municipalities with historically larger responsibilities than most units of rural local government.

Dilemmas of Democratic Decentralization in Africa: The Colonial State, the Early Independence Era, and Their Legacies

The struggle for political power and resources in general frames any major institutional reform, anywhere. As a result, there are many of what we call here "political problems" confronting the development of democratic decentralization and local self-governance in contemporary Africa. Three key ones are discussed here, and they grow from the ideological, institutional, and social legacies of the colonial state and the early independence era. They are: (1) the intellectual model of states and institutional legacy that the European colonial experience imbued in Africans; (2) the patrimonial political patterns that colonialism and the early independence stimulated and sustained in Africa; and (3) the class/elite structure the colonial era left behind. Each of these has had troubling impacts on democratic decentralization and local self-governance.

The African Nation-State Building Project

It is difficult in Africa to reconcile the task of building the nation-state modeled after the European prototype with the principles of democratic decentralization enunciated in Chapter 1. The European, particularly the continental, model of nation and state building is one that historically involved the consolidation and extensive centralization of state power in the face of numerous class and ethnic fissures (V. Ostrom 1991; Davidson 1992). How this highly centralized state structure might coexist simultaneously with a program of state decentralization, involving the deliberate transfer of authority, resources, and accountability arrangements from the central state to the localities, is a real question. In contrast, the transition from the first to a more liberal state in most of Europe was lengthy and turbulent.

Basil Davidson (1992) argued that the attempt by Africans to imitate the European nation-state project is responsible for much of the continent's problems in relating creatively to its past and the failure of its social-reform agenda. The historical idea of the European nation-

state has several key elements that are particularly difficult to implement in Africa. These include the idea of a *homogenous nation-state* as
the only viable state and its imposition of cultural hegemony over conquered groups, and a central government that has firm control over the
national political and economic space (Mazrui 1983). It assumes a *capi-
talist transformation* (Hyden 1983), so that all significant sectors of
society are dependent on, and therefore vulnerable to, the power of the
state for their economic survival. These projects have proven either difficult or premature to actualize in Africa given the continent's history of
four centuries of economic disruption caused by slavery (fifteenth to
eighteenth centuries), followed closely by colonialism in the nineteenth
and twentieth centuries; its continued substantial ethnic heterogeneity;
the disjunction between state aspirations and administrative capacity
and resources; the dependency patterns spawned by colonialism; and
the inability of African countries to attract substantial international capital since independence. As a result, African states are to this day nearly
all institutionally weak, ethnically fragmented, precapitalist, and only
peripherally involved in the global economy. Thus, the model does not
"fit" African realities, and not surprisingly it was largely dysfunctional
as an instrument of governance and development (Wunsch and Olowu
1990a). Nor is the kind of royal and military absolutism pursued by
European elites in their state-building periods from the sixteenth to the
twentieth centuries possible in the ethically oriented, media-linked, and
global-economic world of the latter twentieth and early twenty-first
centuries. However, African political leaders and intellectuals preferred
the centralized nation-state model, perhaps because it assured them a
permanent hold of monopoly power while this project was being implemented.

Besides the intellectual model and tradition of the European state,
there are institutional patterns and power relations that have survived
since the colonial era. Indeed, the continuity between the colonial and
postcolonial states is striking. The most important elements of the colonial state have been summarized as follows:

• Political (policy) direction and control of a subject society by a
foreign power, whether a board of directors like the Royal Nigeria
Company or a Cecil Rhodes company, or by a government agency of
the metropolitan country.
• Bureaucratic elitism and authoritarianism from the beginning of
the twentieth century, where army, police, and civilian departments
were organized in large bureaucracies characterized in principle at least
by hierarchy, continuity, impersonality, and expertise. These principles

were emphasized to the exclusion of the subject population, as key administrative positions were reserved for a small group of political administrators primarily on the basis of race. Furthermore, limited resources and communications severely compromised the integrity of hierarchical administration in the field.

• Use of traditional or customary authority figures in colonial society, not accountable to local dwellers but to colonial administrators, which often allowed petty despotisms to develop.

• The free use of force, first by the military and later by the police, which protected only those in power and the propertied classes while oppressing the ordinary people (Young 1999).

• High levels of statism, in that the colonial state intervened and regulated economic activities in a way that was rarely known elsewhere, to ensure that colonizers profited maximally from the colonial enterprise. In particular, the state created monopoly control over the purchase and export of agricultural goods. This continued after independence, to the benefit of those who wielded central power.

• An ideology emphasizing the colonial masters' benevolence and invincibility, which led to patterns of dependency first by the colonized peoples, and then between the local elites as a dominant group and the African masses (Potter 2000:272–284; Young 1999).

Instead of attempting to build the foundations of an independent African state along more democratic lines, postindependence states in the region sustained these autocratic foundations, only replacing the external power with a domestic single-party, military oligarchy or personal despotism. The reasons for this are in part intellectual (what they were familiar with), political (what was in the elite's interest), and institutional (what were the biases of the operational rules and laws they inherited). Overall, leaders were familiar and comfortable with relations of dominance and control, and not of contestation, flexibility, and respect for others' powers and rights (Wunsch 1990). What made these colonial patterns particularly tenacious is that in colonial times African countries were exposed *both* to institutionalized central despotism, *and* to informal local despotism (Mamdani 1996). How were Africans to build effective systems of democratic local governance with these autocratic, intellectual, class, and institutional legacies?

Within the above-mentioned governance and institutional framework, it might seem miraculous that democratic decentralization anywhere has become state policy. The unwillingness of political and administrative leaders to share the monopoly authority inherited from colonial times, even when the case for democratic decentralization has been overwhelming, has constituted the veritable dilemma of local government reform in Africa (Wunsch and Olowu 1990b; Bayart 1993). Indeed, there may be seemingly well-founded fears behind this reluctance. For instance, leaders have argued that devolution might undermine national cohesion and fan the embers of secession, which are usually real considerations in societies in which ethnic and community loyalties are quite strong relative to national cohesion. In most societies, even national politics are strongly affected and often fragmented by the ordinary citizens' experience in the local community. This leads to a politics that emphasizes electing whoever is best able to promote local community interests rather than who can contribute to the nation's interests as a whole (Hyden 1999:188). There is also the fear that devolution might compromise the integrity of ostensibly nationally delivered services. These dilemmas are particularly acute in Africa because democratic decentralization is often viewed through the lenses of a zero-sum power game, in which local actors gain at the expense of the center, rather than as a possible positive-sum power game in which all players, both local and center, might gain over time (Olowu 2001a; Wunsch 2001a). This is due to the monopolistic and patrimonial nature of governance in many states, an issue we discuss in greater detail in the next section.

Reconciling Patrimonial and Traditional Governance with Democracy

The first problem is closely related to the second dilemma: how to reconcile patrimonial governance with democracy at the local or community level. The patrimonial nature of governance at the central level is well known, but few scholars have devoted attention to the nature of rule promoted in the local community from the early colonial period to the present (Hyden 1992; Crowder 1968). A contemporary scholar working in this area is Mahood Mamdani (1996). He shows how colonial rule promoted local despotism that was comprehensive in giving centrally appointed chiefs high levels of local autonomy. However, they did not have absolute authority, as they were dependent on the central government and its key official in the district, the district officer. The latter was invariably an appointee and national of the metropolitan power. The chief exercised all powers of government in his domain— judicial, legislative, executive, and administrative—in a system of government that was dominated by force. Perhaps the most serious implication of this was the designation of the chief as the customary authority, one that was in effect monarchical, patriarchal, and authoritarian. The absolute authority that many chiefs exercised, including over the private economy, meant that chiefs were responsible for much of the substantial violence and corruption engendered by the colonial economic and political system. According to Mamdani:

> This authority of the chief was like a clenched fist, necessary because the chief stood at the intersection of the market economy and the non-market one. . . . The administrative justice and administrative coercion that were there were the sum and substance of his authority lay behind a regime of extra-economic coercion, a regime that breathed life into a whole range of compulsions: forced labor, forced crops, forced sales, forced contributions, and forced removals. . . . Here there is no question of any internal check and balance on the exercise of authority, let alone a check that is popular and democratic. The chief is answerable only to a higher administrative authority. . . . It is this agent of this fused authority, this clenched fist, who is usually called the chief. To the peasant, the person of the chief is total, and absolute, unchecked and unrestrained. (Mamdani 1996:23, 53, 58)

In fact, at the local level many chiefs were able to manipulate the authority that the colonial state gave them to amass substantial wealth. They then used it during the colonial era, and some after independence, to become important political players, and often to dominate local politics regardless of their formal role and authority (Firmin-Sellers 2001). In the sense that Max Weber used the term *patrimonial,* they perceived and used local government as their personal possession.

A few African countries challenged this pattern of local, patrimonial despotism exercised by traditional rulers after independence. But what many countries did was *replace it* with a local despotism of the party and/or the personal representative of the head of state. This was through an appointed governor or provincial or district officer, one with immense powers over the community. Given these institutional and thus subsequent general behavioral patterns of dominance and submission at the local level, it is a critical question whether local self-governance can reasonably be expected to take root in Africa. This is not to deny that Africans experienced democratic governance before the colonial period, nor to assert that they are incapable of governing themselves democratically. It is rather to note that the institutions and behavior patterns that democratic reforms frequently met, and meet, in the local communities contradict their core principles. An important policy dilemma confronting advocates of democratic decentralization is what can they do to move beyond this (Ekeh 1975).

The Nigerian local government reform of 1976 tried to tackle this problem. In a review of the provisions of the Nigerian reforms for traditional rulers, especially in the northern part of the country where they were most powerful, Joseph Egwurube noted that the reform "radically altered the locus of traditional rulers vis-à-vis local government" as traditional institutions were converted into informed observers of local government (Egwurube 1988:156). Specifically, traditional rulers were no longer to occupy executive positions in local government. What makes Egwurube's analysis particularly insightful beyond Nigeria is his attempt to conceive of traditional institutions within the framework of evolving institutions. According to him, local government systems can be classified along two sets of variables: in terms of *process,* and the *focus* of authority. It is therefore possible to generate four sets of possibilities: *autocratic* or *conciliar* processes; and *personal* or *impersonal* focus of authority. According to him, local government in Nigeria has passed through four basic sequential stages—the "pioneering" stage involving autocratic personal rule; the "bureaucratic" stage, involving autocratic-institutional rule; the "representative" stage involving selected councillors with a traditional or personal administration; and the "responsible" stage involving elected councillors and an impersonal government (see Table 3.2). He concludes, putting this dilemma starkly: "By definition, traditional rulerships are closed systems, characterised by stratification, heredity, legitimacy and personalism. These features are untenable in open, modern, local government systems involving local initiative, universalism, equality and change" (Egwurube 1988:170).

In other words there is a contradiction between the *traditionalization of local government* and the *democratization or modernization of traditional rulership,* but only the latter is consistent with the spirit and letter of a democratic (Nigerian) state. However, such a reform is not easy to accomplish, given the colonial legacy, the intellectual and political bias at the center, and the autocratic and personalistic patterns frequently found at the locality. In Nigeria, at least,

Table 3.2   Stages in the Evolution of Conciliar Local Government

	Autocratic	Conciliar
Personal	Pioneering (traditional chiefs/serfs)	Selected local councillors
Impersonal	Bureaucratic local government (deconcentration)	Elected local councillors

Source: Adapted from Egwurube 1988.

"modern" local governments seemed frequently to fail to move beyond the "pioneering" and "bureaucratic" stages. Sadly, this argument can be applied with equal force to most other African countries. In spite of the strong points in favor of modern local government, disappointing performance has been the hallmark of the institution in Africa, with but a few exceptions (Olowu 1999c; Olowu and Smoke 1992).

This fact has given strength to the argument of those who believe that the modernization of local governments requires first that they be traditionalized—by making the traditional chiefs the wielders of state authority in their localities. This argument rests on several points. First, in spite of the colonial era's impact, many traditional rulers are still held in high esteem by the ordinary local people and are regarded by many as the custodians of peace, order, and stability in the various communities and in the country at large. Second, traditional rulers have provided continuity in government—in contrast to the unstable regimes that take and fall from power at the national level. Third, these chiefs often consult with a variety of citizens through unofficial channels, which actually form the basis of their popularity to both modern and traditional elites. Finally, traditional chiefs often have good information on local conditions and needs.

However, this strategy is unlikely to be sustainable or even acceptable to most Africans. Even though many rural peoples see the utility of some role for traditional leaders, that role has limits. For example, in a period of increasing democratization of all the organs of government, traditional rulers as presently constituted are still generally part of the "state" rather than the "society." This is a carryover from the colonial period. This also explains why some of them are just as corrupt as the formal local governments they claim they ought to replace. Furthermore, their partisanship in aligning with ruling parties in colonial and postcolonial times in many countries has compromised their stance as "neutral fathers of all the people" (Lundin 1994; Nsibambi 1994; Aborisade 1990).

Furthermore, to accept this is to subscribe to the impossibility of democracy in Africa at any level. But this is belied by the achievements of several African states, and the demands for democracy by civil society. At best, such a regime might provide for an urban-centered democracy, where chiefs are weak, but where large numbers of leaders would be selected elsewhere by a closed, oligarchic, and likely conservative rural elite. It is unlikely that a national regime based on these contradicting patterns of governance would be particularly united or coherent in addressing social problems, since the interests of an urban proletariat or bourgeois and a traditional rural elite would seem unlikely to mesh (Huntington 1968).

As a result of all these factors, traditional rulership and local government democratization constitute a dilemma that many countries have yet to resolve. Jocelyn Alexander (1997) comes to this conclusion with respect to Mozambique. She notes that chiefs had strong legitimacy in terms of their roles in mediating with the state. However, she also notes that they had become controversial. They were not always above party politics nor did their interests necessarily reflect those of the wider community. Also common were conflicts between royal lineages, especially as they were recruited as a means of extending the state. Her conclusion was that the Mozambican state and Mozambican society were experiencing a profound crisis of authority and that the nature of that crisis was rooted in the practices and pressures of the past. The postindependence state had failed to "transform Portuguese notions of authority, its coerciveness and militarization, its blurring of distinctions between state and party, attacks on spiritual authority and inability to deliver or protect economic progress" (Alexander 1997:20).

In cases of state collapse or hostile state-society relations, many societies *have* developed alternative structures of community governance based on civic institutions, which they use to govern their economic and social lives. These come in different shapes and modes, but in societies where the state has all but collapsed, Zaire and Somalia for example, they became the main institutions of governance (McGaffey 1992; Shivakumar 1999). Even in countries where the state has weakened, though not collapsed, these civic structures play crucial roles in governance (Olowu and Erero 1996; Monga 1998). Traditional chieftaincy institutions are usually not a major part of these structures. However, *customary* notions of proper and improper behavior, obligations, and decisionmaking are indeed important. Out of these, people create or turn to alternative institutions of governance. Documented evidence from Gambia, Nigeria, and Uganda indicate that these alternative institutions become the de facto local government institutions (Dia 1996; Olowu 1993; Olowu, Ayo, and Akande 1991). Chapter 7 in this volume discusses this phenomenon in Chad. The process through which customary notions of proper behavior and governance are structured into effective institutions of local governance may be a critical topic of study to understand how Africans might genuinely govern themselves and resolve the tension between compromised traditional figures and institutions and effective democratic governance.

To what, then, does this seemingly confused and complex picture add? First, traditional institutions were generally corrupted by colonial administrations into small patrimonial realms. Second, simplistic attempts to "create" modern and democratic governmental units from the top-down on an American or European model are likely to run directly into the local power structure inherited from the colonial era, or put in place in the early independence era. At most, one will have fragile "pseudo-democracies" at the center, with weak roots in the countryside. Third, while traditional leaders are still at times respected and can play important roles in contemporary African affairs, they lack the legitimacy, administrative resources, and skills to become "local governments." Even if they had these attributes, their interests would likely undermine the emergence of national democracy in Africa. Fourth, in cases of state collapse or state-society conflict, indigenous "social infrastructure" has been used to solve local conflict or provide complex local public goods. These, however, were usually not "traditional rulers" in any simple sense, but grew from the use locally of indigenous patterns of organization and rules of action. Still, without formal institutions to structure these actions, local governance may be slow and cumbersome, and lack the ability to provide expensive and technically complex goods. Overall, the intellectual model and habits of the colonial state, the interests of patrimonial rulers, and the shared fears of both local and national elites reinforce one another. Untying this knot may be one of the key prerequisites to achieving local governance.

Local Elite Capture

A third political dilemma is the problem of local elite capture. Logically enough, and as argued in Chapter 2, local governance seems generally to begin with some expansion of authority for local governments. After all, without local authority, there is no local government, nor is it rational for people with serious needs and limited resources to invest in formal local governments. As we have argued in Chapter 1, however, even authority alone, once granted, is not sufficient to make people invest their personal resources into local (or any other level of) governance until that level has the resources to do something: to hire and pay personnel, purchase goods, supply services, build facilities, etc. Although whether Africans are over- or undertaxed is debatable, most taxation systems are, in effect, in the form of severance taxes on agriculture or minerals collected by the center. Rarely are local organs granted broad authority to raise local taxes from the wealthy, especially for those not employed in the formal sector (Smoke 1994; Moore 1998; Fjelsdtad 2001). So, serious decentralization efforts begin by distributing some significant resources downward from the center to newly empowered localities: to jump-start, as it were, local government by giving it some resources to go with some authority. Several states have minimally expanded the tax authority of local units, given them some share of national funds, and transferred personnel to them to perform these tasks.

By remedying, at least in a preliminary fashion, the problems of authority and resources, it might seem likely this would lead to that last element of local governance: accountability through *broadly based political process* to guide and keep accountable local decisions and actions, and set local governance into a "virtuous circle" of performance, legitimacy, and development, as it interacts intensively with local civic organizations and citizens. But it seems substantial empirical evidence suggests that it often does not, and what might be trumpeted as "devolution" is really only deconcentration under another guise.

In Ghana and Kenya, for example, the vast majority of enhanced local government budgets goes into administrative overhead, salaries, facilities, vehicles, and the like, which they must now support. Before decentralization, these were paid out of national coffers. Richard Crook's study of Ghanaian district government showed little was left over to respond to the grassroots dwellers' requests: roads, schools, sanitary facilities, etc. As rank-and-file local residents were paying increased taxes to the district governments, but received only denials of services, or suggestions to raise more money and do communal labor for their projects, cynicism and apathy set in. Meanwhile, because of nationally mandated staff reductions, local services such as sanitation eroded seriously. Locally elected councillors were caught in this conflict and were unable to redirect funds to other needs (Crook and Manor 1998). In two districts, as a result, more than 58 percent of the locally elected councillors intended not to stand for reelection. A local political process that started out with over a 50 percent voter turnout in initial elections in 1988 and 1989 had decayed so that a few years later (1992) only 22 percent felt the elected assemblies were an improvement over the old unelected district council. Seventy percent felt their assembly was incapable of addressing their development needs (Crook 1994:354–355). Ayee found similar problems in local government in Ghana, with recurrent expenditures consuming 85–87 percent of local budgets, and even more negative public opinion regarding the elected councils (Ayee 1994, 1996, and 1997b). Vicki Clarke recently found similar patterns in research during the late 1990s in Ghana's northern region (Clarke 2001). P. Smoke finds similar patterns of expenditure in local government in Kenya (Smoke 1994), and Wunsch found them in Uganda as well (Wunsch 2001b).

Koehn's study of Nigerian local government in Bauchi and Kaduna showed much the same patterns, at least in expenditures (Koehn 1989). A vastly disproportionate share of resources went to urban dwellers, was spent in capital-intensive (rather than labor-intensive) projects, and benefited primarily the staffs of the local governments and other local elite groups rather than the average person. Popular participation did not appear to change this. Wunsch and Olowu found similar patterns in their Nigerian research in 1992–1994 (Olowu and Wunsch 1995; Wunsch and Olowu 1996). There, public members of health advisory boards quite clearly analyzed the cost-benefit calculus of their participation (travel, lost work time) versus their perception that local professional officials utterly ignored them. Their decision: cease participation and cede decisionmaking to the officials. In a parallel study of local government in northern Nigeria, Ita O'Donovan found that localities that wanted development projects were encouraged to pursue "self-help" projects, but had minimal support from local government budgets that were focused primarily on staff support and other "overhead" expenditures (O'Donovan 1992:360–361). Richard Crook and James Manor found similar patterns of elite capture of local government resources in Côte d'Ivoire and Ghana (Crook and Manor 1998), as did Ivan Livingstone and Roger Charlton in Uganda at the district level (1998). Amy Paterson noticed a similar dynamic in rural Senegal's civil society, where state resources were used to co-opt leaders and preempt local challenges to state actions (Livingstone and Charlton 1998). N. D. Muitzwa-Mangiza found in Zimbabwe that the technical specialists posted there by the national government frequently overruled representatives, who "battle[d] for resources . . . to guard their individual department's interests jealously" (Muitzwa-Mangiza 1990:431). O'Donovan felt that the local electoral dynamics in Nigeria were encouraging a fragmented local political process likely to lead to elected councillors who would pursue either narrow vested interests, or simply their own interests (O'Donovan 1992:363–364). Crook and Manor also suggest this in their comparative study of Côte d'Ivoire, Ghana, India, and Bangladesh (Crook and Manor 1998).

Thus, the case literature on local governance, and the decentralization process that is usually pursued to support it in Africa and elsewhere, is replete with this pattern: local elites (bureaucratic, traditional, and economic) appear to capture local resources, spending most of them on salaries, buildings, vehicles, electric generators, and other perquisites for officials. The rest they expend on contracts and jobs for the locally well-connected, and on a few services (Ayee 1994, 1996, 1997a; Smoke 1994; Cohen 1993; Wunsch 1999; Olowu and Wunsch 1995; Wunsch and Olowu 1996; Davis, Hulme, and Woodhouse 1994; Crook 1994; Koehn 1989; Mead 1996; Manor 1995; Blair 1998; Wunsch 2001a). Local social and economic networks at times reinforce this pattern and block effective oversight by elected officials (Crook and Manor 1998:246). In some cases, as in Nigeria, local elected officials appear to run primarily to develop business opportunities (Mead 1996), and the more resources and authority localities seem to have, the larger the portion siphoned off seems to become. Lydia Segal's study of decentralized schools in New York City suggests this may be a universal dynamic (Segal 1997). In the subsequent resource allocation game, broadly based participation remains a nonrational option for most local people. The locality may indeed now have some authority and some resources, but the way in which local governments actually operate soon engenders cynicism and apathy among the general population (Crook 1994; Ayee 1996; Wunsch and Olowu 1996).[4] Even where resignation is not the case, the local elite frequently can and do use some of those resources to co-opt, corrupt, or intimidate possible opponents, and use patron-clientage to preempt any disturbance of this game (Berman 1998; Chambers 1983). All this means that trying to begin a broadly based political process is not rational for most people; and that even when one is begun, it soon decays, as it did in Ghana. As noted above, Ghana's high level of participation in local elections in 1988 was replaced by apathy in the second election cycle in 1994 (Crook and Manor 1998:268).

As discussed in Chapter 1, developing broadly based political organizations to counter these tendencies is difficult. As Mancur Olson demonstrated, organization costs are usually very steep, and the larger and more diverse a potential group (or potential coalition) is, the higher the costs rise. In conditions of severe scarcity, often those groups/coalitions never form, as they face these high costs with very few resources. Indeed, the very ethnic fragmentation typical of Africa seems to engender "big man"–based patronage that sustains local fragmentation (Berman 1998). Smaller, better resourced, and often already mutually cooperating local elites are "cheaper" to organize, "cost less" to manage, and have more resources to pay these costs (Olson 1966). The smaller they keep the local political arena, the larger their share of the pie (Riker 1962). One might hypothesize, then, that the more resources available to local elites the harder they will work to keep control of them. Crook and Manor's comparative work in India and Bangladesh suggests this might be the case in many developing countries (Crook and Manor 1998).[5]

The problem of local elite capture is therefore not only a real but a relatively new political problem confronted by all those engaged in developing local self-governance systems in Africa. It is important that mechanisms are developed to ensure that political forces are generated within the local government system to overcome this problem. One institutional response to this problem of local elite capture is to develop effective accountability mechanisms for local governance. This is explored in the next section.

Countering the Problem of Local Elite Capture: Conventional and New Approaches to Developing Local Accountability[6]

Conventional Approaches to Local Government Accountability in Africa

In view of the potential and real problems associated with local elite capture, most African countries tried historically to resolve the problem of accountability of local governments by asserting hierarchical control over them by central government. They usually designated a specialized ministry or department of the presidency or cabinet secretariat to carry out this function. Control mechanisms have included inspectorates, the requirement that local governments be approved by the central government, deployment of central-level personnel to local governments, central approval of all expenditures, and the regular use of the powers of suspension and dissolution of local government councils. Francophone countries also have required that national officials deal with all finance matters. In all countries, these arrangements are further complemented by internal accountability mechanisms—codes of conduct, financial and establishment codes, budgetary and personnel control, internal audit mechanisms, as well as disciplinary, supervisory, and training arrangements. Professional bodies further supplement these codes with their own professional codes, which have at times been strictly supervised and enforced by professional groups (Stren 1989b; Haque 1997; Ayee 1997c; Olowu 1997). All of these were aimed at reducing corruption in local government—an evil from which neither the national nor the local governments have been immune (Hope and Chiculo 2000).

That these arrangements have not always worked as predicted constitutes one of the most important grounds for democratic decentralization. Central governments often misused their wide powers of control over local governments, using them instead to settle political scores or victimize councils controlled by opposing parties. More importantly, responsibilities of local governments often required the details with which central governments were and are unfamiliar. Furthermore, central governments have preferred to deal with big projects and big companies, which even when they perform successfully, are not well suited to local development. In addition, central immobility and, at times, actual incompetence have delayed and disrupted local government activities. In many instances, central government departments charged with oversight over local governments have not possessed the skills or had the incentives to scrutinize the range of matters or the detailed information necessary to fulfill their responsibilities (Smoke 1994). For instance, central governments frequently fail to approve local government budgets by the deadlines set by those same central governments. This has been encountered in Kenya, Uganda, Senegal, and Ghana—where central governments often approve local government budgets as late as the end of the year or even later. In Nigeria, state governments were to discharge this function, but they were equally unsuccessful. This is not dissimilar to the experiences of other developing countries (Haque 1997; Ayee 1997b; Olowu 1997). A recent report on six countries in the region notes that many of the countries have cumbersome control and approval procedures for budgets and for other key decisions (Steffensen and Trollegaard 2000).[7] In Uganda, burdensome expenditure records were required by the central government, which then was unable even to evaluate the data reported (Wunsch 2001b). At the very best, hierarchical controls help to enhance the illusion of central control over local government, but this is usually neither efficient nor sustainable. Nor are they desirable for nurturing effective local governance in a democratizing milieu (Stren 1989b; Paul 1991). This is also consistent with much of the organizational literature that underscores the ineffectiveness of central controls in complex organizations. These are worse still when conditions (poor terrain, communication, etc.) are dynamic or difficult, as they impede the flexibility organizations must have to deal with these problems, and lead instead to severe goal displacement (Wunsch and Olowu 1990b; Landau 1969).

Alternative Strategies to
Enhance Local Governance Accountability

As the resources and responsibilities of local governments increased, it became even more important to develop effective systems of accountability for localities. There is, however, a growing recognition that centralized approaches have neither been efficient nor effective, as discussed above. Moreover, they have tended to undermine local governance and the public support for local government (Steffensen and Trollegaard 2000:23). Thus in recent years there has been growing openness by African governments to developing mechanisms of local accountability for local governance.

The thrust of democratic decentralization reforms with respect to accountability has been to develop accountability mechanisms using the principles of *exit* and *voice*. The two principles are premised on the fact that the delivery of services is contingent on the activities of three main stakeholders: *service beneficiaries* (customers and citizens); *political leaders and bureaucratic supervisors;* and *service providers.* The effectiveness of accountability mechanisms depends on the influence exerted by the first two on the third. Table 3.3 provides a brief overview of each of these approaches to accountability.

Examples of exit mechanisms include the production of public services such as basic education or basic health services by nongovernmental organizations (both nonprofit and for-profit) and public-sector

Table 3.3 Exit and Voice Accountability Mechanisms

Exit	Voice	Aids to Exit/Voice Accountability Mechanism
Privatization	Elections	Information
Multiple providers	Recall	Incentives
Deregulation	Referenda	Supply-side characteristics
Vouchers/grants	Third-party monitoring	
Contracting out	Auditing and evaluation	
	Pressure by interest groups	
	Public hearings/reporting	
	Mandatory public information	
	Information dissemination	
	Adjudicatory structures	
	Social unrest/resistance	
	Taxation	
	Ombudsman	
	Local government size	

Source: Adapted from Paul 1991.

producers, when local governments give vouchers to citizens to purchase services from any of these producers. The advantages of exit mechanisms are that they are impersonal, neat, and effective. The problem is that few public services delivered by local governments can be subject to the application of the exit principle. Services with low differentiation and high product involvement such as police protection, environmental sanitation, etc., may not be subject to exit. Also, many of Africa's people lack easy options to relocate as an alternative to poor provisioning of services. For such services and people, voice mechanisms are required. Nonetheless, some African countries have embarked upon programs of privatization and deregulation of local governments. Municipalities in Côte d'Ivoire, Mali, South Africa, and Ghana, etc., are outsourcing their services with some positive effects (Wekwette 1997). Water and electricity services have benefited most from exit options, although in Zambia the government simply sold off its public housing programs at great loss to the local authorities.

Voice mechanisms are important for public services for which exit is not possible. But they require personal input from the customer/citizen and such confrontations can predictably be awkward and even lead to conflict, as they involve face-to-face interaction between suppliers and customers. They also require a politically active population that has information and time to pursue these questions. These characteristics make the application of voice mechanisms dependent on knowledge of relevant production/function information, income level, the extent and effectiveness of information barriers, and the public's ability to force those who exercise power to listen to them and change their behavior. The latter is in particular reduced by the wealth and power differentials typical of areas such as sub-Saharan Africa. Nonetheless, given the limits of "exit" as strategy, "voice" has the most potential to enhance local accountability in sub-Saharan Africa at this time. Table 3.4 identifies some of the preconditions necessary if voice is likely to be successful in holding local government accountable.

A number of voice strategies have been developed in Africa. They will be briefly discussed below.

Local elections. Compared to national elections, local elections have not been the subject of serious study. In some cases, multiparty elections are outlawed at the local level even though they are used for political competition at national levels and still affect local races (e.g., Ghana). This approach is defended by arguing that local government matters are bread-and-butter issues on which there can be no division

Table 3.4 Citizen Voice and Organizational Responsiveness

Conditions for Effective Citizen Voice	Conditions for Effective Responsiveness of Local Government to Voice
Broad membership base and alliance with middle-class and elite groups. Technical knowledge. Knowledge of official policy discourses and of effective alternatives. Publicity—ability to effectively utilize the media. Lots of time and starting small. Social capital—where trust and mutual support has been built. Horizontal coalitions with other bodies. Formal standing in policymaking arenas and in oversight agencies. Statutory rights to know and rights to redress.	Internal champions/reform entrepreneurs. External pressure. Vertical slice strategies—commitment of top leadership to reform. Incentive systems rewarding participatory processes and client focus. Involvement of street-level bureaucrats in policymaking and planning of service delivery. Involvement of external actors in local monitoring systems. Linking agency income to performance—user fees, bonuses, etc. Investment in attitudinal change.

Source: Adapted from Institute of Development Studies 2001.

along partisan lines. However, the absence of partisan contests seems associated with lower turnout and with local partisan and other factional divisions that have little to do with local policy issues (Clarke 2001). Multiparty elections are used to fill political positions in Nigerian and Ivorian local governments and communes respectively.

Elections should promote citizens' voice in three ways. They constitute a major form of *participation,* as indicated by the voter turn-out figures. They have the potential to enhance *accountability* and provide *information* on policy intentions and outcomes to electors. The problem is that money, violence, and corruption dominate local elections as they do national elections in many African countries. Some countries have therefore sought to supplement elections into local councils with other mechanisms such as recall by constituents. This is used in Nigeria and Ethiopia, though it is used more effectively in the latter. Other parts of the world use referenda, which are not used yet in Africa. Most countries that have elections for local government use constituency-based systems. Some scholars believe that proportional representation is more desirable to ensure the representation of nonterritorially based groups, associations, and interests in agrarian societies (Barkan 1995).

A recurring problem that impedes effective local voice via elections is the tendency of local participation to fragment into personalistic, religious, kin-focused, or patronage-oriented factions. Further complicating the incentive for local popular organization are situations where a proportion of local council membership is appointed by the central government (one-third in Ghana). Such appointees are often perceived as government representatives, as indeed they frequently are. Members of parliament are ex-officio members in a number of countries (Ghana and Kenya), which also blurs local voice. Women are given one-third representation in local councils in Uganda, but it is not clear this has led to policy outputs any more supportive of women's issues or priorities (Batkin 2001). The case for nomination is based on the need to promote political or social minorities as well as ensure the availability of special skills in local governments. Local elections are a relatively under-researched aspect of local governance in Africa, and many questions remain about how they may be best structured.

Local councils and executives. Elected councillors are expected to represent the interests of their local communities once elected to the council. In particular, local assemblies are expected to provide oversight over the executive. But in a number of countries (Nigeria, Ghana, Uganda, Zimbabwe, and Ethiopia), local executives exercise much more power than the legislature (Barkan 1998; Wunsch 2001a; Crook and Manor 1998). As with the central legislatures, local assemblies are often incapacitated in influencing the policy process or in holding the executive accountable. Budgeting and auditing processes and institutions are not designed to empower councils in carrying out their oversight functions. In most countries local councillors neither have the skills nor support facilities to enable them effectively to scrutinize local budgets or audit reports. They also lack effective sanctions to apply to local government executives. The result is that local government executives often become all-powerful—and use such powers to buy or coerce key legislative support. In this regard, many advocate that central governments should provide budgetary frameworks for localities and separate audit bodies. The latter has proven helpful, but national budgetary frameworks must remain quite general or they will preempt the local autonomy necessary if democratic decentralization is to be real (Ikhide 1995; IMF 2001; Batkin 2001; Steffensen and Trollegaard 2000).

In order to enhance the capacity of local assemblies, some countries and donors invest heavily in training local councillors how to perform their jobs—especially those relating to oversight functions (USAID 2001a; Taylor 1999). It is not clear how helpful this has been without parallel institutional reforms. Some countries also pay full-time salaries to councillors (Nigeria, Senegal) rather than sitting allowances (Uganda). The Ivorian case shows that it is not enough to have structures of democratic governance at the local level. In addition, it is important for political leaders to use such structures to engage organized interests within their constituencies. The local media, civil society, and political parties, when present, can help local democracy in this way, if they work in concert to build a tradition of accountable local executives and governance (Blair 2000).

As discussed in Chapter 1, several issues of council organization also must be addressed. These include the viability of its committee system, concentration of power in its leadership roles, and the autonomy and sufficiency of its resources vis-à-vis the executive. Also important are such mundane factors as its meeting frequency, the planning-budgeting calendar, its right to timely review budgeting documents, the councillors' educational qualifications, and the like. Councils are inherently vulnerable to collective action and principal-agent disabilities vis-à-vis executives, and weakness on any of these matters can leave them largely ineffective in asserting local government accountability to local communities (Crook and Manor 1998; Wunsch 2001b; Ayee 2002b; see also Chapter 6 of this book).

There are different council management systems. The most important forms are the weak-mayor and the strong-mayor systems. In the latter, the whole community elects the mayor or chair of the councils, who then serves in an executive rather than ceremonial capacity. The switch in 1996 from weak to strong mayors in Zimbabwean cities has helped to make local officials more accountable to the political executives. The Municipal Development Program (Eastern and Southern Africa) assisted the process. Neither of these systems has resolved some recurring problems of internal organization of local councils. For instance, Crook and Manor found strong mayors led to mayoral dominations of councils in Côte d'Ivoire, and Wunsch felt this was also the case in Uganda (Wunsch 2001b). The argument in theory has been that strong-mayor systems allow political executives to make the local bureaucracy more responsive (Blair 2000). However, they also may facilitate mayoral coalitions with the civil service to squeeze out local legislatures and sustain local elite capture of local governments. Weak-mayor systems, in contrast, have problems asserting council or mayoral control over bureaucratic personnel (Ostrom, Bish, and Ostrom 1988).

Size of local governments and voice. Large local government units are frequently regarded as better able to facilitate the provision of basic community—and in some cases regional—services. As a result, local government reforms have often consolidated local government units. But several countries have found that large size may stimulate interethnic conflict and widen the social distance between the citizens and the local governments, and thereby weaken public accountability. Nigeria discovered this when it undertook the reforms of 1976. Municipalities in the Republic of South Africa are currently being amalgamated into much larger structures with the hope that this will also achieve objectives of class and racial integration. However, this strategy also takes local government farther away from the people. Also, recent research has shown how it is not necessary to have large size in order to take advantage of economies of scale—as such opportunities can be developed through contracting and joint production of services (Ostrom, Schroeder, and Wynne 1993).

In some cases, sublocal government entities were created, but even those units may not effectively link what people see as their true local community and local government. Uganda's solution has been to create five tiers of local government. While this maximizes participation, as shown in Chapter 8, it is also administratively complex and calls for more trained personnel than are frequently available (Olowona et al. 2000; Wunsch 2001b). At this time, there appears to be no simple solution to this problem. However, it is fairly clear that overly large "local government" units are an oxymoron. Further experimentation with multilevel strategies that creatively allocate various functions to the most appropriate levels should be pursued.

Direct-voice strategies.   Many voice mechanisms discussed above have not performed as hoped, largely because they are indirect and based on the principle of representation. Several factors, some highlighted already, can impede this indirect form of voice-accountability. Direct-voice accountability systems have therefore been developed in a few countries, some of which appear to pay better dividends. They include the following:

• *Participatory budgeting.* This was originally developed in some Latin American cities (with Porto Alegro being the most famous) but is currently being promoted by two World Bank–initiated municipal development programs in Africa. There is one each for southern and eastern parts and the western and central parts of the continent. Under this system, a substantial part of the investment budget of a locality is subject to discussion and debate with members of the public (organized by neighborhoods or civic groups), and the decisions of these groups are binding on local governments. Such groups also hold periodic audit sessions to ensure that their preferences are correctly reflected. Entebbe and Jinja in Uganda are municipalities experimenting with this model.

As these are recently initiated experiments, it is too soon to evaluate their performance.

• *Service delivery surveys.* These have also regularly been used to audit the effectiveness of services received by citizens in Senegal, Uganda, and Ghana. Several developing countries in Asia (Singapore, Malaysia, and India) have used this to advantage in systematically improving the quality of services delivered to citizens by all governmental organs—central and local. While they appear promising, no full-scale surveys of their effectiveness are as yet available.

• *Social funds committees.* The failure of government agencies to deliver services aimed at cushioning the effect of SAPs for the poor has led to the creation of these organizations. These are user groups working in collaboration with government agencies to ensure that services are actually delivered as intended. A study of the Malawi experience shows that they help in effectively targeting social funds, but also have the potential to undermine as well as increase local government effectiveness and accountability. This depends on how they are implemented (Schroeder 2000). Namibia also compels all government agencies, including local and regional governments, to have citizens' service charters. The practice is yet to be evaluated but anecdotal evidence has been positive there, as well as in Uganda (World Bank 2000).

• *Local taxation, revenue sourcing, and "voice."* Local taxation and revenue raising are not organs of voice in the way a local council can be. Nonetheless, they can operate in ways that stimulate residents to exercise voice through local councils, using civil-society organizations, or even speaking as individuals. Unfortunately decentralization reforms have generally relied on central revenue transfers to fund local governments. While this strategy has worked to increase local government spending as measured by its proportion of national expenditures and GDP, it has tended to reduce citizens' voice. This is in part because such transfers are usually not transparent to members of the public. It is also likely that the very low level of local taxation means local residents are not much provoked to exercise voice on how taxes are spent (Wunsch 2002). Finally, since the vast majority of local budgets is spent on staff and facilities rather than services that actually reach the public, it would seem the cost of exercising voice on how that money is spent probably exceeds any probable benefits (World Bank 2000).

In general, African government tax systems are poorly developed both at national and local levels. In fact, local government taxes that are raised are mostly derived from poor people, with the rich excluded from effective taxation if they operate in the private or informal sectors. The introduction of value-added tax (VAT) in some countries has improved matters a little at the national level, but many local governments still do not tax either urban or rural property (Olowu 2000). This is partially due to the poor development of urban management systems but also due to the adverse effect of the intergovernmental fiscal transfers system. Formula are heavily skewed in favor of equality and needs, and provide no strong incentive for local revenue mobilization (Ikhide, Olowu, and Wunsch 1993; Ikhide 1995). However, user charges have been successfully implemented to finance some local services—such as basic education and health. On the basis of these successes, the United Nations Children's Emergency Fund (UNICEF) and the World Health Organization (WHO) worked with African governments to evolve the Bamako Health Initiative, which established revolving loans to finance primary health care (UNICEF 1995; WHO 2001). One important positive effect of this innovation was that it increased the voice of citizens who saw themselves as revenue payers in the management of a service (Guyer 1992; Ikhide 1995; Smoke 1999b). Ironically, this "political" function of local revenue mobilization often leads both central and local governments to shy away from such innovations. It would increase the transparency of government finances and stimulate public voice, and provide the accountability people would expect (Guyer 1992; Paul 1996). Ultimately, increased local taxation and local control over spending choices are critical ingredients to enhance voice in local governance.

• *Ombudsman/complaints bodies.* Many countries in Africa already operate complaint bodies at the national levels that provide opportunities for citizens to report grievances against public officials. Such bodies have been less successful than civil society–based organs such as public media in obtaining redress. Few countries make public hearings a standard practice for regulatory agencies, as is done in industrialized countries. This weakens these bodies' potential for redress of grievances. Burkina Faso, Mauritania, and South Africa make good use of local complaint bodies. In Botswana and Nigeria, as well as a number of other countries, traditional leaders are assigned these roles (Ayeni 1994). This is a promising approach to enhancing voice, but one still generally in its infancy at the local level.

• *Local judicial or conflict-resolving agencies.* The institution of local bodies as judicial bodies—customary courts in many countries since the colonial period—has proven to be an effective governance form (Adu 1964). Field surveys show that such bodies are among the most popular institutions for the poor (Dia 1996). Ghana and South Africa have recently institutionalized local judicial bodies: they are cheap, accessible, and the concept of justice enforced is one of reconciliation rather than punishment (Sa'ad 1995). The Ugandan local government reforms were also praised for devolving adjudicatory powers to local actors (see Chapter 8). The Lagos state government in Nigeria has developed a highly popular conflict-resolution/mediation office staffed by volunteer lawyers to handle family and neighborhood disputes (USAID 2001b). Research in selected Asian and African countries (Nepal, India, Senegal, and Mali) on the decentralization of forestry management describes situations where effective local-level adjudication and conflict-resolution mechanisms have been developed. Marginal actors can make use of them when disputes arise and resolution can be achieved independent from systematic bias toward elite and sectoral interests (Agarwala and Ribot 1999; Narayan et al. 2001). These mechanisms enhance the "voice" of common citizens in local conflict-resolution processes. Their value lies both in enhancing local dwellers' voice in this function of governance, but also in the possibility that policy-relevant issues and decisions they generate will be heard by other institutions of collective choice.

• *Community-level government and social capital.* Local governments in Africa have rarely been based on subjective communities—i.e., the community of persons to which the average citizen feels the greatest ties and where he/she feels he/she belongs. Such communities are often small, but citizens of such communities have strong social attachments to them irrespective of where they actually reside, and share high levels of social capital among them (Barkan, McNulty, and Ayeni 1991; Olowu, Ayo, and Akande 1991; Dia 1996). Instead, local government units have been constructed around objective criteria such as minimum population size for delivering services. As a result, communities with their immense social capital and frequently with existing organs of collective choice are not tapped by the local government system. This is in spite of the generally agreed-upon fact that the single most important explanation for the success of township associations and the survival of communities when the state breaks down, as in Zaire or Somalia, is their social capital (Barkan, McNulty, and Ayeni 1991; Smock 1971). In contrast, large formal local government structures tend to be dominated by administrative personnel, as collective action problems impeding public organization at that level are rarely resolved. Moreover, "local" politics revolves around competition among the smaller communities for the largest share of the resources controlled by the large unit of local government. In some cases, such as Nigeria, the local governments are divided by intercommunity feuds as each community alleges mistreatment by the other communities within the larger local unit. This leads to disaffection and, in extreme cases such as the Rift Valley in Kenya or several local communities in Nigeria, violence erupts. This at times degenerates into national crises requiring intervention by military and security personnel. The case of Chad, as reported in Chapter 7, suggests that much might be made of community-level government and social capital, both to enhance "voice" and to improve local governance. Uganda's village units of governance also suggest this, as discussed in Chapter 8.

This section has reviewed a number of mechanisms that have been developed to enhance public participation and to contain the problem of local elite capture. These are difficult issues in all countries, and thus are in a way not peculiar to Africa. The problems are exacerbated in Africa, however, because of its poverty and history of patrimonialism (Haque 1997; Mitra 2001; Fiszbein 1997). The ineffectiveness of hierarchical controls as accountability strategies has meant that locally accountable mechanisms have become more important. Of these, voice-based mechanisms seem more viable in Africa's circumstances. As Tables 3.2 and 3.3 indicate, the prerequisites for effective exit or voice strategies are substantial, and in much of Africa are only incompletely reached. Adequate information, public organization, institutional openness, and the like are needed. Nonetheless, some successes have been recorded in efforts to build effective accountability structures in local government. However, they are threatened by two trends. First, there is the tendency to retreat to centralized solutions by designating central officials as chief executives of local governments, as seems to be the case in Ghana and in some dissolved Zimbabwean local governments. The second trend is the other extreme of creating elected local government chief executives who become political elephants and dominate local affairs. Either strategy surrenders the hope of effective local governance.

Conclusion

As Chapter 2 suggests, decentralization is not a new governance strategy for sub-Saharan Africa. It has been pursued with greater and lesser success several times. However, as African states weakened and in some cases collapsed during the 1980s and thereafter, as donors exerted pressure for improved governance, as ethnic and regional conflict grew and stubbornly resisted resolution, as civil society began to assert itself and call for democracy and improved governance, as urbanization exploded and more effective service delivery became paramount, and finally as the bankruptcy of centralist, top-down, single-party governance strategies became clear to many and new leadership emerged out of these changes, the *political* calculus of regime survival also changed. To be sure, many political actors at the center continue to resist democratic decentralization because it shifts resources and power away from them. And, in many cases, they will win. However, there are now factors also pushing toward democratic decentralization, and they will not be easily eliminated.

In this positive context, there remain several key challenges for democratic decentralization. These include the conceptual framework through which many of Africa's intellectual and political elites understand the modern state. The centralist, homogenizing, bureaucratic state model, while deeply challenged by the events of the last twenty years, has yet to be replaced by a coherent and convincing alternative. "Democracy," with all its operational complexities and propensity to such problems as immobility, elite capture, patrimonialism, and ethnic-related partisanship, is unlikely to suffice as a political or intellectual road map during these challenging times. In the disaffection that may come after "democracy" fails to solve Africa's problems, democratic decentralization could become a casualty. Similarly, the problems of persistent patrimonialism, the ambiguous position of traditional leaders, and the propensity of elites to capture local governance have yet to be resolved, and can suborn and delegitimize local governance.

In many ways, strengthening local accountability mechanisms is a step needed to resolve these problems. Effective local accountability requires community activism and organization, *and* institutions open and effective in responding to the issues raised. Strong and broadly based patterns of accountability can counteract elite dominance and challenge local patrimonial capture of resources. By implication, strengthened democratic local governance institutions may help sustain national democracy through this difficult era.

However, Africa has not made much progress in developing effective accountability at the local level. Using the "exit-voice" framework, this chapter suggested that exit strategies largely do not fit African conditions. Voice strategies have been utilized in many African states, but are generally in their infancy. Local councils have the greatest experience, and while they face operational problems, progress has been made in some areas. If democratic decentralization can sustain the momentum of the last two decades, this and other mechanisms of accountability may be able to alter the political calculus at the local level in the same way the national calculus has changed.

Notes

1. A UNDP (2000:5) report states that it allocates about half of its resource funds for supporting good governance activities, and that this shift has been accompanied by a recognition "that governance begins in communities, villages and towns."

2. "One important factor in favor of the opposition parties (in Botswana) is urbanization" (Molutsi 1998:370). On this basis he predicts a gradual shifting of support for BDP over time, a prediction that is increasingly becoming real.

3. The six countries were: Ghana and Senegal in the west, Uganda and Zambia in the east, and Zimbabwe and Swaziland in the south.

4. In a few African cases, primarily in large cities characterized by unusually rich associational life, well-resourced and highly mobilized citizens, and extensive revenue bases, Smoke and Olowu find instances where this dynamic seems to have been broken. However, the infrequency of this and the substantial contextual differences seem to validate rather than erode this model. See Olowu and Smoke 1992.

5. Crook and Manor's fine comparative study of decentralization in South Asia and West Africa does find more "corruption" of elected officials in South Asia than West Africa. In South Asia there are far larger "stakes" at hand as local governments in India and Bangladesh spend larger sums than those typical of West African local governments. However, there are also many differences, so the inferences should be tentative (Crook and Manor 1998). Elected officials in Nigerian local government also appear more corrupt than those in Ghana and Côte d'Ivoire, and more funds are also spent by local governments in Nigeria than in these other two West African states (Mead 1996; Ikhide, Olowu, and Wunsch 1993). Again, however, there are many other differences, including the extreme political and economic turbulence experienced by Nigeria over the last three decades.

6. This section benefits from Olowu 2003.

7. The six-nation study was conducted by the National Association of Danish Local Authorities into fiscal decentralization and subnational finance in six African countries. The study was supported by the World Bank and USAID.

4

South Africa and Botswana:
The Impact of National Context

C hapter 1 of this volume outlined a four-part model of the prerequi- sites or preconditions for the emergence of what it defined as "local governance." This model includes:

- Local resource availability.
- Local autonomy and authority.
- Local accountability through an open and public political process.
- Effective local institutions of collective choice.

This working model was applied and tested during a period of exploratory field research on southern African local government in one of the ten provinces of South Africa (Mpumalanga Province), and in several local government units in Botswana. Each research site was assessed in a preliminary fashion for the *resources* available to selected localities, the *autonomy and authority* devolved to localities, the *viabili- ty of the local public-accountability process*, and *effective local institu- tions of collective choice*. Finally, in a preliminary test of the model, effective performance by local governance was also appraised among these units. The last was measured in two ways: management and oper- ations (planning, budgeting, auditing, personnel management), and service delivery in such areas as health, housing, roads, and education. It was expected that the more fully developed local governments were in each of the four criteria, the more effective local government per- formance would be. The variables were measured via a multi-indicator, multimethod strategy. This included over two hundred interviews with local officials, political personnel, leaders of civil society organizations, and academic and donor personnel, and site observation, including equipment, maps, meetings, and personnel and business meetings. It also included a review of appropriate documents, including plans, budgets, personnel systems, audits, minutes of meetings and the like, done over a six-week period in 1995–1996. While South Africa is a quasi-federal system, and Botswana is unitary, the relationship between the local units of government and the provinces in South Africa is not unlike that between localities and the state in Botswana. Thus, while this variable is not held constant, it is comparable.

The evidence presented in this chapter suggests that effective local governance requires the achievement of high levels on each of these variables. Furthermore, it suggests that reaching these requires a gradual and lengthy process, where the center supports localities (though it must not dominate them), and many missteps are likely along the way. It particularly emphasizes that this process cannot be separated from national political context. This includes national commitment to democracy, lawful governance, and consistent policies and administration.

South Africa: Mpumalanga Province

Although the dramatic events in South Africa may be familiar to most people, the laborious process by which a new structure for local government was hammered out in negotiations through 1993 is not as well known. The Local Government Negotiating Forum (LGNF) was often overshadowed by the more dramatic national interim constitutional negotiations, but many believe its results will have as great (or greater) impact on the new South Africa (Pycroft 1996). The major players in the LGNF were the South African National Civic Organization (SANCO) and the National Party. These comprise the national federation body that grew out of the informal "civics" that arose in the black urban areas of South Africa during the 1980s. They both drove the apartheid governmental authorities out of the black urban areas and provided some level of local governance. The Nationalist Party was of course the ruling party of South Africa from 1948 until the African National Congress (ANC) took power in the free election of 1994. Both were galvanized into discussions by the obvious conflict and stalemate that existed between Africans and the minority-dominated local governments. Their search for a mutually acceptable solution led to the Local Government Transition Act of 1993 and relevant provisions of the 1993 Interim Constitution Act, and since then to the final constitutional settlement. The major consequence of these acts for local government was the establishment of varying institutional frameworks for local government (metropolitan, urban, rural), all of which provided for: nondiscriminatory participation in local political affairs; a partial-proportional representation system for local elections in the former white, Asian, "Coloured," and black areas; a guaranteed and substantial role for local government; and a process for amalgamating former white, Asian, "Coloured," and black jurisdictions in an institutional framework that placed most operational responsibility on the formerly white executive and managerial structures, the ones that had been best resourced and were most institutionally developed (Cloete 1994; Pycroft 1996). The final constitution of 1996 essentially maintained this structure (Cameron 1997).

For all this substantial progress, the South African national political framework and context still presented significant challenges to local governance in the 1995–1996 era, and in fact continue to do so into the post-2000 era. While the fundamental transition in power has gone far better than any but the most optimistic would have predicted before 1990, many legislative, policy, and organizational issues critical to providing a stable framework for local governance to emerge are unresolved.

At the time the research on which this chapter is based was completed, the administrative and political roles of the province regarding localities were unclear, the scale and focus of the Reconstruction and Development Program (RDP) was not known, the boundaries of many local governments were unclear, and the scale and pace of efforts to provide a civil service more reflective of the population was ambiguous. Also, little had been done regarding the need to build a more developmental, service-oriented, publicly accountable, and antipoverty-focused culture within the public service. Intergovernmental relations, particularly between the national and local levels, was undefined beyond the vaguest of pronouncements.

Even as this volume goes to press, as Robert Cameron and Chris Tapscott (2000), Paseka Nicholo (2000), John Bardill (2000), Tapscott (2000), Malcom Wallis (1990), Job Mokgoro (2000), C. Pycroft (1999, 2000), and Richard Simeon and Christina Murry (2001) have explained, most of these problems remain, while new ones have developed. As Bardill notes, the pace of change has been slow, there has not been a clear vision for change, leadership has been ineffective at times, and strategic management has not been effective. Tapscott finds particular weaknesses in intergovernmental relations, poor coordination among various levels and departments of government, and thus poor reform and program performance. These findings were underscored by the Presidential Review Commission, established in

1996, which also emphasized the lack of a clear policy framework for intergovernmental relations as well as the continued existence of substantial legislation from the apartheid era as hindrances to developing dynamic and effective local governance. It also noted that personnel and organizational weaknesses at the provincial level worsened these problems. Generally, provincial governments simply could not plan or implement multisectoral programs, thus weakening the support they could offer local governance (Cameron and Tapscott 2000). Mokgoro reiterates the weaknesses of provincial governance, particularly in policy analysis and management (2000), while Pycroft (1996, 1999) emphasizes the numerous structural, personnel, and fiscal weaknesses local governance faces in the current era, and the critical leadership *national* government must provide if these are to be resolved successfully.

Problems at the national level that have affected the evolution of local governance in South Africa include the frequency with which national policy and directives are imposed on provinces and localities without regard for their specific situations, such as the overtime burdens placed on them by the Basic Conditions of Employment Act of 1997 (Mokgoro 2000), and the disruption metropolitan areas have experienced over the abrupt changes in the organizational options from which they were allowed, and then were not allowed, to select for their governance structures. Cameron (2000) feels the central directives that overruled the 1993 Local Government Transition Act two-tier system and then established a compulsory unitary system (Local Government: Municipal Structures Act of 1998) were highly disruptive to metropolitan governance. Also, the ongoing tension between the growth and redistribution emphasis of the RDP and the macroeconomic stabilization emphasis of the Growth, Employment, and Redistribution program of June 1996 have also had a disruptive impact on local governance. The latter's emphasis on cost cutting, right-sizing, and privatization has grown from a far more budget-driven emphasis than local leaders anticipated from the promises of the RDP (Bardill 2000), and has left them uncertain as to what programs they could pursue. Finally, Pycroft (1999, 2000) believes the ANC government faces strong internal divisions in its core support base that threaten its ability to solve these problems.

Nonetheless, in general, South Africa's macropolitical context has remained remarkably stable and consistent in its progress toward liberal democracy, and local governments have certainly not been threatened by challenges to the rule of law or to democracy, nor by wholesale reduction in their powers (Cameron and Tapscott 2000). While the economy has stagnated, it has not experienced the problems of Nigeria or, in the past, of Ghana, Uganda, or Chad. However, the policy, administrative, and institutional contexts were uncertain in 1995–1996, and seem to have continued to be so in the seven years following. This may be expected to hinder, though certainly not prevent, the evolution of effective local governance. In general, then, the rules that structured and organized local governance were in flux, but regarding certain core elements in the postapartheid era, were remarkably stable: rule of law, democratic rights, and regular elections.

Research Site

Nelspruit is one of the municipalities in Mpumalanga Province (formerly the Eastern Transvall). It is located in the eastern part of Mpumalanga Province, a generally fertile agricultural region of rolling hills. Only 50 kilometers from the world-famous Kruger Game Park, it has a diversified economy based on agriculture, services, tourism, and light industry. Formerly a largely white municipality of 24,000 people (22,000 white, 1,000 Asian, 1,000 "Coloured"), following the amalgamation typical of most midsize urban areas in 1994, it grew to an estimated 250,000 with the addition of two former "homeland" townships, Kayanmazane and Matsulo, each with approximately 65,000 people, and various peri-urban areas. Additionally, it has become more of a regional local government then a municipality, as it now stretches from Nelspruit to Matsulo, a distance of some 50 kilometers.

In addition to this substantial growth in population, racial diversity, and size, the new Nelspruit faced several other significant changes. These included the recent election of new legislative personnel and of the (largely ceremonial) mayor, vastly expanded service responsibilities for Nelspruit in the former black townships, and an enlarged personnel system that included personnel from both the former white and black local government units. All this occurred within continued ambiguity regarding the role of the new provincial governments, the status of the former "homeland" areas still under rural council rule, and the size of central government revenue subventions to be allocated to upgrade and develop the former black townships. In all these things, Nelspruit is typical of a large number of nonmetropolitan municipalities in South Africa. For these reasons, it made a good choice for an intensive research site to look in depth at local governance in contemporary South Africa.

In this section, we use the factors outlined in the last section to analyze local government in Nelspruit, Mpumalanga Province.

Local resources. For a long time, the Nelspruit area has been a resource-rich government unit. The personnel staffing local government are highly educated, professionally qualified, and experienced. Their facilities are modern, spacious, comfortable, and equipped with computers, software, and personnel able to manage and use them.

The municipality supports generous services (public utilities, roads, economic development, planning, housing sites, etc.) to the Nelspruit population, which is virtually entirely white, from a local tax base that has typically generated 130 million rand (around U.S.$45 million per year). This budget has been adequate to provide services, to staff the local civil-service personnel slots, and to service whatever capital borrowing the locality chose to make.

Future resource adequacy is less clear. The revenue base, which is composed of property taxes ("rates") and water and electricity service fees, has limited scope for expansion. Rates are set primarily on site value rather than improvements, and payroll taxes, sales taxes, and income taxes are particularly difficult to implement and not under consideration at the regional and national levels that would need to authorize them for local use. Revenue allocations from the national government are uncertain and will almost surely be limited in size to a small portion of local needs. The much-awaited grants from the RDP are likely to meet only a small portion of the needs (Cameron 1996). But local needs will grow *enormously* with the vast increase in local population caused by municipal amalgamation. The possible addition of what was called the "traditional areas"—nearby areas formerly administered by the defunct African "homelands"—will add to Nelspruit's responsibilities (Pycroft 1996; Cloete 1994). Revenue sources in the former black townships are limited given the poverty there and the culture of "non-payment," the refusal of Africans to pay water and electrical charges and any rates/taxes due in urban areas to protest apartheid. Additionally, the municipality has already experienced a substantial increase in personnel costs with amalgamation with the former black townships.

The 1997 budget estimates by Nelspruit's government suggested that capital investment needs (roads, water, sewers, street lights) for the former black townships now added to Nelspruit were 220 million rand (approximately U.S.$75 million). The current capital budget was 35 million rand (approximately U.S.$12 million), leaving a 185 million rand capital budget shortfall. Operating or current costs are estimated to be 150 million rand (approximately U.S.$52 million), which leaves a 30 million rand shortfall from the current operating budget of 120 million rand. This was a bare-bones budget proposal, essentially only to continue those minimal services offered in the townships, not to upgrade the areas to Nelspruit standards. Overall, then, Nelspruit has been a well-resourced local government. However, it faces serious challenges in the immediate future as the ratio of resources to needs has changed.

Local autonomy and authority. Historically, Nelspruit, like other white municipalities, was a powerful juridical body. Working within broad parameters set by central government, it hired personnel, levied and raised taxes, established budgets, set local service priorities and development strategies, borrowed funds (with central Ministry of Finance approval) for capital development, and the like (Cameron n.d.). According to the interim constitution of 1995 (Chapter 10 and Section 245), provincial legislators must not "encroach on local government to such an extent that it compromises the fundamental status, purpose and character of local government" (Cloete 1994:44–45). Broad statutory, regulatory, and executive powers were also established in the interim constitution for local governments to enable them to provide for local welfare, and to raise money through various taxes, fees, levees, etc. (Cloete 1994). The new constitutional framework does not seriously change the authority of local government. However, the amalgamations that grew from the LGNF process fundamentally changed the political dynamics at the locality, as they brought about black majority control. In this regard, Nelspruit is facing many of the same challenges that the many other newly reorganized municipalities face in contemporary South Africa.

The major potential change on the horizon is the newly established Mpumalanga provincial government. While Nelspruit civil-service personnel are almost 100 percent white (except for the generally junior-grade personnel absorbed from the black municipalities), the provincial personnel are virtually 100 percent black. How the provincial government will relate to Nelspruit (and other cities like it) over the long run is unclear, as the agenda of the two groups might well be expected to diverge, and as it might be expected over time to encroach on Nelspruit's accustomed independence.

In the short run, however, in 1996 the provincial government was in confusion stemming from its recent establishment. It was unclear as to its own role and legal authority, preoccupied with hiring personnel, and involved in disagreements over priorities. At this time, the provincial government has had little impact on municipal governments, and personnel interviewed in provincial government did not aspire to interfere much in municipal government. Provincial personnel did not review municipal budgets, personnel decisions, municipal priorities, tax rates, etc. In 1996, the provincial personnel in Mpumalanga believed these were best left to the municipal political process to decide.

Local accountability. The established (and of course historically very limited) process of accountability was largely rendered irrelevant by the "new dispensation" after 1994. The latter has probably quintupled the electorate, and introduced many "new" groups and interests to Nelspruit's government. However, the representative institutions (council) and linkage institutions (political parties and civil society) between the population and the municipality are still underdeveloped. Furthermore, institutional arrangements now in place to facilitate these are flawed in their design, while the interest groups organized at the grassroots level are still weak and fragmented.

The ANC, whose leadership heads Nelspruit's council, is the strongest single political party in the area. Nonetheless, ANC's local strength was compromised by a large Nationalist Party delegation in the council and by alleged tension between it and SANCO. There was a conflict in the former black townships between elected and defeated ANC council candidates. At the time of this research, the ANC did not appear to be developing a coherent agenda for local government and its policies or activities.

A large number of nongovernmental organizations and personnel from the "civics"—grassroots organizations of the antiapartheid era movement—have survived the transition and are more or less active. Though loosely organized, SANCO elected several persons to the council. Their cohesion and cooperation there, and any coordinating role for SANCO, appeared questionable at the time of this research. The political interest and capacity of the local voluntary organizations was also uncertain. Composed of women's groups, sports clubs, student organizations, anti-AIDS efforts, and the like, their organizations often depended on the efforts of a single person or a small leadership circle, and were financially precarious and at times deeply dependent on shrinking donor funding. They and the civics tended to look to the national rather than the local government for their needs. In general, these groups were not yet emergent "local publics" that might attend to local government policy, nor had they been major players in the recent local elections. They had little knowledge of local government policies, programs, and resources they might tap, or that might affect them.

Probably the most coherent and organized component of the African community was a number of black local business owners. They had been working for several years with Asian and some white business firms to increase their access to capital and expand marketing opportunities via a local multiracial chamber of commerce. How their agenda and the pressing needs of the largely poor and unemployed or underemployed black population might cohere into a single political force was also not clear at the time of this research. To summarize, a broadly based and effective local political process after the postapartheid 1995 local elections had not yet taken root in Nelspruit.

Local institutions of collective choice. The municipal council is the only legislative body at the local level. The effective chief executive is a civil servant, the town clerk. The mayorship is an honorary office, filled by election from the council, and without any executive powers. While the council does have full authority over local budgetary and programmatic decisions, in Nelspruit its effectiveness in encouraging and focusing a local political process remains in doubt.

With forty members and a meeting only monthly, the council is a large and only part-time body. It is not clear how well it will be able to connect public wants and concerns with municipal administration. It has no staff, and its members have no offices. Its only committee is a fifteen-person "management committee" that meets three or four times monthly, but it is also without staff or office facilities. Furthermore, the personnel are largely new to public office: in Nelspruit in 1996, thirty-six of the forty members had never held public office before. Debates and discussions at this time remained reactive to executive proposals, and largely ineffective.

Existing municipal procedures reinforce the powers of the town clerk. The council only sees the budget as a finished document. The absence of functionally specialized committees reduces its effectiveness in analyzing the implications of the proposed budget for programs and services. Miscellaneous other problems also appear likely to hinder the council. Most of the members live long distances from the Nelspruit city facilities, and must use unreliable and slow public transport to journey from home to the offices. Furthermore, most must continue employment elsewhere, further pulling them away from time to learn and follow municipal government. At an intangible level, councillors face the challenge of constructing new roles, both for themselves and for a formerly placid, service-oriented city government. They must also deal with a limited budget and constituencies with increased expectations and limited experience in the process of democratic governance. Existing rules regarding council organization and operations did not effectively engage these problems.

In contrast to the weak council, the executive branch of the Nelspruit municipality is a highly organized and sophisticated governance institution. The planning, programming, budgeting, managerial, and auditing functions appeared to be well designed and implemented. Municipal officials were knowledgeable about the details of their budgets, one another's responsibilities, the general budgetary implications of the spatial reorganization, and the challenges of training and working with a town council that has many members entirely new to politics.[1] An effective balance between the legislative and executive arms does not appear to exist. In part this may be seen as a result of poor design of the legislative body.

Local government effectiveness. Budgeting, planning, and management support services (human resources, property management, purchasing) function well for this historic Nelspruit local government. Its inclusion of the new former "township" areas is less developed. Budgetary figures (estimates, expenditures, operating capital, and revenue budgets) were easily available, and estimates and actuals were very close, reflecting good planning and performance. "Structure Plans" (general land-use plans) and "Town Planning Schemes" (zoning regulations) were available, up-to-date, and of professional quality. Revised plans were in progress. The Management Service Office had accurate and timely data on personnel budgets and was trying to solve the management problems of integrating civil-service personnel from the old homelands (black townships) with the Nelspruit personnel. The town planner was occupied with the challenges of planning for the new areas of responsibility. Offices were well organized, well staffed, and had sufficient resources. However, as noted above, operations had not developed to nearly the same level regarding Nelspruit's new borders and responsibilities.

The town clerk (city manager) was well versed in the conditions and priorities of the newly added areas.[2] He could discuss the challenges he faced: balancing revenue versus expenditures; strengthening personnel management; reconciling traditionally European versus African communication patterns (i.e., formal/gazette style versus grassroots consultations and discussion); educating the new town council; and developing working relationships with the new mayor and the new chair of the Council Management Committee (the key legislative-oversight role). In 1995, the relationships among all three were positive and cordial. All these patterns are indicators of a stable bureaucracy, with the capacity to identify problems, set priorities, develop programs and budgets, and implement them in a relatively transparent and efficient way. Nonetheless, neither words nor actions had yet to be reflected in a redefined and refocused bureaucracy.

As well as these incomplete managerial and organizational dimensions, Nelspruit was not at all effective in delivering services to its new constituents. It was not even preparing to begin doing so. Specifically, while local officials maintained they were thinking frequently about this "new era," they did not appear to be engaging in serious reprogramming of *resources* to meet their new responsibilities. So far, some personnel had been redeployed, but only from the former black areas to the Nelspruit office, a 50-kilometer distance. There was no clear plan to reconfigure those offices to improve and expand services to the new areas, and adjust to becoming in effect a regional government. Similarly, officials appeared to be approaching the coming budgetary process with largely incremental assumptions. Existing programs and investments that focused on Nelspruit town would be marginally modified to reflect the reorganization, but there was no evidence of a fundamental reconsideration of resource or service flow, or of changed personnel responsibilities. Officials in Nelspruit repeatedly emphasized the need for revenues to expand in the new areas before services could be expanded. There were no plans to reconfigure service priorities to reflect the needs of the new areas.

This lack of plans to improve service delivery could be considered in light of the fact that officials had already swallowed a substantial increase in fiscal responsibility in absorbing and achieving salary parity for the former homeland personnel with only a one-time grant from the provincial government to help. And with the new area-wide council that was to begin functioning in January 1996, any specific planning might have been premature. Additionally, ambiguity regarding possible national development grants and such specific problems as the town's authority in traditional areas had also worked to leave the civil servants in uncertainty. Even so, the embrace of the status quo by Nelspruits' executive personnel appeared rather unrealistic and improvident. This difficulty in adapting to a new, development-oriented role has been noted elsewhere in Africa by G. Mutahaba (1989).

Botswana

Botswana is an important case for any study of decentralization, as it has sustained at least a limited form of democracy since independence, as well as some twenty years of commitment to decentralization. In fact, in October 1994 Botswana marked its sixth open and more or less competitive election since independence, a record unmatched throughout Africa (Danevad 1995). With an equally impressive economic growth rate, the highest in the developing world from 1965 to 1989 (World Bank 1989c), Botswana offered an environment that was to prove supportive for local and democratic governance.

While observers debate the nature and extent of democracy in Botswana (Picard 1987; Holm 1987; Tordoff 1988; Parson 1991; Danevad 1995; Good 1996), none deny that Botswana has been exceptional in its political openness, competition, and adherence to law (*Africa Today* 1993). It is particularly notable and unusual in its acceptance of political competition at the local level, and has established a climate where a local political process has been unusually viable. Even given the elite's capture of a disproportionate share of Botswana's growth proceeds, it has offered an unusually high flow of resources to local governments.

As Picard (1987) and Tordoff (1988) note, local government has a long history in Botswana. While it suffered in the early postindependence era from many of the same problems local government faced elsewhere in Africa, strategic choices made by the political center avoided the centralization seen in most of Africa. In 1970, with central government confidence in local councils at a low point, and with a bureaucratic battle raging over the future of local government between the Ministry of Finance and Development Planning and the Ministry of Local Government and Lands, the Tordoff Commission recommended that council staffing and finance be substantially improved. Its recommendations were adopted, and since then local government has been a major component of Botswana's political system (Picard 1987). In these regards, the rules that structured Botswana's local-governance system have been largely stable and supportive. However, as this case study will indicate, and as other scholars agree (Sharma 2000), local government there still faces challenges and has substantial room for improvement.

Local resources. While overall resources are higher than found in most of Africa, local revenue sources are currently very limited. Rural districts raise funds primarily through fees for services, small business licenses, and rents for council-owned housing. Urban districts also have these sources, but their primary source of funding is property rates. Urban authorities cover their budgets better than rural districts do, mainly because of their use of property rates. Nonetheless, if Gaborone is typical of Botswana's urban authorities, even urban revenue collection is weak (Peters-Berries 1995).

A serious problem is the failure to levy service fees comparable to service costs. One of the causes of this failure is the absence of an effective system to determine the actual costs of these services. Another is the limited authority that local government has to set fees, as the Ministry of Local Government, Land, and Housing (MLGLH) or other central ministries control fee levels for most local services. Another problem is a tendency of local personnel to assume that national government will cover their financial shortfalls (Peters-Berries 1995). The local government tax, an income tax, was previously in place but was rescinded at the height of the diamond-mining boom. A new local government tax and the extension of rate authority to the district councils appear to be the most viable options for new local revenue. For the moment, national revenue transfers are substantial and cover extensive local programs. Botswana's ability to sustain these in the future, though, may be a problem.

The quality of local government staff is quite impressive with regard to diversity of personnel slots authorized and filled at the local level (medical officer, planner, attorney, economist, chief of staff, etc.), their paper qualifications, and their demonstrated competence and professionalism. With the exception of "industrial class" employees (primarily laborers and other unskilled personnel), all local government personnel have been hired and managed by the Unified Local Government Service (ULGS) since 1973. ULGS is managed by an establishment secretary and secretariat, housed in MLGLH. The salaries of these personnel (about 23–35 percent of local government personnel) are also paid by the national ULGS, which eases the local budget burden. Other personnel are the responsibility of local councils (SIDA 1993; Dahlgren et al. 1993). The effectiveness of these personnel seems likely to be a result of the effective intergovernmental systems that link MLGLH and the local governments. Of course, as noted below, this same ministry as well as the Finance Ministry appear as well to circumscribe local autonomy.

One concern regarding personnel and administrative systems is the breadth of coverage with qualified personnel. Other researchers have noted that less competent personnel are in place in the remote areas, and that many intermediate posts are vacant throughout the ULGS. If these vacancies are widespread, they will weaken local governance (SIDA 1993; Dahlgren et al. 1993).

Local authority. This case deserves more-detailed attention than South Africa's because the issues regarding local authority in Botswana parallel closely those of local governments throughout Africa. Botswana's experience shows how apparent "authority" can be illusory, and the consequences of this.

The MLGLH is the "parent" ministry of all local government in Botswana. As Botswana is a unitary state, local government has no constitutional status and is a purely statutory creation. Within these statutes, MLGLH plays key roles in virtually every aspect of local government. These include controlling or supervising most key decisions regarding local personnel, budgeting, development planning, self-help projects; ensuring conformity with national policies and priorities; providing training; developing new revenue sources; and developing new managerial systems and procedures. Even when local governments seek greater autonomy, their primary spokesperson and advocate (and occasionally, foe) is MLGLH. Thus this ministry is critical for all aspects of local governance in Botswana.

The ULGS hires, assigns, promotes, disciplines, discharges, and transfers all nonindustrial personnel. This system is responsible for ensuring that all areas have adequate personnel and discouraging any tendencies toward ethnic concentration of personnel. However, there are numerous criticisms of the system's appropriateness for local governance. Specific problems are the lack of control that local governments believe they have over selecting congenial and committed personnel, and the disruptive impact that the transfer system has on local affairs and the lives of local personnel, particularly of women.

In our interviews at three local governments, the same complaints were made by legislative and administrative personnel: arbitrary and abrupt transfers of personnel were disruptive to local projects and programs, smooth administrative functioning, team building, morale, and to the employees' lives. Town secretaries and councillors in particular complained about being unable to ensure that they were assigned personnel committed to their goals and familiar with their particular needs and problems. These patterns were also noted by Picard (1987). Since ULGS's control extends to personnel training, development, and performance appraisals, local authorities rely on government training centers that are managed by MLGLH. Supervisors must receive permission from the ULGS to send employees to training workshops. The result is that a request for training must compete against similar requests made by all other local authorities. Limited resources lead to many requests for training being denied or delayed. Recent changes, however, are gradually expanding local control over junior appointments. By the end of the current national development plan, 85 percent of local government posts are to be filled and administered by local authorities. However, this does not address the most pressing concern of local officials: the senior staff. Some type of national-local civil-service system may be needed to give security and homogeneity of service, to help ensure professional competency, and to maintain links between sector ministries (i.e., health and education) and local officials. However, an end to arbitrary and rigid transfers, greater deference to hiring choices of localities and personnel, and improved status vis-à-vis the national civil service are also needed.

From one perspective, local governments already largely control their budgeting. Localities are entirely responsible for preparing their annual estimates. MLGLH reviews budgets primarily for arithmetic accuracy, to ensure that none are in deficit, and for conformity with national policies regarding personnel (that certain posts are filled, certain teacher-pupil rations are followed, certain health facilities, etc., are staffed). Of course, pay levels must be met, along with other benefits. Emergency conditions such as a recent drought may require certain extra activities and funding by local governments. And new and existing centrally directed capital investments (schools, boreholes, sewage systems, clinics, roads) must be staffed and maintained. Still, within these guidelines, local governments prepare their own budgets.

But what does local governments' control over their budgets really amount to? At every site visit, local officials (both professional/administrative and political) agreed that MLGLH's oversight actually left them with little autonomy. In fact, recurrent commitments are so high and so driven by policy decisions made in Gaborone that local officials believed they had virtually no latitude at all to identify and respond to their own unique priorities and problems. Local needs that they deemed to be particularly pressing (such as absence of storm drains to solve flooding problems in one area, health initiatives in another, low-cost housing in a third, etc.) were ignored because all revenues were already committed elsewhere. Salary and vehicle costs alone were so high that little was left over for any local initiatives (Peters-Berries 1995). If a problem was not on the agenda of a national ministry with the ability to channel funds to meet the need, it was not addressed. If such ministries felt that something should be done, it was usually accomplished regardless of local priorities (Briscoe 1995; Chanaux-Repond and Kanengoni 1995). Local professional personnel felt discouraged by this. Local political leaders felt that their work was futile and that they were unable to respond to their constituents. J.R.A. Ayee found similar problems in Ghana (1992b, 1997b), as did Vicki Clarke (2001).

In contrast to recurrent budgets, the status of capital budgets was unambiguous. These were clearly determined through a top-down process, with the Ministry of Finance and Development Planning (MFDP) telling the MLGLH how much was available in each sector area (health, education, roads, etc.) for local projects. MLGLH then apportioned it to the local governments. They, in turn, reported that most of these grants were consumed by investments required by national ministry norms. In any case, MLGLH decided which projects would be funded, so that local governments were uninvolved in policymaking, despite the fact that these decisions also had significant implications for local governments' recurrent budgets (Picard 1987). This is similar to patterns noted elsewhere in Africa by Olowu (1990a).

Central regulation and oversight also impede the timely completion of capital projects. Before starting a project, local authorities must submit a project memorandum to the MLGLH. The ministry then forwards the memorandum to the MFDP for approval. There is no assurance that the project will be funded in a timely manner or in its entirety. For example, in Kweneng, 20 million pula (approximately U.S.$8 million) was requested for an approved capital project, but the district received half that amount. Lobatse often experiences a six to seven-month delay in the receipt of capital funds after it submits project memoranda. Once a project memorandum has been approved, ceilings are provided for each capital project. The limits are often incompatible with the financial requirements of the proposed project. The central government also requires authorization and appropriation for each certificate of payment to release funds. Thus, projects with multiple contractors often force local authorities to make repeated requests and trips to the center for payment of invoices. The tedious and time-consuming process can be costly to local authorities, since contractors who have not been paid within twenty-one days of the execution of a contract may assess interest against the amount they are owed. Delays in the receipt of funds or the payment of invoices for contractors often cause problems for development projects. This of course follows the "repetitive budgeting" model noted by Caiden and Wildavsky (1973).

Thus capital projects have remained a cumbersome, centralized process for local governments. A local process ostensibly designed to register, assess, and encourage local development (i.e., each locality has a senior economic development officer and engages in a grassroots development process) has in effect been prevented from fulfilling this promise, making local government appear rather irrelevant to any critical eyes.

In the past, district and urban planning were not at all coordinated with the national development plan. The district and national plans covered different periods and were prepared at different times. The consensus is that district plans rarely affected national plans, which ultimately controlled all investment decisions (Chanaux-Repond and Kanengoni 1995). Indeed, local planning was mostly ignored (Briscoe 1995). One highly placed respondent reported that local development projects essentially were approved when they fit into the national ministry plans. However, national and district plans (in 1995) were being prepared simultaneously for the National Development Plan–8, and it appeared that efforts were being made to incorporate some local priorities via what they were calling "matrix planning." Strengthened input for localities in the capital investments of sectoral ministries is desirable if local governance and decentralization are to progress in Botswana.

As noted above, the MFDP plays a major role in local government. Because of local governments' overwhelming dependence on the central level for subventions to cover recurrent budgets, MFDP's role in determining the amount to be allocated to these grants (subventions) is extremely important. MFDP, of course, determines the amount of the capital development budget. While MLGLH allocates the shares to go to each local government, MFDP retains final authority to approve or deny any specific project (through the project memorandum requirement) and controls disbursement of revenues for each invoice as projects are implemented. In virtually every respect, local governments are subject to decisions made at the central level, through complex and often cumbersome processes.

Other ministries with major impact on local government include health and education. Unlike most African countries, Botswana's local governments are responsible for elementary education and primary health care. Personnel involved in delivering these services are employees of the local governments. Day-to-day management is provided by the local authority, which appears to discharge it rather competently.

There is, nonetheless, a strong ongoing role for the "parent" ministries in the area of health and education. They set staffing levels and standards, determine minimum equipment levels, provide ongoing training and professional support, and set conditions of service. In the case of the most professionally qualified service-sector employees (medical doctors), their subordination to the local governments' chain of command is not entirely clear to the parties concerned. Much of the redundancy of this situation is desirable. When primary health care was essentially separated from the national Ministry of Health in Nigeria, standards and morale were severely reduced in the field, and local government support was often inadequate (Olowu and Wunsch 1995). Still, too much central interference saps the vitality of local governance, as it becomes a meaningless exercise.

Local accountability. Local accountability is more developed in Botswana than in South Africa. Botswana has had uninterrupted democ-

racy and civilian rule since independence even though a single party has
dominated until recently. Nonetheless, the local public political process
is still unevenly developed.

Councillors employed several strategies to keep attuned to constituents. In Lobatse, they sponsored meetings in their wards to
exchange information with constituents. Councillors also held membership in civic organizations and reported that they use these affiliations
to stay informed of the concerns of the community. The Lobatse town
council is attempting to develop a newsletter on local government to be
widely circulated in the community. Councillors in Gaborone sponsored
forums in their wards. The mayor of Gaborone also toured the city with
members of parliament and visited each ward. In total, the mayor con-
vened twenty-five meetings and used the occasions as an opportunity to
gauge public sentiment on a variety of issues. Kweneng District councillors met with constituents in conjunction with regular sessions of the
council. There is little coordination of effort, however, between district
councillors and members of parliament.

Presently a number of civic and voluntary organizations function in
Botswana. Civic organizations such as the Lions Club, Rotary Club,
Youth Council, and church-affiliated organizations encourage self-help
and provide some limited local assistance. In Lobatse, the town council
awarded grants up to 18,000 pula to these small, community-based
organizations. The Gaborone City Council recently received permission
from the Ministry of Local Government, Land, and Housing also to provide small grants to civic organizations. Some of the larger organizations have offices, but most do not. It is not clear that these organizations, in 1995, were serving as serious linkage mechanisms between
citizen, elected official, and administrator. Some were dependent on
donor grants to survive. However, a base exists on which such a process
might develop.

Political parties were quite active at the local level at the time of this
research. Indeed, in each of the two urban sites visited, the majority of
the council was composed of the national opposition party. However, it
is not clear from our interviews that this was energizing governmental-
grassroots interaction, or leading to any new policy directions. There
appear to be few ideological or class differences between the two major
parties (Danevad 1995). Like civic and voluntary organizations, it
appears as more a latent structure that might become vitalized, perhaps
if local governments were to have more programmatic and policy discretion.

In Kweneng District councillors were articulate and clear as to their
roles in local government. The district councillors identified the follow-

ing functions as their primary responsibilities: meeting constituents and seeking feedback, informing the council of the needs of constituents, defending the council's decisions before constituents, advising constituents of council actions, meeting with village committees and village extension teams to determine needs, encouraging self-help among the constituents to avoid dependence on the council, increasing knowledge of government policy, and supporting each other as councillors.

Local institutions of collective choice. Municipal (urban) councils are the most developed popular institutions involved in the local political process. Councillors interviewed at three research sites seemed well-informed and interested in local administration. Nonetheless, they face challenges (as part-time officials) in keeping abreast of and contending effectively with full-time professional administrators whom they do not hire or fire, nor over whose programs they really have much control. The three councils visited utilize a similar committee structure to conduct business. Committees focusing on education, health care, social services, trades and licenses, and finance exist in Lobatse, Gaborone, and Kweneng. Committee members select the chairperson, and in Lobatse and Gaborone the mayor sits as an ex-officio member of all committees. The frequency of committee meetings varies. In Gaborone, council committees meet once a month, while in Kweneng the district council's committees meet in conjunction with the formal council sessions. However, as noted above regarding authority and autonomy, it does not appear that these bodies are actually effective in setting local priorities and leading significant collective action. They appear more ready to act when the central government appears willing to twist them to act. The position of mayor currently has little authority in Botswana.

Councillors are not as well prepared as administrators to discharge their duties. The separation of powers is unclear, and councillors do not have a command of pertinent public-policy issues. The fact that citizens do not have a direct financial stake in local government makes it less likely they will involve themselves in council oversight activities. Citizens who do not see a direct link to local government may simply discount the importance of local authorities. Councillors must simultaneously seek to solidify their position in local government and increase confidence in their representation among constituents.

Local government effectiveness. Local governance in Botswana presents a complex and mixed picture of local personnel and institutional capacity. On the positive side, a workable and working administrative structure is in place and, at least in the more accessible areas, is generally filled with competent personnel. In the governance of city, town, and district council affairs, this structure has been able to prepare and execute budgets dealing with the personnel, supply, and maintenance functions of several large, complex departments and activities. For the most part, they appear to manage these functions well, although often requiring supplemental payments and allocations to complete each year. Several written studies validated our findings (Peters-Berries 1995; Picard 1987; Tordoff 1988; SIDA 1993; Dahlgren et al. 1993).

Local authorities engage in local physical planning, prepare development plans with specific project proposals, and manage the implementation of a large number of capital projects on an annual basis. In doing so they must, among other things, deal with a slow, cumbersome bureaucratic process to obtain funds from MFDP, and balance the requirements of contractors, MLGLH, and MFDP. Achieving this balance in itself reflects substantial institutional and personnel capacity. In general, personnel interviewed were professional, knowledgeable about their responsibilities, and articulate about the problems of the local governance system. As a result, perhaps, local governments in Botswana have an excellent record of delivering such key services as water, education, and health care (Tordoff 1988; Holm 1987).

Another area of local activity is implementing relatively small, labor-intensive projects connected with the drought relief effort. According to several interviews and one study (Meyer 1995), local authorities exhibited some skill in doing this and in resolving personnel, fiscal, managerial, and technical problems in the process.

Consensus exists among written sources (Peters-Berries 1995; Chanaux-Repond and Kanengoni 1995; SIDA 1993) and local respondents that financial administration is the weakest point in local governance. Budget projections are frequently inaccurate, audits often as much as three years behind, and funds sometimes misallocated (i.e., capital funds into recurrent expenditures). In 1989–1990, only three of fourteen urban and district councils produced their final accounts on time. Only two received unqualified approval by auditors. Also, district councils have exerted few cost-saving measures, probably in part because of absence of incentives as well as shortfalls in capacity (Briscoe 1995). Other problems include minimal capacity to collect local revenues and little evidence of ability to analyze expenditure efficiency. The extremely poor cost recovery system for local services is an example of this. Also, estimates and actuals regarding locally collected revenues often differ by 100–200 percent (Briscoe 1995).

Local governments regularly apply for supplementary grants. Since these appear to be regularly approved, this may be as much a financial strategy as a problem of competent budgeting and expenditure control. Also, the need for grants often results from unpredictable natural events such as drought (Briscoe 1995).

The second area of weakness is personnel management. Respondents agreed that local governments were able to accomplish some routine tasks but believed them incapable of the range of personnel functions that complex personnel departments pursue. Personnel development, discipline to resolve difficult personnel problems, efficiency studies, reconfiguration of personnel assignments, and the like exceed present local capacity (SIDA 1993; Dahlgren et al. 1993). If there were to be a phased increase in local personnel responsibilities, such capacities would need to be enhanced.

A final concern at the local level is weak management information systems and a lack of programmatic focus at the local level in the various sectors. Local personnel, one key study found, did not conceptualize their areas in a strategic, problem-focused, and systematic sense. This may stem from the habit of expecting direction from the center and the reality of central dominance over planning and capital investment decisions. Regardless of the cause (central preemption or local passivity), there is little local strategic or programmatic initiative (Langlo and Molutsi 1994; SIDA 1993). These, however, are relatively sophisticated functions, and many local governments in the developed world could be similarly criticized.

Conclusion

Local governance in South Africa is entering a dynamic era of change. In applying this chapter's analytical framework to it, one finds it characterized by high levels of resources and authority, but with embryonic accountability processes undergoing rapid change. Historically, *local* accountability was viable, but only for the enfranchised and empowered white minority. That political process is obsolete, though remnants of it are still visible. The current postapartheid political process is weak at this local level in all respects: civil society, political parties, the legislative arena, information flows, and informed and active publics. National institutions, while becoming more democratic, were still embryonic and preoccupied with national problems. They were, in 1995–1996, exerting little leadership at the local level, while the very institutional structure local governments were to work within was still ambiguous.

Local government performance in Nelspruit reflects this transitional pattern. It has, for the moment, retained the managerial and organizational capacity of the old well-resourced system, but it has yet to begin redirecting its services and activities to the populations for which it is now responsible. In these regards, it confirms the model offered in the introduction to this chapter. Its performance, at least in delivering services, must be regarded as weak.

It is unlikely this situation will last for long. Popular expectations for help from local government are high. What is unclear is what, if anything, will emerge to create the new political process for Nelspruit's local government. Absent that, the technical and organizational excellence could be destroyed by public frustration and political rancor. Much of the local hesitancy by all players could be logically linked to the policy and organizational uncertainty of the national political framework. While the survival of constitutional democracy in South Africa seems highly likely, exactly what role, options, and opportunities might be available to local governments seemed uncertain in 1995–1996, as indeed they still seem in 2003.

In the second case, Botswana, local government displays unusually high levels of performance, both in its internal management and its record of delivering services (schools, water, roads, relief, health care) throughout most of the country. In each respect, it is unusual for Africa, and indeed for most of the developing world.

Contributing to this success are several key factors: a substantial and sustained flow of fiscal and personnel resources; a national climate that tolerates local party politics, an open and critical media, and activity by diverse voluntary and civic organizations; a stable legal environment and a sustained commitment from the center to maintaining real local government; and significant responsibilities (though limited authority) for local governments. The outcome of these factors are local governments able to perform many activities and functions, but personnel (both political and professional) frustrated by the encumbrances that prevent them from doing more. As a result of this last problem, it is not clear that the "time and place" information, which is the relative advantage of local governance units, is being used by the national ministries in their policy pronouncements. Nor is it clear that national ministries are inspiring localities to take initiative. It appears there is little or no flexibility for unique local problems, needs, and priorities, whether in diverging from national guidelines or in shifting resources from health and education into other areas. For example, health or education might be better served in an area by upgrading transportation rather than by building additional facilities or hiring more staff. Under the current system, recurrent budgets are largely prescribed by national policy, and capital budgets are entirely under national control.

Nonetheless, while local autonomy is limited and there are still personnel and operational weaknesses in Botswana's local government, it clearly has made vast strides, and appears the best of the two cases studies in providing quality local governance that responds to local needs.

This chapter began by reviewing the four-variable model developed in Chapter 1. It argued that four factors were necessary for effective local government: resources, authority and autonomy, an effective system of local accountability, and well-designed local institutions. Greater levels on each of these were expected to be positively associated with improved local government performance, with the latter including internal operations and delivery of services appropriate for local needs.

With only two case studies, it is of course impossible to test the many logically possible combinations of these variables. However, the two case studies did allow a preliminary test of the general hypothesis: the higher the levels on these four variables, the better the performance of local government. Table 4.1 summarizes the chapter's findings. The table supports the chapter's and this book's working model of local governance, particularly for service delivery.

Beyond the general hypothesis, the cases offer insight into some subpatterns. In South Africa, for example, strong resources and authority, in a technocratic and legalistic political community, led to local governments that were efficient but decoupled from the majority of their constituents. At the time of this research, 1995–1996, the city surveyed in South Africa seemed almost robotlike in its continual attention to doing what it had historically done in the way it had historically done it. Professional city personnel seemed aware of the need to change direction, even anxious at times, but no real redirection had occurred. Perhaps the momentum of any large bureaucracy (habits, policies, standard operating procedures, existing clientele) explains this. Absent an

Table 4.1   Evaluation of Summary Findings: South Africa and Botswana

Country	Resource Availability for Local Governance	Local Authority, Autonomy	Open and Accountable Local Political Process	Local Institutions of Collective Choice	Performance: Service Delivery	Performance: Operations
South Africa	Medium	Medium	Low	Medium to low	Low	Medium
Botswana	High	Medium	High	Medium	Medium	Medium

external "push" from an active, sustained political process, Nelspruit (and perhaps South Africa generally) appeared likely to continue as it had in the past and thus fail to provide effective local governance in the long run. With the new constitution only briefly in place at that time, the political framework can at best be assessed as "ambiguous."

Botswana, overall, ranks higher on our four independent variables, and has a stronger performance by local government. Nonetheless, its relative weakness in local authority seems closely related to serious discontent expressed by local officials (both professional and political) regarding their ability to fine-tune national programs to local needs. Weaknesses in planning and local initiative may also be related to this. Also, the still low level of local resources mobilized in Botswana for local government may at least in part be explained by the still incompletely developed local political process. As for continued shortfalls in management and operations, they can be explained by the relative youth of Botswana's local government systems, and overall continual weakness of the nation's personnel base. For Botswana's local government to reach the next plateau of performance, locally raised resources and local authority must be expanded. These might enable local administration at the same time that they energize a local political process. Nonetheless, the relative stability and openness of the Botswana political system have allowed local governance to grow and evolve slowly and steadily for nearly thirty years.

In summary, local government in these two cases presents a mixed but not discouraging picture. The variance between them can be explained by their respective environments and policy choices, and tends to confirm the model as hypothesized. South Africa must develop viable local accountability, develop and sustain a stable and clear national policy framework, and continue the reforms of the postapartheid era. Botswana has the "easier" challenge: gradually to enhance the authority and responsibility its localities already have, and to continue strengthening local institutions, while it sustains and enhances its national democracy.

Regarding local governance, the lessons seem clear. It will not develop overnight. A stable, constitutional, democratic context, as well as a stable economic context at both the national and local levels, are extremely important. They provide a structure within which local governance can gradually be learned. Missteps such as local elite capture of local governance, corruption, etc., can be avoided, while political leaders and publics can learn how to govern themselves. National governments must be prepared for mixed local governance performance during the early years of decentralization, but if they neither abandon nor smother localities, gradual progress may be expected. Ample resources, as in Botswana, make many things easier, but they are not a guarantee of the success of local governance, as in Nigeria (see Chapter 5). Still, as Botswana suggests, local governance can be achieved in Africa.

Notes

This chapter is a revised version of an article that first appeared in *Africa Studies Quarterly* 1, no. 1 (May 1998).

1. These findings are consistent with those of Pycroft (1996) regarding local government generally in the former "white" areas.

2. In U.S. terms, Nelspruit had a strong city manager but weak mayor-council system. The size of the council plus its lack of staff made it a weak legislative body.

5

Nigeria:
Local Governance and
Primary Health Care

Throughout its turbulent postindependence history, Nigeria has continued to experiment with its federal and local government systems. At independence, the federal structure was highly regionally decentralized, with most developmental responsibilities shouldered by the three large regions. Local government was placed under the regions and this led to the diverse development of local government in each region. Since the mid-1960s, when the military initially took power, the general trend has been to expand the number of states and local governments (LGs). Nigeria has moved from twelve states in 1967, to nineteen (1976), twenty-one (1987), and thirty (1991) under General Babangida. Not to be outdone, the last military dictator, Sani Abacha, raised the number of states to thirty-six in 1996. Similarly, local governments grew from the 299 at their creation in 1976 to 593 in 1991 to their present number of 774. In general, while the trend line has been irregular, the pattern has been progressively toward weakening the states, strengthening the national government, and expanding the authority and responsibility of local governments. These structures have been largely financed from the country's large earnings from oil (Oyovbaire 1985; Olowu 1990d; Osaghae 1998).

The efforts to strengthen and democratize local government within the Nigerian federal system dates to 1976. The decentralization and democratization of local government was part of a general program to restore civil rule after a decade (1966–1976) of military rule. The reform had three main elements. First, it reasserted local government as a system of democratically elected local councils with their own resources, personnel, responsibilities, and autonomous legal existence. Second, local governments were distinguished and separated from deconcentrated structures of the state or national government. Third, the reform and subsequent constitutions (1979, 1989, 1995) empowered local governments legally and transformed them into the third tier of government in the federation (Adamolekun 1984; Gboyega 1991). This meant that not only were they to take an active part in public sector development programs but also to initiate contractual and partnership arrangements with state and nonstate (private sector and nongovernmental) organizations.

The reforms recorded positive gains, especially in their earliest years (1976–1981): the fiscal and human resource capacities of local governments were transformed by large infusions of federal grants. These led to major infrastructure investments all over the country. The quality of officials, both political and administrative, was also enhanced and some beginnings were made in developing the idea of responsive local governments. The new local governments built and maintained a wide variety of infrastructure for basic health, schools, rural roads and water supply, agricultural extension, and adult education programs (Oyeyipo et al. 1989; Olowu 1990b; Idachaba et al. 1981). During the Second Republic (1979–1983), however, local governments experienced serious problems, especially with state governments. The latter diverted federal transfer funds meant for local governments, and refused to hold elections for local government councils. Instead, they appointed the party faithful to LG offices, refused to pay state statutory allocations to local governments, and did not comply with the constitutional mandate that devolved specific responsibilities to local governments.

Beginning in 1988, the federal government took several drastic measures to strengthen local government autonomy. These actions included:

- Abolition of the state ministries of local government and their replacement by bureaus of local government matters within the deputy governors' offices, the latter to serve as information clearinghouses for local governments as well as to render technical assistance to local governments (1988).
- Direct payments of federal allocations to local governments instead of passing them through state governments (1988).
- Reform of local government political/management structures. Each local government was to have four "operational" or line departments (works, education, health, agriculture) and two "service" or staff departments (personnel management and finance and planning) (1988).

- Creation of new LGs in 1976, 1987, and 1991, bringing the total number to 593 in 1991, and to 774 in 1996.
- Creation of the office of local government auditor (1988).
- Announcement of local government autonomy with respect to operational and financial matters. Local government budgets were to be approved by local government councils, no longer by state governments (1990).
- Increase of local government revenues allocated from 3 percent of the nationally collected revenue to 10 percent of the federation account (1981), 15 percent (1990), and in January 1992 to 20 percent. State government allocations from the same fund dropped from 34 percent to 24 percent while the federal government retained 50 percent. When the value-added tax was introduced in 1995, local governments were entitled to 30 percent of the proceeds.
- Transfer of primary education and primary health care to local governments (1990).
- Adoption of a presidential or strong-mayor system universally in all local governments. In effect, this meant the complete separation of executive and legislative branches (1991).

At the same time that these reforms were occurring in the general framework of Nigerian government, parallel reforms were developing in the health sector. The constitutions of 1979 and 1989 devolved health responsibilities on local and state governments. However, local governments became the key actors in this process during the 1976–1980 period with the national government's "basic health services scheme," which developed into the primary health care program (PHC) in 1984.

In 1988, the Ministry of Health articulated and aggressively pursued a comprehensive, locally focused health policy that made the local governments the key actors. The policy focus was a community-based health system in which primary, secondary, and tertiary health care were organized at local, provincial, and national levels, with each mutually supporting the other. Actually as far back as 1986, a total of fifty-two model LGs had been selected as pilot project sites for strengthening PHC at the LG level. Each was given 0.5 million naira, together with material and technical assistance to reorient and develop the local health system. Each of these model LGs was linked with a college of medicine or school of health technology to assist with the training of local government health officials.

Up to 1986, most state governments managed and delivered PHC.

In June 1988, however, under the leadership of the federal health minister, Olikoye Ransome-Kuti, who had a long-standing interest in the development of community-based health care, the federal Ministry of Health directed state governments to devolve all PHC responsibilities to local governments over a three-year period terminating on June 30, 1990.

State governments had responsibilities under the new health policy for the supervision and coordination of PHC and for playing an advocacy role. The Ministry of Health carved the country into four broad zones for the purposes of supervision. Each zone was under the leadership of a zonal coordinator. These zonal coordinators formed the core personnel of the newly created National Primary Health Care Development Agency. PHC activities were to revolve around several core functions:

- Public education.
- Improvement in nutrition.
- Adequate safe water and basic sanitation.
- Maternal and child health care, including family planning.
- Immunization.
- Prevention and control of endemic and epidemic diseases.
- Provision of essential drugs and supplies.
- Elderly and handicapped care.
- Accident and injury care.

Below the LGs, district and village health committees were to be established to provide inputs such as information, suggestions for improvements, complaints, control, etc., for the new system down to the grassroots level.

Why did the Nigerian federal government embark on these radical reforms—ones that were aimed at boosting the capacity of local governments to deliver services? One explanation is that Babangida wanted to boost his popularity as a benevolent dictator by identifying with some of the popular policies of the Murtala/Obasanjo military regime, which put in place concrete measures to restore civilian rule, a goal that was attained within only five years (1975–1979). The only difference was that in this case the regime wanted to use this as the justification for ensuring that Babangida stayed on in power (Osaghac 1998). An explanation more generous to the regime would argue that the local government reforms were the institutional elements of the regime's ambitious economic and political reform program (Olagunju and Oyovbaire 1989).

Whichever explanation one accepts, what is significant is the impact of the reforms on the goals of decentralization and local governance. Did these reforms lead to improved service delivery, higher levels of accountability, and an empowered citizenry? There may be no better sector to analyze to respond to this question than the health sector, where a spirited effort was made to effect decentralization.

Decentralization and Primary Health Care in Nigeria

The PHC/LG system in Nigeria is an important subject of study because it is a major field experiment in decentralization and potential local governance. The evidence gathered regarding PHC's performance in the field allows the analyst to focus on specific problems and successes, and thereby to begin evaluating the problems one might expect to experience in other and broader service, decentralization and local governance efforts. It also allows the analyst to evaluate central government policies and strategies for their impact on decentralization and local governance, and to suggest specific recommendations for future such efforts.

Among the advantages the Nigerian case offers is the scale of the effort (over seven hundred local government units), the duration of the effort (nearly ten years from the initial PHC pilot study), and the breadth of the reform. Specifically, the changes had real substance. Personnel, resources, and authority were all actually transferred to the LGs, and the states (whether by default or design) were put on a serious "diet" as resources were reallocated to the LGs. LGs received the authority to raise taxes and levy fees for service, to let contracts, to hire and fire personnel, and to establish and manage their own budgets. They also held local elections, electing an executive (LG chair) and legislative body (LG council). The reform seemed rather clearly to be an instance of devolution rather than merely deconcentration, with great promise for the emergence of local governance. In all this, it was quite remarkable for such efforts in Africa.

Much progress was made in PHC by 1992. Personnel were deployed, buildings were built, and programs were begun. And, in strictly medical/technical terms, much was in place (training, donor activity, supplies, epidemiological data analysis, help in vaccination campaigns) to support the program. Indeed, PHC provided millions of Nigerians with their first access to any professional health care, and for many it was one of the first government programs to reach out to them. Undoubtedly, many Nigerians were helped by it. Many survived malaria, childbirth, and respiratory and digestive tract diseases because of its efforts. Expanded Programme of Immunization coverage increased from 30 percent in 1980 to 55 percent in 1992. Some LGs such as Barkin Ladi in Plateau State performed very well and together with a few others in the country, such as Owo LG, attracted international attention. The reform was particularly successful in those parts of the country where a strong civil society or communities worked actively with these new local governments (WHO 1992, 2001).

Nonetheless, there was concern among the donors and key Nigerian health personnel as to whether or not PHC overall as an organization, and the LG as the key supporting organization, were operating as well as they might, particularly in developing, managing, and revising PHC programs and operations.

The concern led to a field study of twelve PHC programs and their host LGs. Research was also done in six states, three governmental offices, and the national Ministry of Health. This chapter reviews the highlights of this study, with particular emphasis on its implications for our understanding of the policy and other prerequisites of successful decentralization.[1]

While PHC/LG operations varied in quality, with some working rather well, the following problems were disconcertingly frequent:

- Planning, programming, quality control, problem identification and solving, and the like were haphazardly done by most LG/PHC staffs. Conscious and systematic programs to perform these functions were virtually nonexistent.
- Management awareness of field conditions and needs was quite low in most LG/PHC programs. This was particularly clear in the areas of personnel management and facility supervision.
- Training programs were intermittent, nonsystematic, often too brief to achieve desired goals, and lacking in follow-up.
- Field supervision was generally sporadic, and lacked any overall plan. Often it was virtually nonexistent. Vehicles were frequently out of service because of breakdown or lack of funds for fuel.
- Facilities were frequently inappropriately located and designed, given available infrastructure, underserved areas, and existing facilities.
- No cost-effectiveness or utilization studies could be found through which LG/PHC personnel had assessed their programs.
- Guidelines for supervision had been developed by the federal Ministry of Health, but were not in use in most LGs.
- Resources did not appear rationally balanced among supply,

salary, and capital budgets, so personnel facilities lacked supplies and sometimes facilities lacked personnel, while other
facilities appeared overstaffed.

- Poor "housekeeping" existed at most health facilities, including
erratic opening and closing hours; poor record keeping; unreliable staffing (particularly by upper ranks); epidemiological data
in disarray; lack of cleanliness; dilapidated, broken, and poorly
maintained equipment; absence of basic medications; lack of
knowledge of the local community, etc.
- There was evidence of poor (occasionally dangerous) medical
practices at health facilities.
- Budgets poorly reflected the actual expenditures of PHC, and
had to be frequently revised; there were often no funds for key
supplies or basic medications, and salaries were often paid late.
- There was little evidence of state or federal support or awareness
of PHC operations at the LGs. There was little contact between
state or federal personnel and LG personnel.
- LG/PHC personnel had made no or very little use of community
organizations in setting local program priorities, troubleshooting
health problems, assuring facility quality control, etc.
- Relations between the PHC office and community health committees appeared haphazard and disorganized, including absence
of minutes, reports, or other records of the committees' activities.
- There was evidence of declining confidence by members of
local health committees that their deliberations and recommendations were taken seriously.
- Many local residents regarded the PHC system as unreliable,
ineffective, and unresponsive to their needs.

The remainder of this chapter will review the causes of this disappointing performance, its implications for Nigeria's policy on strengthening local governments for health care delivery, and for local governance in general. It will analyze the causes at two levels: first, the
factors that have caused these shortfalls in performance, and second, the
strategic and institutional nature of these problems and how they interacted to create stubborn obstacles to improving PHC. Then it will
review a number of government policies that appear to have negatively
affected PHC, and suggest the implications for decentralization strategies and local governance in general.

Despite this generally negative appraisal, it is important to highlight the fact that some local governments managed to perform cred-
itably. Our research showed that two factors were crucial to explaining
such successes in the midst of widespread failures. First, leadership at

political and managerial levels was critical. Leadership of the right quality was able to surmount the variety of problems highlighted above. Moreover, where such leadership operated in a community that was responsive to these positive initiatives, as happened in Barkin Ladi LG (Plateau State) and Offa LG (Kwara State), the community not only provided resources in terms of donations from sons and daughters of the community to support their health services infrastructure (Barkan et al. 1991), but also used their connections with the state and central governments to ensure that some of the worst management problems highlighted above were attenuated in their communities (Olowu et al. 2000). This synergy of exemplary leadership resonating with the community underscores the significance of social capital for the successful development of local governance systems, an issue adequately discussed by Robert Putnam (1993) with respect to the evolution of Italian municipalities.

Explaining LG/PHC Performance

Explaining the problems of the LG/PHC system requires multiple levels of analysis. These include the context in which it operated, the way it was designed, and the impact of certain key national policies on it.

The LG/PHC system faced a number of contextual challenges that would be daunting for such a complex human services system in *any* country. These included a harsh and unforgiving physical environment, serious shortages in human and fiscal resources, weakness in the "attentive publics" that are important to lobby for resources and constructively critique programs everywhere, and a turbulent local political scene. While these would have been serious challenges anywhere in the world, several aspects of the design and organization of the Nigerian LG/PHC system made these worse, as did some key decisions and policies made by the national government. First, let us consider these contextual problems in more detail.

Nigeria's natural environment is a challenging one. The country's immense size, poor roads, weak communications system, largely rural and dispersed population, and incomplete coverage with electricity and safe water, combined with endemic malaria, poor nutrition, and high incidence of preventable childhood diseases, create a severe challenge for a primary health care system. Patients are scattered about wide areas where secondary and primary roads are extremely bad; extremes of climate (rainy season–hot, dry season cycle) make transportation difficult; information on regional needs is limited or absent; and there is little or no redundancy in human or physical (vehicles) resources. Thus, if a vehicle breaks down, or a key worker is ill or absent, there are no replacements. If the electricity fails, vaccines, which require refrigeration, are ruined. The absence of redundancy in a harsh environment means the organization is frequently disrupted, and the disruptions erode its morale and the public's confidence in it.

Human and fiscal resources are of course a primary way of managing and overcoming a harsh environment. However, Nigeria's local governments have been starved of all sorts of resources that might have helped them, virtually since the inception of PHC. Personnel have improved compared to the prereform period but remain inadequate, both in numbers and in training. Only a few physicians and registered nurses were found at the twelve research sites visited, most of whom were largely in managerial roles at PHC/LG headquarters. Many service delivery personnel had only a few weeks of training, and with that were trying to make complex clinical decisions. Funds were equally short, as primary health care's needs greatly exceeded the limited federal grant to LGs, which must in any case be divided among such activities as education, public works, agriculture, and administration. Federal funds often arrive late and are erratic in amounts. Furthermore, as no effective local taxes or user-fees have been developed, local revenues did not exist to supplement these shortfalls.

Public constituencies for PHC are quite weak. Even though elaborate structures of grassroots participation nominally existed in the policy framework and in reality in many local government areas, it was difficult to regard these as active or informed constituencies on the local level. Local persons were found to be generally uninformed regarding PHC, or involved only in an individual and reactive manner. Nor were there any health-related professional associations to act as surrogates for local communities. Finally, the LG, village, and ward communities met only erratically, were poorly organized, and seemed ineffective in influencing local programs.

Some of the most serious contextual problems for the PHC/LG system came from a political environment that was marked by instability, both of regimes and policies relating to local government. Between the introduction of the local government reforms of 1976 and the conduct of our field research, there had been four changes of government, two of which were nonconstitutional and involved military putsches. In addition, there was a major unsuccessful coup attempt in 1990. A transition to civilian government, which commenced in 1986, ended abruptly in 1993 with the July cancellation of the presidential elections of June 12, 1993, and a military coup in November. The election was eventually regarded as free and fair but the presumed winner of that election was placed in detention, paving the way for a new military dictator who then sought to become a civilian president. In the midst of this national turbulence, local governments witnessed many policy changes and much institutional turbulence. Indeed, while conducting our field research in 1993, all local government elected officials were removed in one fell swoop, four months ahead of the end of their terms. Later, when the military putsch of November 1993 took place, all democratic structures were dismantled, including the local governments. Such turbulence is hardly conducive to the development of stable expectations and accountability among local political leaders, civil servants, or the public.

The repeated creation of new states and new LGs from old ones introduced great institutional instability. The relationships between LGs and states, already weak, were additionally disrupted. Also, budgets, personnel, vehicles, and equipment were transferred and divided to follow these changes, disrupting relationships between civil servants and political personnel.

Additional problems were created by policy instability at the national level. Supplies, budgets, and allocations have been disrupted as national priorities shifted. Institutional relationships have also been unclear and unstable, as the national government has failed to define clearly the respective responsibilities of the national ministry, the four "zones," and the states vis-à-vis the LGs. In all this, LGs were unclear about to whom they were accountable, whom they should look to for technical assistance, and the like. Finally, the national decrees regarding local government established a single institutional structure for all local governments throughout Nigeria, regardless of area, population, urbanization, or possible cultural differences.

The second general set of problems that impeded the PHC/LG system were those of its design and organization. Briefly, these dealt with structures for local participation, continued centralization, ineffective local supervision, internal confusion regarding hierarchy, the speed and top-down way in which this was established, and the funding system. All these aspects of its organization worked to impede its success.

The LG/PHC had a structure of grassroots participation that involved local representation at village, ward, district, and LG committee levels. While the village-level committee is popularly selected, for the most part, the ascending tiers are made up of the chairs of the respective subordinate tiers. There are also traditional leaders, community leaders, and various local organizations represented—women's and men's improvement and benevolent organizations, teachers unions, etc. In some areas, PHC personnel sought out traditional and natural community leaders to form the grassroots base of the PHC committee system. For example, in Ife central, the village committees were built upon the compound elder system. Similarly, in Sokoto State, the district and village heads were the chairmen of the district and health committees respectively.

On the positive side, several of the committees' intended roles seem to be working well. Both PHC directors and leaders interviewed highlighted the information-disseminating abilities of these committees positively. They supported immunization campaigns and many of them had selected village health workers for training by the PHC program. They also facilitated house-numbering and survey activities, and assisted in the implementation of the Bamako Initiative on revolving health funds. On the other hand, there were two main areas of concern. First, there were signs of meeting fatigue. Turnout at meetings was beginning to erode as attendance at meetings did not seem to lead to any visible changes and participants tended to see this as a waste of the time they could spend on their farms and professions. Second, the incentives for participants to attend these meetings were weak: they were neither paid nor did their opinions seem to be taken seriously. They tended increasingly to see their roles as purveyors of the ideas and policies of the PHC teams to the community rather than vice versa.

Problems also grew from the roles allocated to superior levels of government. Specifically, the national and state governments retained key functions in purchasing and distributing key supplies, gathering and analyzing data, selecting and assigning senior personnel, providing training and quality control, and of course in finance. All things being equal, many of these functions might indeed be better handled by a capable center: these tasks provide economies of scale, usually utilize known technologies, and have few coproductive aspects to them. But in Nigeria in the 1990s, the center (federal and state) was understaffed, underfunded, and just unable to do them. Instead, LG/PHC largely languished, cut off from the expertise it needed, unable to purchase supplies on its own, and left without guidance when the data it gathered and sent to the center received no analysis.

At the same time, supervision at the LG level worked poorly. It was hindered by broken vehicles, petrol shortages, and lack of funds. In fact, the linkages needed to sustain PHC as a system were everywhere largely absent. Furthermore, at the LG level a defective organizational structure left field personnel without a clear supervisor, and no one (except the overall LG/PHC director) with clear responsibility for and authority over field personnel.

The lesson here is that organizational linkages and responsibilities must be sensitive to the capacity of the levels involved. When they cannot take on the task contemplated, then alternative arrangements need to be made. A second lesson is the need for clear focus of responsibility up and down the organization, so subordinates know who they are responsible to, and superiors know what they are responsible for.

General problems also included incomplete socialization and training for new roles; adaptation of new organizational models without time to experiment, learn, and adjust; the coordination problems (and cost) of building many new facilities; shifting and relocating personnel into jobs for which they were sometimes unready; and developing whole new systems of budgeting, planning, data gathering, and personnel evaluation. These all grew in part from the rapid implementation of the PHC programs. Simultaneously, of course, the LG system was also being put into place, including establishing elections at local levels, which had hitherto not occurred.

A slower pace of change would have helped, as well as mechanisms to listen and learn from the bottom up, and some systematic capacity to review, analyze, and spread the lessons of experience across the country. Instead, some 770 LGs, spread across thirty-six states, were simultaneously trying to "discover the wheel" and make it work, all without a system of learning from one another. This of course is typical of the consequences of the exclusively top-down, regimented mechanisms that African national governments usually pursue during decentralization.

Funding was another area where organization and structure proved to be problematic for LG/PHC. Briefly put, there was little incentive for LGs to try to raise their own monies, so they did not do so. By not doing so, *all* local government activities (except perhaps administration) were starved for funds. The major reason for this is that all local governments in Nigeria receive major funding from federal revenue grants: 90–96 percent of LGs' revenues come from this source. While LGs have the authority to levy several taxes on such things as local enterprises, homes, licenses, fees for service, and markets, virtually none do so, or they do so at absurdly low rates. Several reasons, along with the federal grants, have been offered for this:

- Local leaders would be required to pay more taxes, and are close to many of the small-scale businesspersons who would be the most cost-effective sources of tax.
- Local revenue sources are relatively cost-ineffective, or at least cumbersome to collect.
- The federal or state revenue reward or penalty associated with

raising or failing to raise local revenue is small and largely ineffective.

- User-fees/charges are politically unpopular and viewed with sus-
picion by local dwellers who have seen local funds disappear
suspiciously in the past.

As a result of these, and perhaps other factors, LGs raise virtually none
of their own funds. This has led to not particularly surprising consequences (to be discussed below) for spending patterns and for local
inattention to LG affairs.

Finally, the national decrees regarding local government established
a single institutional form for all local governments throughout Nigeria,
regardless of area, population size, urbanization, or possible cultural
differences. This has been the source of numerous difficulties.

Accountability, PHC, and Local Governance in Nigeria

Overall, then, the physical context, and the human, organizational, and
policy arrangements created numerous obstacles for success by
Nigeria's PHC/LG system. Growing out of these, and making several of
them worse, is a general pattern of low accountability throughout the
system. Richard Crook and James Manor, in their major study of decentralization in West Africa and South Asia, found accountability to be
one of the key factors affecting performance of decentralized entities
(1998). Even when public interest and participation are strong, that
often does not translate into effective control of the executive branch
and its programs by the legislative branch. Accountability is in fact
weak throughout the Nigerian system, and helps explain many of its
problems.

To begin with, the instability of the local political process has
meant that developing a viable pattern of public accountability has been
difficult. Second, the design of the LGs, with a strong-mayor type of
system elected by the public, has meant that local elected councils have
been generally quite ineffective in influencing the budget, or in holding
the mayor or the professional staff accountable. This is consistent with
findings elsewhere in similar systems in Africa (Cook and Manor
1998). Finally, and compounding all this, the absence of any local-level
organization among the public to support or "push" public health has
reinforced the disengagement of PHC from the public.

This weakness in public accountability was reinforced by a weak culture of professional accountability within PHC. The turbulence of the personnel system, the weakness of the local supervisory systems (including the absence of resources to keep the PHC headquarters in touch with field personnel), the poor training of most PHC personnel, and the severe shortfalls in supplies and equipment combined to lead both to weak professional expectations in the system and to very low morale. Little could be done easily, little was expected, and thus little was done.

Finally, what one might call bureaucratic or administrative accountability was also weak. The absence of clearly defined roles for states, zones, and the center left LG/PHCs pretty much on their own. Training, technical support, and other responses to local needs had largely ground to a halt. This, of course, followed much the same pattern that shortfalls in resources, the ineffective PHC/LG supervisory structure, and the weak clinical knowledge of supervisory personnel had led to within the LGs.

The outcome of this was that LG/PHC was largely a system in name only. The support different levels of governance must give one another was absent. Whether it be in encouraging, demanding, or facilitating appropriate professional standards, providing key resources, helping to develop strategic and management plans, or whatever else, most PHC actors were largely on their own. Furthermore, PHC was a system without steering from the public or political leadership. Where there was a strong PHC *leader,* one with a vision, some managerial skills, and some political support from the LG chairman, PHC operated fairly well. But where those elements were absent, there were no mechanisms to get PHC back on track.

Incentives and Reward Systems

To understand how the contextual and accountability problems created such difficulties for LG/PHC, one must consider the issue of *incentives and reward systems.* In a variety of ways they worked to discourage the actions necessary for an effective PHC system. At times these problems were intensified by Nigeria's poverty and political turbulence. Areas of activity where incentives and reward systems were particularly problematic were revenue, supervision, professionalism, grassroots participation, and political support for PHC. Each will be discussed below.

In funding, several policies acted as disincentives to strengthen PHC resources. First, the fact that the national grants, which are the primary funding mechanism for all LG activities, are linked only to such aggregate characteristics as area, populations, and need, and pay no heed at all to local effort, gives localities no incentive to levy or collect taxes. Second, there are no requirements or even incentives for localities to develop revolving funds for medications or supplies, nor user-fees for facilities, personnel costs, or other operating costs. LG accounting systems do not routinely facilitate sequestering PHC funds from other LG resources, so this also discourages PHC revenue enhancements. Finally, the fact that the LG grant is in effect a common pool resource for all LG agencies does not encourage any single sector to "bite the bullet" and charge for services, nor does it encourage prudent spending. As has long been recognized, the dynamic associated with scarce common-pool resources is "pump" as fast as you can, before your neighbor gets your share, and perhaps so you can capture his.

Similarly, there are few incentives for close supervision. To begin with, simply engaging in supervision is difficult, time-consuming, and exhausting, given the significant distances that must be traveled under usually harsh conditions. Second, the dominance of seniority in advancement means that there are few clear career rewards for supervision. Also, inflation has caused little salary differentials between supervisory and rank and file personnel, giving little incentive to take on the burden of management or to work very hard at it. Third, there are so few well-trained personnel available that it is not clear what close supervision, were that even possible, might accomplish.

The incentives for professionalism and service delivery in the field are also unclear. Strong intrinsic motivations alone might suffice for some personnel. But with supervision virtually nonexistent, with salaries and salary differentials eroded by inflation, with seniority the primary method of promotion, and with the public largely passive, there are few if any *extrinsic* motivations for professionalism and superior service delivery. Furthermore, with supplies woefully inadequate, training incomplete, and technical support largely absent, it seems that pushing for excellence would be a recipe for crushed morale. Finally, as budgets and supplies do not grow with need, serving more clients only exhausts one's supplies sooner.

There are also few incentives for grassroots participation. Health officials readily admit that they see their role as delivering "professionally managed" programs, and cannot recall any instance where they changed any program or policy in response to local public input. If this futility was not enough, members of the local health advisory committees receive nothing to cover travel or opportunity costs to attend meetings where they say there is nothing but "talk, talk, talk." Similarly, for health service personnel who believe they are delivering a less than bare-bones program, the absence of any slack resources to respond to additional local demands means there is no incentive to encourage any.

For political leaders, the incentive to strengthen PHC is also unclear. While increases in local taxes will (they believe) cause a serious uproar, they see no constituency that will respond favorably to increased funding for PHC. User-fees are also regarded as politically impossible. As for the national grant, there appear at the localities to be other, better organized constituencies competing for the funds: teachers, merchants and drivers using the poor roads, contractors interested in construction projects, etc. Local competitive elections have never had a chance to develop through more than two election cycles, which might have led to some pattern of accountability to the public. Nor, as noted above, is the LG chairman particularly accountable to the LG council. For these reasons, perhaps, politicians seem to respond to the wants of LG staff and organized constituencies rather than to the public's needs.

In general, then, reward and incentive structures in the LGs do not work to encourage expanded funding, supervision, or professionalism. Neither do they build support for this service, one that caters to the poor majority rather than to the locally well-off.

We may well argue that the Nigerian LG/PHC system nonetheless accomplished much during its short operational life span (1988–1995). However, these achievements fell short of its potential to reach even more of Nigeria's poor population with basic health services. A demanding and turbulent environment interacted with constant resource shortfalls, an unsupportive national policy context, and poor design of PHC and LG institutions to create serious operational problems. At a strategic level, one can see how the policy and design problems worked to weaken accountability throughout the system, and to create reward structures that tended to make the operational problems worse. For example, localities had really no incentive to raise funds locally (given the federal grant and its terms), supervisors had little incentive to follow their personnel more closely or upgrade their programs (without money or authorization to purchase more supplies or reward better performers), the public and locally elected councils had little incentive to try to influence policy (given the dominance of the LG chairmen and the disengaged publics), personnel had no extrinsic incentive to try particularly hard to improve services (absence of rewards or sanctions), and the states had little incentive to try to support the LG/PHC program. Of course, the whole system was vulnerable to the turbulence that continues to characterize Nigeria's economy and polity.

Some of these problems are more easily fixed than others: the LG executive could be easily made more accountable to elected councils; LGs could have more authority to purchase supplies on their own, develop their own supervision systems, and to reward performance rather than seniority; and federal monies could be made contingent on certain levels of local revenue and/or user-fee systems. Others, like public ignorance of local programs, lack of public involvement, better training for PHC's many personnel, and state passivity regarding the LGs, are more difficult to resolve, given the lack of education and the poverty widespread in Nigeria. Still, their solution is imaginable through serious efforts in public education and a new culture of service and attentiveness to the public by PHC personnel. Other problems, however, such as the turbulence of the national economy and polity, seem beyond anyone's control. And Nigeria's, and Africa's, poverty will continue to drag down many of these efforts. Nonetheless, as comparative research has shown in South Asia, local governance *is* possible among even very poor areas if commitment is there at all levels (Crook and Manor 1998).

Conclusion

The Nigerian experience of local government reform, particularly dramatized by the LG/PHC reforms, raises a number of significant lessons for the construction of effective local governance systems in Africa. First, it underscores the sustained attention attached to the effort on the part of several administrations since 1976 when the local government reforms were first introduced. Interestingly enough, throughout Nigeria's political turmoil, no central government has found it in its interest to abolish local government. Not every administration was as supportive, but generally there has been a sustained support for the idea of a local government system that is substantially autonomous and yet in constant interaction with the central state. Second, it highlights the fact that efforts to introduce democratic decentralization and local governance raise crucial problems of design, context, resources, policy, and accountability. However, these problems can be analyzed to determine what constitutes feasible solutions. Incentives can be altered, sometimes by changing organizations, sometimes by changing policies, and sometimes by shifting resources and authority within a system. Success in building local governance will not be accomplished unless such nuts-and-bolts issues and problems are confronted and addressed. Yet again, the "devil is in the details." Third, and finally, these nuts and bolts constitute the institutional preconditions for building a democratic local governance system with clear articulation of responsibilities, provision of resources, and structures of accountability. These same issues can be found in the other case studies in this book.

Notes

Two brief sections of this chapter are reprinted with the permission of Transaction Publishers—James Wunsch and Dele Olowu, "Regime Transformations from Below: Decentralizaion, Local Governance, and Democratic Reform in Nigeria," *Studies in Comparative International Development* 31, no. 4 (1996–1997): 71–72 (copyright 1996 by Transaction Publishers); and with the permission of the Institute of African Affairs—Dele Olowu and James Wunsch, "Decentralization, Local Government, and Primary Health Care in Nigeria: An Analytical Study," *Journal of African Policy Studies* 1, no. 3 (1995): 6–8 (copyright 1995 by the Institute of African Affairs).

1. The results are reported in detail in Olowu and Wunsch (1995); Wunsch and Olowu (1996); Ikhide, Olowu, and Wunsch (1993); and Olowu et al. (2000).

6

Ghana:
A Top-Down Initiative

Joseph Ayee

Overview

This chapter is an overview of the Ghanaian decentralization program since its introduction by the Provisional National Defense Council (PNDC) government in 1988. It addresses the politics of policies regarding decentralization and how the broader political strategies and those in power are served by decentralization policies. Specifically, it deals with the problems that the district assemblies (DAs) have had in working effectively, the continued weight and consequences of central influence through appointed members, the ineffectiveness of local bodies in raising local funds, the difficulty in getting local professional personnel out of the influence of centralized ministries, the negative impact of national political parties on local affairs, the problem of getting national laws and regulations revised to reflect decentralization policies, and the general performance of the district assemblies. In this connection, the chapter will address the following three questions: How have central practices, policies, and procedures affected the ability of the district assemblies to really "get going"? How are the broader political strategies of those in power served by decentralization policies? How has decentralization in Ghana affected the quality and sustainability of local governance? These questions will be answered on the basis of four conditions that are important to the success of decentralization. They are: (1) devolution of authority; (2) deconcentration of resources; (3) development of local political process and local accountability, and (4) development of effective local institutions of collective choice.

Methodology

Data was gathered from primary and secondary sources between December 1999 and March 2001. Interviews based on questions relating to the devolution of authority, deconcentration of resources, and development of local political process and local accountability were conducted with five officials of the Ministry of Local Government and Rural Development, two officials of the Office of the Administrator of District Assemblies Common Fund, four randomly selected district chief executives, ten members of parliament (MPs), ten district assembly members, and heads of selected decentralized departments. In all, one hundred randomly selected respondents were interviewed. In addition, the questionnaire requested information on:

- The functions and legal powers of the DAs.
- The needs of the people in the districts.
- Revenues, expenditures, sources of funding, and revenue generation and sharing.
- Manpower and training needs.
- Progress of composite budgeting and other actions programmed to implement the decentralization program.
- The weight and consequences of central influence.
- The problems that faced the DAs.
- The relationship between the DAs and the so-called decentralized departments.
- The problem of getting national laws and regulations revised to reflect decentralization policies.
- The general performance of the DAs.

Secondary data was gleaned from published and unpublished government documents such as the 1992 constitution, acts and laws relating to decentralization, and reports and financial statements of some selected district assemblies.

National Political Context

Decentralization has occupied successive governments in Ghana since independence from British rule in 1957. This is evidenced by the number of commissions and committees of enquiry that were appointed (ten in all) and the legislation enacted (twenty in all) coupled with local government elections (six in all) during the postindependence period. The concern for and preoccupation with decentralization may be explained by the fact that decentralization was not only regarded by successive governments as a necessary condition of economic, social, and political development, but also was one way of achieving their political objectives—for example, recentralization of power and legitimacy (Ayee 1994).

Ghana's current decentralization program is a continuation of the one initiated by Jerry Rawlings's Provisional National Defense Council, which took over power through a military coup d'etat from the civilian government of Hilla Limann's People's National Party government in December 1981. The government's initiative in reform of decentralization started in 1988 with the promulgation of PNDC Law 207. The initiative for reform was inspired by the government's political philosophy of "power to the people" and its structural adjustment program (SAP), whose principles concern the role and responsibilities of the state and the expanding role of the private sector, both in the sense of private commercial entrepreneurship and voluntary community initiatives. These principles have been reinforced by the 1992 constitution, which stipulates the establishment of a sound and healthy economy, with a reduction in the role of the state in the economic life of the country through shifting more responsibility to the private sector, and developing an environment of investor confidence.

In November 1992, the PNDC government led by Flight Lieutenant J. J. Rawlings held multiparty presidential elections to return the country to constitutional rule. It was won by Rawlings's National Democratic Congress (NDC). Although international observers such as the Commonwealth Observer Group declared the elections as "free and fair," the outcome of the democratic transition was highly disputed by four opposition parties, namely the New Patriotic Party (NPP), the People's National Convention, the National Independence Party, and the People's Heritage Party. Consequently, they boycotted the parliamentary elections in December 1992. Therefore, during Ghana's first four years of its fourth attempt to establish constitutional government, the government party, the NDC, virtually controlled all (189 out of the 200) seats in parliament.

On December 7, 1996, the Ghanaian electorate went to the polls, where the NDC was once again elected. Although there were some irregularities in the elections, the opposition parties did not regard them as serious enough and so conceded defeat (Ayee 1997a).

Under the 1992 constitution, the Rawlings government understood good governance to mean a neopatrimonial system of governance that consists of the following:

- Highly centralized personal rule sanctified by periodic elections leading to personalism.
- The distribution of state-generated benefits to political followers leading to pervasive clientelism.
- The selection of public officials on the basis of personal rather than institutional loyalty.
- The unmediated and uncircumscribed control of a coercive apparatus (Sandbrook and Oelbaum 1997).

In December 2000, presidential and parliamentary elections were held. They were the third successful poll under the 1992 constitution and Ghana's Fourth Republic. The elections were won by the main opposition party, the NPP, whose presidential candidate, John Kufuor, was sworn in as the second president of the Fourth Republic on January 7, 2001. Jerry Rawlings, who dominated the Ghanaian political scene for nearly twenty years and introduced the local government reform, did not contest the elections in accordance with the two presidential terms as prescribed by the 1992 constitution (Ayee 2002a).

Objectives of Ghana's Current Decentralization Program

The 1992 constitution and various legislation on decentralization[1] have articulated the explicit objectives of decentralization such as empowerment, participation, accountability, effectiveness, efficiency, responsiveness, decongestion of the national capital, and the checking of rural-urban drift. Specifically, the decentralization program has been designed to:

- Devolve political and state power in order to promote participatory democracy through local-level institutions.
- Deconcentrate and devolve administration, development planning, and implementation to the district assemblies (local government units).
- Introduce an effective system of fiscal decentralization that gives the district assemblies control over a substantial portion of their revenues.
- Establish a national development planning system to integrate and coordinate development planning at all levels and in all sectors.
- Incorporate economic, social, spatial, and environmental issues into the development planning process on an integrated and comprehensive basis.

The 1992 constitutional provisions with respect to decentralization are quite specific concerning the ultimate responsibilities of parliament. However, with respect to specific responsibilities of district assemblies, the constitution's language is quite broad. More importantly, the structure of relationships between the so-called decentralized central government ministries and departments, statutory public corporations, and the DAs is not substantively addressed. Also, no differentiation is made in the constitution of the choices made among different forms of decentralization.

Some of the objectives of decentralization could be, however, incompatible. For instance, popular participation could mitigate against local revenue generation and mobilization on the one hand, and/or demands for increased expenditures on the other hand. Similarly, what might most likely foster popular participation in discretionary decision-making might suboptimize managerial efficiency.

Moreover, the government has not been able to indicate the implicit objectives of decentralization, that is, what one might call the politics of decentralization—for instance, either using decentralization as an instrument of mobilizing support for specific objectives or as a form of political patronage.

Devolution of Authority

Ghana's DAs—local government units—have been designated the highest political and administrative authorities, planning authorities, development authorities, budgeting authorities, and rating authorities. Consequently, the DAs have been given eighty-six functions that empower them to provide deconcentrated, delegated, and devolved local public services. For instance, a deconcentrated function of the DAs, as agents of the Ghana Highway Authority, is the maintenance of trunk roads lying within the boundaries of their areas of authority, while a delegated function is the provision of an adequate and wholesome supply of water throughout the entire district in consultation with the Ghana Water and Sewerage Corporation. Similarly, a devolved function of the DAs is the mobilization and management of revenue as well as the construction and maintenance of feeder roads, streets, parks, cemeteries, and other public utilities. Indeed, the devolution of authority to the DAs has made them take on added responsibilities, such as the provision and maintenance of secondary schools, which were hitherto performed by the central government.

Some progress has been made toward the devolution of authority to the DAs. Specifically, the DAs, on the advice of the district tender boards, have been given the power to award contracts not exceeding U.S.$100,000; they are the sole taxing authority in the districts; they make bylaws, which are subject to approval by the Ministry of Local Government and Rural Development before they become operative; they prepare their own annual budgets that reflect their estimated and actual recurrent and capital expenditures; they are corporate bodies that can sue and be sued; and they are the sole district planning authorities, charged with the overall development of the districts (Ayee 1997b, 1997c).

In spite of the devolution of authority, the DAs suffer severe limitations in the exercise of such authority. First, they cannot hire and fire staff. Although legislation stipulates that staff of the twenty-two line ministries and departments at the district must be controlled by the DAs, the staff of the departments still owe allegiance to their parent bodies at the national level. This is because their recruitment, career progression, and dismissal are done by the national headquarters of the departments and the DAs.

Second, the exercise of the authority is subject to two things. First is the monitoring of performance of the DAs by the Regional Coordinating Council (RCC), chaired by the regional minister, an appointee of the central government. Although the RCC is to play a secondary role in Ghana's decentralization system, it is in practice very powerful, especially when there has generally been no agreement on its coordinating and monitoring functions. On several occasions, the RCC has controlled the activities of the DAs. Sometimes the power to approve or reject the bylaws of the DAs is delegated to the RCC by the Ministry of Local Government and Rural Development. Second, it is subject to the general guidance and direction of the president on matters of national policy. The most important reserved intervention of the central government is the power of the president to "cause to be investigated the performance of any function of a district assembly and where necessary in the public interest declare a district assembly to be in default and transfer to a person or body as he may think fit such functions of the district assembly" (Republic of Ghana 1993a:26). This is a big stick that has been held over the heads of the DAs by the central government. The minister of local government has defended this as being intended to ensure a strong central government presence at the DA. Nevertheless, the practical implication has been that the dependence of the DAs on the central government has become so extensive that it would not be out of place to talk of decentralization in Ghana as local administration of the intentions of the central government (Ayee 1997c).

Furthermore, although the DAs have been given the power to borrow money and obtain overdrafts within Ghana, they cannot do so without the approval of the Ministry of Finance. No such approval is, however, required where the loan or overdraft to be raised does not exceed U.S.$10,000 or has a guarantee by the central government. Most DAs were not able to take advantage of this provision because no bank has been willing to grant them credit facilities.

Even though the DAs are budgeting authorities, they are required to submit to the regional coordinating council (RCC), before the end of each financial year, a detailed budget for the district stating the revenues and expenditures for the ensuing year. After collating and coordinating the budgets of the districts in the region, the RCC submits the total budget to the minister of finance. In other words, it is the Ministry of Finance that eventually approves the budget estimates of the DAs. Furthermore, although the central and local government treasuries at the district level have been merged into one district finance office, the idea of a district composite budget remains a fiction. Under the composite budgeting system, the budgetary allocations due to the so-called decentralized departments such as health, education, social welfare, community development, and town and country planning, are to be sent directly to the DAs. The rationale behind this is that since the district officers of the departments will no longer go to Accra, the national capital, they will develop loyalty to the DAs through which they will receive their funds. The idea of composite budget has therefore been promoted to curtail the central control over the DAs. In practice, however, nothing has happened. Central ministries continue to direct how the local departments should use funds and organize their work. Furthermore, the Ministry of Finance has refused to relinquish control over approval of estimates. Indeed, it has been found that central financial control over capital spending and official payments as stipulated by the Financial Administration Decree of 1979, and the Financial Administrative Regulations of 1979, has become tight. Perhaps even more importantly, the subordinate staff of the DAs are not fully at their disposal. The DAs have been given instruction since 1990 on personnel levels by the Office of the Head of the Civil Service and the Ministry of Finance. Even the transfer of a grade-I typist has to be done through the civil-service machinery (Ayee 1994). All these have worked to the diminution of decentralization. The president, in his 1998 Sessional Address to Parliament, directed the Ministries of

Finance and Local Government to operationalize the idea of composite budgeting, but the minister of local government doubts whether it will be possible.

Fifth, the devolution of authority to the DAs has also been circumscribed by the Ministry of Local Government and Rural Development (MLGRD). This ministry monitors the decentralization process and the effectiveness of the DAs and also advises the government on all local government issues. Consequently, it approves all bylaws of the DAs, issues guidelines for the making and levying of rates in the districts, and issues instructions, after consultation with the Ministry of Finance, for the better control and efficient management of finances of the DAs. Most DAs have constantly complained of directives from the MLGRD that have undermined their autonomy and independence.

Planning has remained largely under national government control. Under the National Development Planning System Act (Act 480) of 1994, the top-down planning approach with planning officers located at the center planning for the entire country was to give way to a bottom-up approach. Under it, the DAs are planning authorities with power to ensure participation, coordination, and integration in the preparation of district plans. They were also to conduct a public hearing on any proposed district development plan and consider the views expressed at the hearing before the adoption of the plan. Indeed, it is a requirement that district plans being submitted must be accompanied by evidence that the required public hearings were held. The plans are then sent up to the RCC for harmonization into a regional plan, which in turn goes to the national capital where the National Development Planning Commission integrates all the regional plans into a national plan. In practice, however, the national plan and the annual budgetary allocations hardly bear any resemblance to the proposals made at the district level. What assumes importance in the planning process are the sectoral plans, which are submitted by the central ministries. Thus planning in Ghana remains as central as ever, in spite of the rhetoric on bottom-up planning.

The DAs have been accused of not being enthusiastic about planning. The explanation is that they do not do so because in the experience of the DAs, no one ever takes their plans seriously, and it is a waste of their resources. In addition, the DAs are accused of repairing buildings instead of building new ones. This charge may be true, but it may not be a justifiable criticism, because repairing the buildings may be the best way to spend resources given local needs. These might not be examples of the failure of decentralization, but of its success. The

DAs may be making their own rational decisions based on what is best for their needs. Criticisms of the DAs for these sorts of deviations from nationally determined priorities reflect implicitly the attitude that these changes are only deconcentration.

The reality of devolution of authority to the DAs reveals the centralizing features of Ghana's decentralization. The responsibility of the DAs is restricted to local issues. They make recommendations to the central government. But through official clarification, directives, and exhortation, the DAs have been made to understand that their domain is a very narrow definition of the district. They have no power over matters that can even remotely influence national policy. Insofar as the practical powers of the DAs are concerned, decentralization has been turned into recentralization. In fact, with the exception of assisting local development through the provision of finance and materials, the DAs have not, in practice, been entrusted with any major responsibilities at all. They remain on the sidelines of central government activity. Their confinement to local issues has constrained their role. They transmit the purposes of government to the people. Their ability to persuade the government to modify its policies to conform to popular opinion has been severely curtailed (Acheampong 1995; Ayee 1997a, 1997b).

The DAs also do not seem to have any direct influence on national policy. This is, however, unfortunate because the DAs are designed to provide opportunities for ordinary people to participate in decisionmaking and the general process of development. The devolution of power affected through the DAs is also seen to facilitate the responsiveness of government agencies and organizations to local people's needs and preferences. But the interpretation of the powers of the DAs rests with the central government. Thus, any act of a DA that the government considers to be irreconcilable with the law is declared illegal. All bylaws are approved by the minister of local government while the president has the power to dissolve defaulting or nonperforming DAs without consulting the electorate.

Admittedly, every government has to contend with the balance between local autonomy and central control for the sake of political stability, coordination of development projects, and harmony between local and national aspirations. In Ghana, however, the problem has not really been one of maintaining a balance but one of avoiding closer central government supervision and control. Such an encumbrance clearly does not advance any devolution of genuine authority to supposedly democratic and autonomous bodies such as the DAs (Ayee 1994, 1996).

Deconcentration of Resources

Decentralization in Ghana consists of two main elements, namely, the transfer of power and the transfer of means, which implies resources such as finance and personnel. Without the latter, the transfer of power would not be effective.

Finance

The weak financial position of the DAs vis-à-vis their extensive responsibilities has been recognized by the government of Ghana. The government's response to these financial inadequacies has been essentially twofold. The first is the device of "ceded revenue" under which a number of poor-yielding taxes—entertainment duty; casino revenue tax; gambling tax; betting tax; advertisement tax; income tax payable on registration of trade, business, professional, or vocation; daily transport tax payable by operators of commercial transport; and income tax payable by specified categories of self-employed persons in the informal sector—have been transferred to the DAs.

Monies generated from the ceded revenue were centrally collected by the Internal Revenue Service and the total collected for a year was transferred to the Ministry of Local Government, which then shared it among the 110 DAs. It used a revenue-sharing formula approved annually by the cabinet, based on equality, population, and assessed development status or level of deprivation of each district. The revenue-sharing formula, however, seems unclear because it does not detail the factors used and the weighting assigned to them, nor the criteria employed for determining the degrees of deprivation of the districts. In other words, there was no fixed formula designed for sharing proceeds from the ceded revenue.

Ceded revenue added U.S.$403,000 to the total revenue of the DAs in 1989, U.S.$442,000 in 1990, U.S.$782,000 in 1991, U.S.$4,150,000 in 1992, and U.S.$1,800,000 for the first half of 1993 (Ayee 1995). In all cases, the yield from the ceded revenue exceeded the total revenue mobilized internally by the DAs.

This notwithstanding, the ceded-revenue approach did not much improve the capacity of the DAs to perform functions assigned to them, as most of these revenues were consumed by administrative costs: salaries, district government buildings, and vehicles. The DAs still looked to the central government to provide grants for their development projects, which were not forthcoming. Furthermore, the DAs had only limited success in increasing revenues from rates and other forms of local taxation for a number of reasons. First, most DAs are located in impoverished areas, which limited the total amount of mobilizable resources. Second, even if resources were there to be mobilized, elected DA members naturally hesitated to impose fresh taxes on their constituents since they made the representative unpopular. They were particularly reluctant because most of the resources that might be tapped were (and are) in the hands of local elites, from which most DA members come and on whom they often depend at election time (Crook 1994). Thus efforts to mobilize local resources often amount to attempts to persuade local elites to tax themselves. Or they bring elected DA members into bitter conflict with their electorate. Third, the long history of the failure of local government in Ghana and the misuse of locally mobilizable resources has made taxpayers cynical about what the DAs may do with local contributions or tax revenues. They are therefore generally unwilling to pay taxes. Fourth, the scope of functions allocated the DAs in relation to their size and resources almost guarantees that large numbers of the electorate will be disappointed. Even if the DAs made a better job of revenue collection, it is impossible that every community in the 110 districts could have its demands for large-scale infrastructural and social development met (Ayee 1995, 1996; Crook 1994). In fact, Richard Crook and James Manor's research suggests that very few of these local hopes were fulfilled (1998).

The second approach at revenue transfer is the District Assemblies' Common Fund (DACF) under which the 1992 constitution directs that not less than 5 percent of the total revenues of Ghana shall be shared among the DAs on the basis of a formula approved by parliament annually. The formula for 1998 is based on several factors, namely: need (35 percent); equalization (30 percent); responsiveness (20 percent); service pressure (10 percent); and contingency (5 percent). The DACF is administered by the District Assemblies' Common Fund Administrator (DACFA), who is appointed by the president with the prior approval of parliament.

The 1994, 1995, 1996, and 1997 disbursements from the DACF show that they greatly exceeded revenues generated locally by the DAs. In 1994 this was U.S.$19 million, representing 19.6 percent of the central government's total domestic development budget for the year. In 1995, 1996, and 1997, disbursements of U.S.$28 million, U.S.$41 million, and U.S.$45 million, representing 28.5 percent, 25.5 percent, and 26.7 percent respectively of the total domestic development budget, were transferred (Ayee 1995, 1997b).

That the DACF has tremendous impact on the operation of the DAs cannot be denied. Nevertheless, from the point of view of central-local relations, the DACF has been operated in such a way that it increased central control, not reduced it, as it was conceived to do. Under Section 9 of the DACF Act (Act 455) of 1993, the minister of finance (MOF), in consultation with the MLGRD, is authorized to determine the category of expenditure of the approved budget of a DA that must be met out of the DACF. After areas have been drawn, the DAs select projects according to the value of their share and communicate this to the DAFCA and the MLGRD. This stipulation has been carried out in 1994, 1995, 1996, and 1997 by a directive from the MOF, in consultation with the MLGRD, to all the 110 DAs to concentrate their allocations from the DACF on specific projects in the areas of health and education and central government undertakings. This directive has been seen by the DAs as undermining their autonomy. The government, however, has explained that the directive is not meant to control the DAs, but rather to serve as an interim measure designed to manage the interface between the period of centralized project funding and a decentralized one. In the view of the government, if the directive were not issued it would be difficult to complete projects the central government had begun but not yet completed in the districts. However, this directive has become a permanent feature of the DACF, especially since the act that establishes the DACF stipulates that no expenditure from the fund may be made without the consent of the MOF acting in consultation with the MLGRD. In short, therefore, through central institutions such as the Ministry of Finance, Ministry of Local Government and Rural Development, and the District Chief Executive (DCE), which represents the central government at the local level, the decisions on the allocations of the DACF have been usurped by the central government so that the DAs remain talking shops without finance to implement their decisions. Consequently, the DAs have not been able to validate to their local citizens the value of the local, democratic processes. Continued central control has prevented the DACF from being an instrument of decentralization and democratization.

Even though one concedes that the DACF has substantially increased the financial base of the DAs, the financial viability of the DAs is still in doubt. For example, the 110 DAs and 10 RCCs, as well as some MPs, have, since the introduction of the DACF in 1993, constantly drawn the attention of the central government to the inadequate disbursements from the DACF, and accordingly appealed for an upward revision of the percentage, with limited success. In addition to the low proceeds from the DACF that affected the financial buoyancy of the

DAs, there is evidence to suggest that some of the proceeds have been embezzled by DA officials. In the award of contracts for development projects, some DCEs had colluded with contractors to inflate the costs of projects. In April 1997, twenty-five DCEs were dismissed for rent-seeking practices. Indeed, in August 1997, the regional minister for Ashanti refused to commission a clinic in one of his districts because the cost was inflated. The rent-seeking activities of DCEs have been deplored by Vice President John Mills. Speaking at the closing session of an induction course for twenty-seven new DCEs held in August 1997 in Accra he warned that:

> If any of you has the notion that the office of the district chief executive is for amassing wealth at the expense of the people, I invite him or her to step down now. Severe sanctions, not excluding criminal prosecutions, would be imposed on any district chief executive caught dipping his hands into the District Assemblies' Common Fund or any funds of the assemblies. (*Daily Graphic,* August 29, 1997:1–2)

Furthermore, the reports of the auditor general for 1995, 1996, and 1997 also pointed to disturbing accounts of improper allocations resulting in the mortgaging of the Common Fund for several years, some as far forward as the year 2020, as well as poor contract management, resulting in poor construction works, overpayments, corruption, and, in a few instances, misappropriation. In the view of the vice president, "This malfeasance must stop, else the noble idea of the Common Fund will be discredited" (*Daily Graphic* 1997). Consequently, regional ministers were asked by the MLGRD to closely monitor the operations of the DAs in their regions. A temporary ban, in effect from January 1997, was imposed on the award of new contracts by the DAs except with the prior approval of the RCC.

The introduction of the DACF seems to have made the DAs over-rely on its proceeds rather than acting as an incentive to mobilize resources locally. Most DAs raised less than 45 percent of their projected revenue from traditional sources since the introduction of the DACF. This poor state of affairs has been confirmed by the reports of the RCC monitoring teams that toured the 110 districts in 1996 and 1997, and the report of the auditor general for the same period. Even though the factor of responsiveness in the revenue-sharing formula was meant to stimulate local mobilization of funds for development, there is evidence to suggest that the collection of locally generated revenue has gone down considerably. Consequently, the factor does not really have the desired effect (Ayee 1997c).

Personnel

The other important resource of decentralized government, and perhaps one of the universally cited problems that confronts the DAs, is lack of competent personnel. While the devolution of authority to the DAs imposes increasing demands for services at the district level and requires well-trained local functionaries, at the same time Ghana's economic conditions, administrative reform, and structural adjustment all require less government spending and fewer government agents. These two conditions are, of course, contradictory. The poor quality of staff at the district level has been acknowledged by all, including the Ministry of Local Government. At a workshop on "Budget Planning System in Local Government in Ghana" in 1994, the minister for local government admitted that 65 percent of the local government inspectors at the Inspectorate Division of the MLGRD were not qualified (Ayee 1997a, 1997b).

The poor quality of staff at the district level has been attributed to a number of factors. First is the refusal or reluctance of some staff to accept postings to some districts, particularly the deprived ones, which some Ghanaian bureaucrats refer to as "the bush." Such assignments have been viewed as difficult, unrewarding, and an important impediment to personal mobility, since they remove the incumbent from the center of activity in Accra, the nation's capital. The reluctance to serve away from the capital is also tied to the general unwillingness, particularly of senior bureaucrats, to oversee or directly supervise the implementation of work. This Ghanaian problem is reminiscent to the one described by R. Vengroff and H. B. Salem in Tunisia:

> Service in the regions or in the municipalities is not regarded as positive from a career standpoint by most functionaries. In the smaller, more isolated municipalities, the quality of life, access to schools for their children, good quality housing for themselves and the variety of cultural attractions in Tunis are lacking. Opportunities for salaried employment for their wives are also limited in that environment. . . . The opportunity for training and participation in seminars is considered to be a very important perk. Many functionaries feel that those outside the capital rarely receive timely information on, or invitations to participate in, workshops and seminars. (Vengroff and Salem 1992:486)

The second factor is the low image of local government in the mind of the public. The subject of local government is associated with public latrines, sewers and cesspool emptiers, sanitation and garbage disposal, dirty markets, and slaughterhouses. Consequently, in a society where many people by reason of their education and upbringing have no inclination to "soil their hands," service in local government is not an attractive option. Local government service has had to rely mostly on people who lack the administrative ability and capacity for the work. So low is the status of local government service in Ghana that no one plans or seeks a career in it. People drift into local government service with no specific plans. S. N. Woode (1989) has demonstrated that among civil servants, transfer from a "plum" ministry to district or local government service excites resentment or irritation.

The third factor is the resistance of the twenty-two line ministries and departments to their placement under the DAs. This shift was to enable the DAs to perform their functions effectively. However, considerable difficulties have been experienced in the integration of the line ministries and departments. They include:

• Reluctance of the national and regional-level officers of the line ministries to accept the redefinition of their roles and relationships with the District Chief Executives (DCEs)—the political heads of the districts who are appointed by the central government—and with departmental district heads in terms of the decentralized system. Instead, the central and regional heads of departments have refused to instruct their district officers to work through the DCEs.

• Holding on to funds and controlling programs in the districts by staff of the line ministries and departments without the knowledge of the district officials. Some line ministries and departments continued to operate independently of the DAs and refused to acknowledge the authority of the DAs over them.

• The various instruments that set up the various ministries and departments have not been amended despite the policy changes, so the district heads of departments attend meetings of the DAs more out of respect or fear than out of legal obligation to them (Ayee 1997a, 1997b).

• The line ministries and departments, in spite of "decentralization," continue to report to Accra through the regions, while their staff are appointed, promoted, remunerated, and disciplined by their national and regional offices because the DAs lack the financial resources to hire and fire staff. The furthest the DAs can go in controlling the staff of the line ministries and departments is to request their respective headquarters to remove the recalcitrant officers. The headquarters, in turn, has frequently responded by delaying replacement of such officers, or sometimes actually refusing to transfer them. The frustration of the DAs in dealing with district-level officers has been amplified by President Rawlings:

> Government is aware of the tendency of some departments to under-mine the authority of the District Assemblies, claiming to report only to their head offices. There have been cases where requests by the district assembly for vital information have been turned down because the personnel of the departments concerned still refuse to understand the new order in local government administration. Some attitudes being displayed by the bureaucracy have tended to impede the process of grassroots participation and actions will be taken to make the bureaucracy responsible enough to work for the people, and with the people. (Rawlings 1991:14)

Even though President Rawlings spoke of "remedial action" to get the line ministries integrated under the DAs in 1991, as of the middle of 1998 nothing concrete was achieved. What has been done has been a retreat from this commitment, or has been cosmetic. For instance, under the Local Government Act (Act 462) of 1993, instead of each district having twenty-two decentralized departments, metropolitan assemblies, municipal assemblies, and district assemblies are to have sixteen, thirteen, and eleven decentralized departments, respectively. The Ghana Education Service, which was on the list of twenty-two departments, disappeared from the list of departments and organizations now to be decentralized under Act 462 for unexplained reasons.

Like the president, the minister of local government and rural development has also pointed out that

> the non-establishment of the decentralized departments as integrated departments of the DAs represents one of the major shortcomings of the entire decentralization program. In the event, what has happened is that the various sector Ministries have established committees at the district level in order to establish a linkage with the District Assembly, and virtually all the committees are chaired by the District Chief Executive. (Ahwoi 1998:16)

In spite of the intentions of the 1992 constitution, the Civil Service Law (PNDC Law 327) of 1993, and the Local Government Law (Act 462) of 1993 to promote democratization through decentralization, the bureaucracy is as centralized as ever, and the DAs are far from being served by a competent, loyal staff. The source of continued centralized administration lies in contradictory legislation passed by the same government that has proclaimed abiding interest in decentralization. While the Civil Service Law and the Local Government Act provided for a decentralized civil service, legislation such as the Education Service Law and the Health Service Law have been passed that continue to place the staff working with the DAs under the control of their headquarters in Accra. An example of central interference was exhibited in June 1998 when the director general of the Ghana Education Service signed a performance contract with the district directors of education when they were supposed to be working for the DAs (Nkrumah 1998). Indeed, the minister for local government has blamed the failure of decentralization on the bureaucracy, particularly the top management personnel of the civil service. "Every impediment has been placed in the way of implementing the decentralization program. Top civil servants do not know about the program and do not want to know. Some have deliberately confused it with an exercise of deconcentration" (Ahwoi 1992:24). This accusation may be true or not. Nonetheless, the heart of the matter is that administrative reform of any kind encounters resistance, and policymakers and implementers must take measures to neutralize or minimize it. To simply blame someone for resisting it misses the issue.

How does one reconcile Rawlings's statement blaming the bureaucracy and the realities of continued and expanding centralization? This could be explained from the viewpoint that decentralization fitted into the overall political tendencies of Rawlings because he saw it as a plank for the achievement of political legitimacy.

Perhaps the greatest problem in this whole scheme of things is the position of the MLGRD vis-à-vis the other sector ministries, notably finance, health, and education. The MLGRD was expected to operate as a local government secretariat for the purposes of the decentralized local government system. Resistance to this role by the ministry is a summation of the resistance to the decentralization program. Nevertheless, this resistance could be broken down if three things are done:

- The decentralization of the national recurrent budget prepared by the Ministry of Finance, which will relocate the remuneration of the district level staff to districts.
- An increase in the percentage of the national revenue that constitutes the Common Fund, which will have the effect of expanding the scope of coverage of the decentralized development budget.
- The establishment of a local government service with its concomitant decentralization of staff recruitment.

Developing Accountability, Representation, and Effective Institutions of Collective Choice

A local political process is important to ensure the accountability and responsiveness of district government to the local public. The key institution in this may be presumed to be the DA. It mediates between the public and the district executive. It must be able, then, to assert some control over the executive to provide for accountability, as well as be accountable to and represent local opinion. Both of these dimensions are now considered.

Accountability of the District Executive to the District Assembly and Effective Institutions of Collective Choice

Effective accountability of the district chief executive (DCE) to the DA has yet to be achieved. The problem is that the DCE is centrally appointed, is far more powerful than the presiding member (PM) of the DA, and understands himself to be both the local chief executive and the representative of the central government. Through all this, he exerts great influence over the DAs and simultaneously precludes development of effective institutions of collective choice.

Specifically, his office is the conduit for transmitting central government concerns to the district, and thus has weight vis-à-vis the DA. Also, he is chief representative of the central government in the district and continues through this role to exert undue influence over the DAs. In addition, the DCE is the most influential member of the DA, as reflected by his chairmanship of the Executive Committee (EXECO), the nerve center of the DA. It exercises executive and coordinating responsibilities. Neither in law nor practice does the PM, the chairman of the DA, ever present a real threat to the dominance and preeminence of the DCE. For example, the PM is specifically excluded from the membership of the EXECO, on the assumption that this would provide a balance when the DCE makes reports on the activities of the EXECO to the full DA (Ayee 1994, 1997a, 1997b). However, this has not worked. Instead of a "check or balance," the PM is essentially removed from these key decision processes of EXECO, and the DA is ineffective in influencing EXECO decisions.

The dominance of the DCE in decisionmaking in the DA is not in doubt. This being so, the consensual style of decisionmaking prevalent in most DAs really works only to strengthen his/her control. Perhaps partially as a result, there has been a tendency for the DA members to accept decisions made in the interests of the DCE and the central government, rather than of the public. Indeed, while addressing the Mfantsiman District Assembly in June 1996, the central regional minister was appalled at the lack of promotion of the interests of the electorate by the DAs, and noted that "it would be better for the District Assemblies to consult the people for their views when development projects are being initiated" (*Daily Graphic,* June 20, 1996:3). Most DA members the writer interviewed in June 1997 complained of the authoritarian style of leadership of their DCEs. Given the role of the DCE in Ghana's decentralization program, any official who replaces him will not merely be a titular head but will become a power broker. In short, the extremely active role of the DECs has undermined the democratic orientation of the decentralization program.

Aside from the DCE, the central government has a wide array of human and material resources with which to cajole and otherwise influence the DAs. For instance, districts that voted against the government in general elections were denied provision of basic amenities such as roads, clinics, and schools. In addition, the continued weight and consequences of central influence through appointed members cannot be ignored. The president appoints 30 percent of the DAs and committee members in consultation with chiefs and interest groups in the district. More often than not, the president did not consult anyone before the appointments were made to the DAs. Although the appointed members were to bring knowledge and professional and technical skills to bear on the DAs, they are people who were predictabley loyal to the central government. Their inclusion in the DAs was political: it was meant to give the DAs some "political direction" (which has meant serving as central government "watchdogs") and to ensure that the presence of central government was felt in the DA forum. This emphasizes the politics of decentralization, which sees decentralization policies as serving the broader political interests or strategies of those in power.

Still, and giving some hope of signs of local accountability, the government's hope of using the appointees to its own advantage has not always fully materialized. Some have lived up to their image of providing expertise to their DAs. Others have been active critics of the local administration and the central government itself. Nevertheless, despite some appointees having successfully confounded the public's view of them as "government stooges," one cannot fail to acknowledge the threat by the appointed members to the autonomy of the DA. In some DAs, decisions taken in the absence of some appointed members were revisited and sometimes reversed when they later showed up at meetings (Ayee 1994, 1996).

Accountability of the District Assemblies to Constituents

To be sure, ensuring accountability of the DCE to the DA is of little value unless the DAs are accountable to the public. Two requirements were meant to promote accountability of Ghana's local government officials. The first was a broad set of responsibilities assigned to DA members. They were to:

- Maintain close contact with their electoral area, consult their people on issues to be discussed in the DAs, and collate their views, opinions, and proposals.
- Present the views, opinions, and proposals to the DA.
- Attend meetings of the DA and meetings of subcommittees of which they are members.
- Meet their electorate before each meeting of the DA.
- Report to their electorate the general decisions of the DA and its executive committee and the actions that they had taken to solve problems raised by residents in their electoral areas.
- Maintain frequent liaison with organized productive economic groupings and other persons in the district.
- Take part in communal and development activities in the district. (Republic of Ghana 1993a)

In short, DA members were to discharge their responsibilities having due regard to the national interest and the interest of the people in their districts.

The requirement that the DA members should meet their constituents before and after DA meetings has, in most cases, not been met for obvious logistics problems. DA members were only paid meager sitting allowances, an average of U.S.$10 per sitting, while at the same time monetary demands were made on them by some of their constituents. Consequently, DA members decided not to meet the electorate regularly. Having said this, the DA members were under an official injunction to be responsible for the development of their areas, and are to be judged by their success or failure in encouraging development. They were also to be judged by how closely they maintained contact with the electorate, a task facilitated both by their local residence and the closeness of representation built into the system—an average ratio of one member to two thousand electors. Much pressure was therefore on DA members to act as delegates for their communities. This was reflected in their approach to their roles on the DA: to fight for a share of the DA resources for their area to the exclusion of all else (Ayee 1994, 1996; Crook 1994).

The second requirement meant to promote accountability is the potential revocation of the mandate or appointment of a DA member. Section 9 of the Local Government Act (Act 462) of 1993 provides that the mandate of an elected member of a DA may be revoked by the electorate if they lose confidence in him. This can occur on any of the following grounds: that he had abandoned the ideas and programs for which he was elected; that he had systematically neglected his duties; or that he had committed acts incompatible with his office as a member of the DA.

The procedure for the removal of an erring DA member is laborious, which in practice deterred the local people from taking any action against their DA members. First, when the electorate loses confidence in an elected member of the DA on any of the above grounds, 25 percent of the registered voters in the electoral area may petition the District Election Committee (DEC) for the revocation of that member's mandate and his recall from the DA. Second, the DEC shall, upon receipt of such a petition, determine whether a prima facie case has been made for the recall of that member. Third, where the DEC determines that a prima facie case for the recall of a member had been established, the DEC should organize a referendum to decide whether or not such a member must be recalled. The issue at any such referendum is decided if at least 40 percent of the electorate vote on the issue, and 60 percent of the votes cast are in favor of the revocation of such mandate.

Appointed or nominated DA members were also subject to removal. Section 9 (6) of Act 462 stipulates that the president may revoke the appointment of an appointed member either in the exercise of his discretion, or upon the recommendations of three-fourths of the members of the DA, or upon a complaint made by a registered voter in the district on stated and proven grounds.

In reality, no local citizen was able to initiate any action to remove an erring DA member because of the cumbersome procedure involved, even though there is substantial evidence that the electorate was dissatisfied with the performance of DA members. What the electorate has done is wait for four years and vote against the DA member in the DA elections. This happened in the 1994 and 1998 DA elections. DA members who were removed administratively were removed on grounds that they absented themselves from more than three consecutive ordinary meetings of the DA without the written permission of the presiding member of the DA, contrary to sections of Act 462.

The development of a local political and accountability process also depends on the ability of the DAs to cooperate and work with civil-society organization (CSOs) at the district level. In recognition of this, the legal framework of decentralization stipulates that the DAs should coordinate, integrate, and harmonize development programs promoted or carried out by CSOs as well as act in cooperation with them in the district. However, there is no evidence of coordinated activity between the DAs and CSOs. The CSOs, without consultation or coordination with the DAs, frequently carried out projects. There is mutual distrust between the CSOs and DAs over questions of funding. The DAs felt that the CSOs were better funded by donors and therefore were able to provide more and better-quality basic amenities, thereby creating real legitimacy problems for the DAs in the districts. On the other hand, the CSOs had the impression that they were better than the DAs in terms of the provision of projects because of their superiority in terms of human and financial resources. Another dimension of the problem is that the DAs often did not grasp the important role that CSOs play and did not consult with their leaders. For their part, the leaders of the CSOs generally did not make the effort to place their legitimate demands before the DAs (Ayee 1992a, 1994, 1997b). Consequently, there are nonreciprocal relations between Ghana's CSOs and the DAs, which have had the practical effect of leaving local-level issues unresolved and not encouraging democratic practices.

The beneficial work of the donors, often through nongovernmental organizations such as World Vision or Adventist Development and Relief Agency, has ironically further eroded the potential for a local political process focused on DAs. While the DAs were involved in providing basic community services such as classrooms, health posts, markets, hand-dug wells, and electricity extension, the large role played by the donors and the NGOs led many local people to mistakenly credit NGOs and donors for every project done in the districts. The visibility and legitimacy of the DAs was thus eroded.

Political Parties: A Solution?

Clearly, an effective political and accountability process has yet to emerge at the district level in Ghana. Problems of central dominance of local institutions are compounded by the often-noted challenges of mobilizing public participation, aggregating public interests, and building stable coalitions in legislative bodies. Partisan politics ought to be considered as a partial solution to these problems.

Insofar as central control reflects a sincere desire for policy coordination rather than simply squashing criticism and dissent, political parties have long been one way that democracies achieve harmony between local and national opinion among political activists. Party philosophies help encourage consistency in program proposals across all levels of political office. Party platforms are shared at every level of government where the parties are contesting seats. But in Ghana, political parties are proscribed from local politics. In the words of the Article 248 (Sections 1 and 2) of the 1992 constitution, "A candidate seeking election to a District Assembly or any lower local government unit shall present himself to the electorate as an individual, and shall not use any symbol associated with any political party. A political party shall not endorse, sponsor, offer a platform to or in anyway campaign for or against a candidate seeking election to a District Assembly or any lower local government unit." Two reasons for excluding partisan politics from the DAs have been given by the PNDC government and the Committee of Experts that drafted the 1992 constitution. First it was argued that in the past, elected governments in Ghana cynically exerted influence on local government bodies to win political advantage. Second, the nonpartisan nature of the DAs facilitates the mobilization of the people and is more conducive to consensus formation, factors that are crucial to development at the grassroots (Republic of Ghana 1991). However, the evidence already discussed suggests that the second reason has been stillborn.

Of course the option for political parties is controversial and debated. The lists of advantages and disadvantages is long, and the evidence is incomplete.

Advantages of nonpartisan politics in local government. Nonpartisan politics do not suffer from one key disadvantage of partisan politics. In partisan politics, policy proposals tend to be formed in party meetings rather than in open government council. True debate can be stifled by the presence of party whips, thus depriving the leadership of public ideas and opinions of merit.

The savagery with which partisan elections and campaigns are often conducted may discourage able individuals from standing for office, and thus deprive the district of their services (Ayee 1992a).

Nonpartisan politics permit candidates of the same party to stand against each other. In partisan elections, through primaries, political parties reduce the number of member candidates for any given seat to one. This deprives the nation of many able voices. Under nonpartisan politics candidates from the same party can run against each other.

Advantages of partisan politics in local government. In the complex society of today, opinion needs to be organized to be effective. Ordinary individual opinion cannot possess the specialized knowledge or the weight to command attention. By aggregating interests, parties produce both the specialized knowledge and the weight of numbers needed to effect policy. The involvement of major parties in local government tends to increase the national significance of local government. Effective decentralized government is still a goal in Ghana, yet not a reality because local government does not have a clear relation to national government. The key to making local government more effective and to linking it more firmly to national politics may lie in letting parties compete in local elections.

By successfully contesting elections at every level of government, politicians rise through the ranks of their parties. In countries with partisan local politics, most MPs rise through the ranks of their parties and enter office already knowledgeable about parliamentary procedures. Partisan politics thus strengthens a nation's top leadership by seasoning.

In Ghana, many currently registered parties have little support. In partisan politics at the local level, parties with no grassroots support are soon identified as such and die off. Partisan local-level politics thus sharpens the focus of the national political discourse by eliminating unrepresentative parties from the debate.

Effective agenda setting is possible in democratic government only if there is consistency in points of view. Without some form of party discipline this may be difficult to achieve. Party organization helps develop definite policy and furthers its aims. Political parties provide focal points of local affairs and partisan candidates for DAs running as members of a political party would have manifestos and platforms to guide them. Currently, as nonpartisan candidates, members of DAs are elected on the basis of their personal popularity and seldom for the force of their ideas. Thus many elected representatives in the DAs come to office with little or no idea of what to do.

*   *   *

In short, Ghana's nonpartisan local government elections produce local governments full of people with no formal agenda, while through lack of party affiliations local politics are not linked to the national level. In other words, administrative decentralization alone does not seem to have advanced the cause of local governance in Ghana. One is tempted to believe that there is a place for partisan politics in Ghana's local government. Indeed, as is widely reported in the media, in actual practice Ghana's DAs are not free from partisan politics. It is an open secret that in the district assembly elections of 1994, 1998, and 2002, most, if not all, political parties either sponsored or supported individual candidates to win seats in the DAs, contrary to the constitution. This is because the parties wanted to control the grassroots in order to boost their chances of winning national elections (Clarke 2001). However, since this was unofficial and did not involve the public, the mobilizing role parties can play did not occur.

In general, a local political process and effective institutions of collective choice have yet to develop in Ghana's districts. Central government dominance, DA weakness, and public fragmentation and disengagement seem to be the major problems.

The NPP Government's Ideas on Local Governance

The New Patriotic Party (NPP) administration that took over power in January 2001, although it has brought new ideas on how to improve local governance in Ghana, has not been able to implement them because it has been in power for a short period and almost all the ideas involve constitutional amendments that will take some time to become law. The new ideas are contained in the manifesto of the party entitled "Agenda for Positive Change." In the manifesto, the NPP government believes not only in the decentralization of government and bureaucracy but also re-echoes the point that much of the political frustration since independence can be traced to the excessive centralization of government and governmental power in the nation's capital. The NPP government blames its predecessor government, Rawlings's National Democratic Congress, for its inability to live up to the spirit of the 1992 constitutional provisions on decentralization.

To correct the anomalies that have undermined effective decentralization in Ghana, the NPP administration has made its intention known to do the following things, which are yet to be implemented and some of which, as indicated earlier, need constitutional amendments:

• Amend Article 248 of the 1992 constitution to make local government elections partisan. To the new government, a partisan local government system is congruent with the existing constitutional requirement of a partisan central government system. It believes that a partisan local government with elections held at or near the middle of the term of office of the country's president has the effect of sending a signal to the ruling party regarding the people's assessment of its performance; and can thereby jolt the ruling party to improve its performance.

• Disagree with the present arrangement for the appointment and removal of the district chief executives and ultimately will amend the constitution to have them freely elected.

• Review district boundary lines and, where necessary, create additional districts to ensure effective and evenly spread development of the country. For similar reasons, the government may, subject to the constitution of Ghana, consider the creation of new regions.

• Provide more resources for the local authorities at the regional, district, and local levels to support their planning functions and in the delivery of health, education, and other services, such as providing good drainage and sanitation and managing the environment. Toward this end, the government proposes to increase the share of resources going to the districts from 5 percent to 7.5 percent, while encouraging the districts to raise and properly manage their own funds.

• Embark on a massive manpower development program for meeting acute staff shortages in the fields of financial management, planning, and engineering. Under this program, a large number of unemployed graduates in the country will be absorbed in the DAs. However, to avoid overburdening the DAs with unduly large work forces, contracts of specialized services to qualified consultants by the DAs would be encouraged.

• Halt the abuse of the District Assemblies Common Fund (DACF) prevalent during Rawlings's NDC government and ensure transparency and fairness in its use.

• Improve organizational structures for carrying out development projects in towns and villages to strengthen involvement and active participation of chiefs (NPP 2000).

Since the government took over office in January 2001, it has taken some measures that reinforce the status quo. First, 105 district chief executives (instead of 110 because five of the district assemblies had rejected the president's nominee) were appointed by the president and approved by the DAs. This is no departure from the existing practice. Of course, the government has indicated its intention to change the practice by referring the matter to the parliamentary subcommittee on local government and rural development. The appointment of the DCEs by the president was, as usual, fraught with intense lobbying by groups (such as youths; national, regional, and district party executives; parliamentarians, etc.) within the ruling party and groups outside it (such as traditional leaders and ethnic loyalists who would like the DCE to come from their own areas).

Second, the NPP has ordered the payment of outstanding DACF

proceeds to the DAs, which were in arrears for nine months. For instance, the government released U.S.$27.5 million and U.S.$10.6 million (out of the U.S.$42.7 million budgetary allocation to the DACF for 2001) for disbursement to the DAs as the last quarterly and first quarterly installments of the DACF for 2000 and 2001. The delay in the release of proceeds from the DACF is due to the long disbursement process, the availability of funds in the consolidated fund, and the fact that the constitution does not give dates on which the DACF should be released. Payment into the DACF is authorized by the Ministry of Finance to the controller and accountant general. It is then forwarded to the central bank, the Bank of Ghana, for a check to be prepared in the name of the office of the administrator of the DACF, who in turn issues a check to the DAs. To get around the delay involved in the disbursement of the DACF, the minister of local government and rural development met the stakeholders (the Ministries of Finance and Local Government and Rural Development, the Bank of Ghana, the controller and accountant general, and the administrator of the DACF) at the end of August 2001 to find a way of making the period for the release definite.

Third, auditing of accounts of the former DCEs by the auditor-general is in progress. Some DCEs have been surcharged and given thirty days to pay up or face court action. DCEs who have been cleared will be paid their ex gratia award. The action to surcharge and subsequently to prosecute DCEs who have embezzled or misappropriated money is new. Under the Rawlings NDC regime, DCEs who engaged in such nefarious acts were either dismissed or redeployed. The new government's action to surcharge or prosecute DCEs found to have embezzled DA funds is in line with its policy of "zero tolerance" for corruption.

The government has articulated clearly and repeatedly its commitment to decentralization. There has been a comprehensive review of issues, challenges, and constraints to decentralization while time-bound performance targets have been set in various official publications such as the Ministry of Local Government and Rural Development's *Decentralization in Ghana: Implementation Status and Proposed Future Directions, the Ghana Poverty Reduction Strategy* (2002), the 2002 Presidential Sessional Address to Parliament, and the 2002 budget. These notwithstanding, there is the perception that decentralization is a low priority relative to the "president's agenda" outlined in the 2002 Sessional Address to Parliament, which includes vigorous infrastructural development, modernized agriculture, enhanced social services with emphasis on health and education, good governance, and private-sector development. This may be due to the inability of government to commit or implement a comprehensive decentralization program. Knowing that decentralization involves major political and technical trade-offs, the NPP government seems unprepared to undertake in its first term extremely difficult and comprehensive reforms (such as the establishment of a local government service and the election, rather than the appointment, of DCEs), which are not considered important in order to win a second term in office. Consequently, the government is interested in tinkering with activities to strengthen the local government system without having to develop and commit to a risky and complex decentralization program.

The hope is that the government, in implementing its "new" ideas on decentralization, does not, like its predecessor, involve itself in a self-legitimating deception or engage in an elaborate public-relations hoax.

Conclusion

Ghana's decentralization program is a top-down one, initiated by the central government, that has transferred some of its power and authority to the districts, but little to the DAs. It has some sort of ulterior political motives of a centralizing nature, in the sense that it is intended to strengthen, rather than weaken, the role of the central government. In other words, the decentralization of government machinery has in fact strong elements of centralization. That is because the central government gives with one hand and takes back with the other (Conyers 1989)—the politics of decentralization. For example, central funding grows with the introduction of the DACF, and so does central control. Without local autonomy to manage resources, there can be no genuine accountability, something reflected in the weak local political process found in the districts. However, given the limitations on local mobilization of resources, which afflict all the DAs in Ghana, a significant element of transferred central funding in fact appears inevitable.

The central-local government relationship in Ghana is not one of cooperation and partnership, but rather a principal-agent relationship. The central government in Accra (the principal) still tries to maintain tight control by treating the DAs as agents of (that is, under) central authority. The interpretation of the powers of the DAs rests with the central government, particularly the MLGRD. Any act of a DA that the central government considers irreconcilable with the law is declared illegal. Either the MLGRD or the regional coordinating councils, as indicated earlier, approves all bylaws. The president has the power to dissolve or suspend any defaulting DA in the "public interest." Such encumbrances do not advance the devolution of decisionmaking to the DAs, nor do they encourage the emergence of the DAs as viable agents of local governance.

Limited procedural decentralization at the district level has not led either to a major improvement in the service delivery capacity of the DAs, nor to the promotion of a democratic ethos. The responsiveness of the DAs to demands from below is largely a function of the linkage mechanisms operating at the local level. Where villages or towns were represented in the DAs by "native sons"—whether elected or appointed—they have been better positioned to extract resources from the district than those communities that had no one to speak on their behalf. However, in those instances where a local community claimed a national-level minister or a "big man" as a native son, the flow of patronage resources far exceeds what can be obtained via DA members. When this happened, DA members were under severe criticism for inability to deliver. Indeed, with the minister or "big man," who needs a DA member?

Decentralization has also not been able to reduce congestion and overconcentration of power in the nation's capital. Despite "decentralization," officials in the regions and districts visit Accra, either once or twice a month, to chase funds or ask for certain favors for their regions or districts, which they cannot receive if they remain in their rural areas. Although the minister for local government has pointed out that the practice has been discouraged and is a hangover of centralization of administration, the evidence on the ground points to the contrary. The fact remains that Ghana has not yet moved from a centralized system of administration. Despite the claim to have decentralized power by setting up the DAs, the government has in fact brought about a form of supervised or centralized decentralization in which the central government is omnipresent and has the last say not only in important issues but even in a wide variety of matters relating to the day-to-day running of the DAs. Continued central control has therefore undermined the main objective of the decentralization program, giving "power to the people" and consequently encouraging democratization.

Overall, Ghana's program of top-down decentralization has hitherto not been effective in laying a foundation for local governance. The absence of an effective local political process and local accountability, the absence of resources with which localities can make choices and implement plans, and the lack of any real authority has meant little foundation has been laid for effective local governance.

Note

1. See the 1992 Constitution (Chapters 8 and 20); PNDC Law 207, 1988, which has been repealed by the Local Government Act (Act 462), 1993; the Civil Service Law (PNDC Law 327), 1993; Legislative Instrument (LI) 1514, 1991, which has been repealed by LI 1589, 1994; District Assemblies Common Fund Act (Act 455), 1993; the National Development Planning Commission Act (Act 479), 1994; the National Development Planning (System) Act (Act 480); and the legislative Instruments of 1988–1989 that created the 110 district assemblies (DAs). In addition to these, there are eight administrative regulations, e.g., the Financial Memorandum (Section 81) of the Local Government Act (Act 54), 1961; Financial Administrative Decree (FAD), SMCD 221, 1979; the Financial Administration Regulation (FAR), LI 1234, 1979; bylaws of the 110 district assemblies; Model Standing Orders for Municipal and District Assemblies, 1994; and Legislative Instruments of the Ministry of Local Government and Rural Development.

7

Chad:
Governance by the Grassroots

Simon M. Fass and Gerrit M. Desloovere

Talk about African politics during the past decade has turned increasingly to decentralization, local government, grassroots and intermediary organizations, civil society, democratization, and other variations on the theme of participation and its benefits. Behind this talk is the firm belief, nurtured by a generation of painful experience, that most if not all central governments, as presently constituted, are structurally incapable of delivering durable social, economic, or political progress to the majority of citizens (Wunsch and Olowu 1990a). It follows that these states need more than cosmetic changes in stewardship. They require profound structural reformation, generally in the direction of operational transparency, responsiveness to citizen interests, and other features of broad-based participatory democracy (Nyang'oro 1994).

Unfortunately, indigenous forces at hand to engage in state reconstruction are few. Accordingly, the need in the immediate future would seem to be emergence and growth of a wide array of self-interested institutional actors that could so engage themselves. The hope here is that some or all of these entities, acting autonomously at the local, regional, and national levels as elements of larger systems of societal governance, may at the same time also help to restructure the state. Viable systems of local governance would seem to be critical elements in this process. However, given the many problems faced by Africa's formal local government structures created from the top down, some of which are discussed in other chapters of this volume, there is also the need to build local governance systems from the bottom up. Notwithstanding references to nonstate entities of various kinds and to their presumed promise for the future, such as by P. Landell-Mills (1992), empirical evidence on what such organizations have done to hasten emergence of local governance systems, and on why and how they emerge in the first place, remains scarce.

Such evidence does exist. Chad, with a central apparatus too weakened by three decades of recurrent fighting to provide much in the way of services, is a good example. Unable to rely on the center, this society has built Africa's most decentralized systems of health, water supply, and other public services. In education, for instance, indigenous local associations have financed an increase of more than 835,000 school seats during the last twenty-five years. Government, in contrast, supplied less than 45,000 places. Communities now contribute more than 3.8 billion Communauté Financière Africaine (CFA) francs per year to schools and pay salaries between CFA 5,000 and 15,000 per month to nearly 60 percent of the country's 15,000 teachers. The Ministry of Education (MEN), with a primary education budget of about CFA 6 billion, pays another 27 percent, a monthly average of CFA 115,000 (while the rest work in private schools).

This fiscal decentralization (by default, rather than by policy; see Chapter 10) has been accompanied by a gradual shift in control of public services from the state to the localities that pay for them: a shift to local governance. In the case of education, an early sign of this shift is emergence of a type of public facility that is relatively new to the country—the "community" school. Now constituting more than one-quarter of the country's schools, it differs from a state facility in only one respect: the director is not a state employee. As a result, the school operates under authority of the locality. Teachers answer to parents for their performance and not, as in state schools, to education inspectors. Likewise, construction, procurement, number of grades offered, student-teacher ratios, financing mechanisms, curriculum, and other decisions are made by the community alone. And they create their schools without seeking prior state approval.

A second sign, closely related to the first, is penetration of local control into state schools, especially where all teachers but the director are paid by the community. Here inspectors, abandoning the tradition of enjoining parents to follow the director's instructions, are beginning to order directors to work with parents. Writ larger, a third sign is the irrelevance of state teachers' strikes and, as in 1992–1993 and 1993–1994, of government declarations of *annees blanches* (aborted academic years). Because community teachers in state schools lose their jobs if they strike, their classes continue. Students in classes taught by state teachers simply move to those of community instructors, or to nearby community schools. If there are no community teachers or schools in the vicinity, then villages create them overnight.

In other words, the MEN's role in primary instruction has diminished to the point where its disappearance would likely have little effect on the quantity and quality of basic education. The MEN and other service ministries in similar circumstances—i.e., a goodly portion of the central apparatus—have become marginalized. In their place to supply not only local but also national public services today are thousands of village and other associations that, if not juridically then certainly empirically, operate as local governments.

Relying mainly on data from interviews in more than ninety villages during 1992–1998, in this chapter we use the case of schooling to describe a relatively successful system of local governance, focusing on how and why it has succeeded—not so much in terms of better schooling but rather, and more generally, in terms of a better system to set goals, mobilize funds, and manage resources.[1] In this framework we look closely at several things. First is the confluence of factors that launched the society on its path to local governance: the unsettled nature of the state, which has underwritten its inability to respond to demand for public services; man-made and natural disasters; and economic development projects, which stimulated rapid growth in demand.

We then examine institutional aspects. Our look focuses initially on how individual communities have organized to finance and manage their schools—which are usually just one element of a wider set of local service activities. Next we take a close look at why and how intermediary organizations emerged to build bridges between localities, and between localities and the state, and at how the organizations have helped local institutions, via lobbying and other means, to speed the growth of effective local governance.

Turning to the state and its foreign-aid agency assistants, we explore some of the ways in which centralized, top-down thinking, such as blatant disregard of the reality of operating local governance entities, inhibits the ability of the state and aid agencies to collaborate with communities in improving services. To illustrate that there is much to gain and little to lose in shifting from centralized to local-governance and collaborative modes of reasoning, we describe a schooling project for nomads. It demonstrates clearly that state–aid agency–community collaboration is possible, productive, and beneficial to all concerned.

After reiterating that what we describe for the case of schooling applies as readily to other public services, we conclude that the associations' services—by their tasks, functions, and decisionmaking processes—operate very much like local governments elsewhere. Even though the associations lack appropriate juridical status, it is useful to accept them as governments because, as we show, the state and donors have much to gain by treating localities as full partners in provision of services, and by actions to strengthen their capacities.

The Unsettled State

Chad, a territory covering almost 500,000 square miles, contains 8 million people spread across a complex array of different languages, ethnicities, and religions that is remarkable even for Africa.[2] In addition to French and Arabic, the official languages, there are twelve major linguistic groups containing more than a hundred different languages and dialects. This variety reflects an ethnic and religious composition of considerable diversity: six major ethnic groups in the largely Christian and animist south; twenty-two groups in the mostly Muslim north-central region; and an assortment of other nomad tribes in the far north (also Muslim).

Before French colonial penetration in 1899, this heterogeneous zone was home to several powerful states. Kanem-Bornu, established in A.D. 800, reached the height of its power during the late sixteenth century. The kingdoms of Baguirmi and Ouaddai emerged early in the seventeenth century and thrived in the eighteenth. But by the end of the nineteenth century, these states were in decline, torn by decades of war and internecine feuds. Weakened by constant fighting, one after the other fell to Rabih az-Zubayr, a Sudanese adventurer, during 1883–1893.

By 1900 the French had defeated Rabih, and the Kanem-Bornu dynasty reestablished itself under French protection. The territory became part of the federation of French Equatorial Africa in 1910, but stiff resistance from northern populations delayed pacification of the present area of Chad until 1917.

The next half century, during which the country changed status from colony to overseas territory (1946) and then to independent republic (1960), was modern Chad's most stable period. During this time, administrative and economic development was concentrated in the south. One reason was that the south contained more exploitable resources than the north. Another reason was that northern populations, like their Muslim counterparts elsewhere and unlike southerners, passively resisted colonization long after fighting stopped. For example, they refused to work for the administration, serve in the army, or enroll children in French schools.

In the 1940s and 1950s the northern populations, especially in towns, began to notice that their resistance had allowed southerners to outclass them educationally, economically, and politically. The bulk of cadres in the colonial administration, civilian and military, were from the south. Northerners then began to collaborate with the French. But having come late to the game, at independence they were still underrepresented in the state apparatus. For many, particularly those tracing their ancestries to the precolonial kingdoms, this implied that independence would not bring autonomy. It would only bring a shift in subservience, from French to southern people.

The country's political fissures, however, as in other African nations, were more entangled than a simple north-south divide. Political parties that established themselves before independence showed a tendency, irrespective of ideology, to have specific ethnic foundations. As a result, and camouflaged as they might be by fancy names given to parties and movements, politics after independence degenerated into a constant struggle for control of the state among ambitious leaders of various ethnic factions—initially between northern and southern leaders, later almost exclusively among northerners.

Francois N'Garta Tombalbaye, a southern trade union leader who became the country's first president in 1960, showed the way. In 1961 he merged his political party with that of the principal opposition to form a broad-based government. It was short-lived. Alleging a coup conspiracy by Muslim elements in the government, Tombalbaye dissolved the National Assembly in 1963, declared a state of emergency, arrested top ministers drawn from the merged opposition party, and established a one-party state.

Troubles began in earnest during 1965–1967, when suppression of northern protests against arbitrary taxation and intolerable behaviors of public officials and the Chadian army—mostly southerners—catalyzed emergence of several armed opposition groups. Often led by adherents to the parties banned in 1963, some of these groups banded together to form two guerrilla movements. The Front for the National Liberation of Chad (FROLINAT), established in 1966, operated primarily in the far north. The Chad National Front operated in the east. The stated aim of both groups was to overthrow the government, reduce French influence, and build closer relations with Arab states. Heavy fighting occurred in 1969 and 1970, and French military forces helped the Chadian army suppress the revolt. But with Libyan backing, the rebels resumed fighting in 1971.

President Tombalbaye was deposed and killed in a military takeover in 1975, and General Félix Malloum, Tombalbaye's chief of staff, became head of state. Soon thereafter, in 1977, Goukouni Oueddei, leader of a major FROLINAT faction, launched a new offensive. In an effort to stop the fighting and consolidate his position,

Malloum invited Hissène Habré, leader of another FROLINAT faction, the Armed Forces of the North (FAN), to serve as prime minister in 1978. This moment marked the beginning of the shift from a north-south conflict into a struggle among northern factions.

In a bid to unseat Malloum, Habré's forces attacked the capital's radio stations in early 1979. But Goukouni Oueddei seized the city. Under a Nigeria-brokered Transitional Government of National Unity, which accorded roles to Habré and to Colonel Wadel Abdelader Kamougue, head of what remained of the Chadian army, Goukouni Oueddei became president late in 1979. The following year brought renewed fighting, with Goukouni's Libya-backed forces pushing those of Habré to the Sudan while Kamougue and the army, abandoning the contest and the capital, headed south.

When Libyan troops left Chad in 1981, Habré's forces reoccupied all important eastern towns. After peacekeepers of the Organization of African Unity withdrew in 1982, Habré formed a new government while Goukouni, with Libyan military support, established an opposition government in the far north. Habré's forces, aided by French troops, prevailed over Goukouni in 1983–1984. They then turned their attention to reestablishing central authority over the whole country, which they accomplished in the south by 1986 and in the north by 1987.

The FAN cracked along ethnic and family lines soon after this consolidation. In April 1989, Habré's interior minister and two military advisers led an unsuccessful coup attempt. One of the advisers, Lieutenant General Idriss Déby, escaped and began new attacks in 1990. By the start of 1991, his Movement for Chadian National Salvation had taken the capital and forced Habré into exile in Cameroon. Déby suspended the constitution and formed a new government with himself as president.

In 1993 there were two failed coup attempts, one on behalf of Habré and the other on behalf of Abbas Koty, a rebel leader. There was also recurrent fighting with Déby's opponents in the north, and a flight of 15,000 people to the Central African Republic following massacres by troops fighting the south-based Armed Forces for a Federal Republic (FARF).

By this time the country's persistent instability had driven various observers to suggest that Chad was not a political entity. For some, such as S. Decalo (1980) and R. Lemarchand (1986, 1992), it was little more than a patchwork of competitive microcosms that governed itself through fleeting religious, ethnic, and regional alliances that always dissolved into factional squabbles. For others, such as R. Jackson and C. Rosberg (1986), it was a state without civic or socioeconomic concreteness, which survived almost entirely through external recognition and support. Going further, W. F. S. Miles (1995) claimed that though Chad might be a juridical state, it was certainly not an empirical one.

Such reactions, perhaps understandable in the circumstances, bordered on hyperbole. The Chadian state might not have performed to observer standards, but if not all then most or at least much of the time after 1960 it displayed the five elements that W. J. Foltz (1995) suggests constitute a state: central political authority; protection of national boundaries; establishment of order across the national territory; capacity to extract internal and external resources sufficient for the state to function and reproduce itself; and control over actions of state agents sufficient to coordinate and execute policy. Instability may have caused it to be weaker and less pervasive than elsewhere, but unlike the case of Somalia in recent years, the central state and its apparatus remained in place.

Indeed, though sporadic fighting has continued to the present—the most recent a 1998–2002 insurrection in the far north by Youssouf Togoimi, former comrade-in-arms of Déby in the fight against the Libyans during the 1980s as well as former minister in Déby's government—1993 marked the start of a process of democratization, reconciliation, and institutional development that might eventually establish a central state meeting the expectations of outside observers. In that year President Déby opened a national conference to chart the country's political future. Participants included forty opposition parties, twenty other organizations, and six rebel movements. By 1996 voters had approved a new constitution, and the first multiparty presidential elections under it gave Déby 69 percent of the vote in a runoff round, and his nearest rival, Colonel Kamougue, 31 percent. At the next presidential election, in May 2001, Déby prevailed again, winning 63 percent of the vote.

On the reconciliation front, all major military actions ended after the government signed peace agreements with fifteen rebel groups, including the FARF, most of which transformed themselves into political parties. And legislative elections in 1997, which international observers said were free and fair, gave Déby's Patriotic Salvation Movement 55 seats in the 125-member National Assembly. Three decades after Tombalbaye dissolved it, there was once again an alternative to armed opposition.

Time will tell if these constructive signs give way to durable outcomes. In the meantime, as we detail below, the weakness of Chad's central apparatus has turned out to be a disguised blessing, first because it has forced localities to find alternative means of supplying themselves with public services, and second because over time the process of planning, financing, and managing these services at the village level has established an effective system of (relatively) democratic local governance that, if accompanied by state and other external actors in intelligent ways, bodes well for the future.

Demand—The Crucial Factor

As elsewhere after independence, the French-language public school surfaced when a neighborhood or village advised the district school inspector that it wanted one. If convinced that the community could organize an association of parents of students (APE) or other entity able to construct and equip a school, collect funds for supplies and repairs, and assure enrollment, the inspector found a teacher. The teacher, always a state employee, then took charge of the school while the APE focused on assuring its part of financing. For brief periods APE financing could sometimes include the instructor's salary, for example, when a new teacher started work before the MEN completed the hiring process, or when political perturbations disrupted routine ministry operations.

These periods grew longer as events, which at the same time caused state resources to stagnate and demand for schools to accelerate, made it increasingly difficult for the MEN to hire new teachers. The first event, in 1979–1980, was the spread of fighting to the capital. Together with Colonel Kamougue, all southern residents of the city retired to their native towns and villages. This exodus included the bulk of government employees because the south, as noted earlier, had schooled a much larger proportion of children than the north and produced the largest share of cadres for the central administration.

During the next two years, until peace in the capital in 1982 allowed their return, the refugees maintained public services they valued, including schools. Availability of teachers was not a problem. The difficulty was financing. Functioning autonomously under Kamougue while fighting raged in the north, the south had its own sources of public revenue, such as state enterprises. But receipts were sufficient to cover salaries of only a small number of individuals. The rest pursued farming, trade, and other economic activities. Because it was already accepted practice for parents to pay part of the cost of schooling, including teacher salaries for short periods, they merely extended the practice by paying salaries for the whole school year. Other than this, there was no change to the procedure by which schools came into being.

The scale of this phenomenon was small at first, concentrating mainly in places where there were enough displaced urban families to support a teacher. Most other villagers were not involved because they had little interest in schooling. Some even mocked those that had been to school. What good is it, they asked, when people with advanced diplomas not only do the same things as unschooled villagers but also show themselves less competent in farming and other work?

This skepticism faded as the schooled population demonstrated a heretofore unheard-of capacity to organize in order to reach specific goals. This included not only APEs but also, more importantly, village associations to create and manage marketing and storage coopera- tives, dispensaries, wells, and sometimes improvements in agricultur- al production. In other words, though people who had been to school were no more adept at doing what villagers already did, they showed a talent for reaching beyond the boundaries of the village to introduce new things. By indirectly raising interest among parents that gave lit- tle thought to it before, the fighting heightened rural demand for schools.

A second event in the south, establishment of "self-managed mar- kets," gave rural demand a further boost. Cotontchad, a state enterprise that promotes cotton production, introduced these markets in 1975 as a way to lower its operating costs. In exchange for rebates, which were separate from payments to producers for their cotton, the markets per- formed weighing, classification, maintenance, and other functions that would otherwise require more costly use of Cotontchad personnel. Access to these rebates, however, was restricted to communities with village associations that could organize self-managed markets and con- tained at least two officers literate in French. The market thus accom- plished two things at once. It increased the incentive for rural communi- ties to have people who were literate in French in their midst. Through the rebates, it also provided them with resources to realize this objec- tive, by creating schools, for instance.

Spread of the markets accelerated when the National Rural Development Office (ONDR) launched an animation program to help villages organize associations, receive recognition from Cotontchad, and, with the rebates, initiate collective actions with respect to social assistance, wells, dispensaries, and other communal services. This pro- gram gained momentum as hostilities subsided, with ONDR animators reaching most corners of the south by 1990. In that year, self-managed markets in 2,000 villages processed 62 percent of total cotton production (Gouvernement du Tchad 1990).

By this time the incentive for schools extended well beyond the need to satisfy Cotontchad. Thousands of communities had opened themselves to the world outside. They were more aware of new possibilities and of the utility of French literacy in gaining access to them. Even if a government post was unlikely, a community still needed people with French literacy in order to interact more effectively with state officials in the search for state goods and services. And an individual could aspire to become a small functionary, secretary of a village association for example, and thus earn the esteem of the community. People were also more aware of what illiteracy had cost them. They now understood that buyers, including Cotontchad purchasing agents, tricked them at the scale and deliberately miscalculated payments, and that inability to read things such as a summons from the police or directions for use of medicine could cost them dearly. French literacy was a method to defend individual and community interests.

These things did not mean that all adults had to learn French. A literate child in effect made its parents literate. Nor did it mean that all children should attend school. The experiences showed only that parents would benefit from having at least one child succeed in school and that communities would benefit from enrolling more children in the future than in the past, either by expanding existing schools or by creating new ones. But because schooling produces more schooling through the logic of demand, i.e., the success of graduates raises demand for schooling among parents of future students, these small beginnings were a major factor in the explosion of primary enrollment from fewer than 215,000 in 1975 to more than 1.1 million in 2002.[3]

Though not nearly as strong as in the south, growth of demand for French schooling in the north was also important. Here the initial push came after evacuation of southerners from Ndjamena allowed northerners to perceive increased state employment possibilities. The key event in many areas, however, having essentially the same character as in the south except for the direction of movement, was the uprooting of rural people and their relocation to towns. There were small movements whenever fighting erupted in a zone, but the big shift came during the drought and famine of 1984.

Forced into larger centers, refugees from isolated villages found themselves in worlds that they never imagined to exist. Ndjamena, Abeche, and other places confronted them with new perspectives and for the first time introduced them to populations, in most respects similar to themselves, who were literate in French as well as Arabic. Many had never met a state employee, let alone one who was native to the north. Together with others who had similar experiences in Sudan, many refugees concluded that schooling was useful in preparing people for the unknown, and that it did not necessarily undermine their Arab-Islamic identity—a consideration that kept Muslim parents from enrolling children in French schools since the start of colonization (Kyayar 1969).

The heart of the matter was defense, however. It was frustrating, not to mention life-threatening during a famine, to be unable to directly communicate with local populations, government officials, and relief agency personnel that did not understand Arabic, to be unable to read important announcements and other French documents, and, most importantly, to have no one of the village in positions of influence to act on behalf of community and family interests. People deeply affected by these circumstances returned to their villages resolved to take steps that would prevent repetition of what had happened to them and, at minimum, assure that their children did not suffer the same fate. Though it was still secondary to Koranic instruction that prepared children for everyday life, French literacy did have some practical use. What they now had to do was convince others of this fact and then, when there were enough potential students to justify a school, ask the state for a teacher.

But by this time the state had passed the point where it could respond to every request. To stretch the budget as far as feasible, the MEN adjusted to fiscal realities by abandoning the notion that all teachers had to be state employees. At least temporarily, only one state teacher was required in order for a school to have official status as a public institution. Aside from this individual, who served as school director, other teachers could be paid by the communities they served.

This adjustment sufficed for a short time only. Parents, tired of waiting for a state teacher before initiating a school, asked inspectors and canton chiefs to help them find individuals willing to serve as community instructors in the interim. As the interim grew longer, some places decided that while they would eventually inform authorities of what they had done, they did not need help in finding teachers. These places, especially in the south, had ample supplies of young men, and sometimes women, who had returned to their communities after receiving some secondary education. Many were willing to take time from (or even abandon) their main occupations as farmers, herders, traders, and so forth to teach in exchange for modest compensation. A state teacher with more advanced training might offer better instruction, give the school official status, and relieve parents of a heavy financial burden, but in the circumstances something was better than nothing.

As the interval between creation of a school by a village and receipt of a state teacher widened, an increasing share of them operated only with community teachers. Though the procedure by which they came into being was little different than before, the MEN called them "spontaneous" schools to distinguish them from public schools with state teachers/directors and from private schools. In 1994, under pressure from parent groups arguing that these schools were "spontaneous" only in the eyes of government, not in the eyes of parents, the MEN changed the name to "community" schools.

Organization and Management

Localities manage their schools and other services in similar ways. By election or by consent at general or special meetings, male heads of households with students choose a small group of men, literate if possible, to take charge on behalf of the community.[4] Names of these groups vary, the most common being the already-mentioned APE. Localities that organize to promote wider objectives, such as village associations to operate self-managed markets or other development activities, may also have APEs. But here the group is one of several committees that the larger entity establishes to supervise school activities. If resembling state schools seems important, the committee is an APE. If resemblance does not matter, if it is important to stress that the school benefits all families and not just those with students, or if it is important to underscore that the group runs the school (because by law an APE is subservient to the director of a state school), it remains the school committee.

All groups, which we call APEs for simplicity, have the same basic structure and perform the same basic functions. Individual members, though they may not have formal titles, take specific roles as treasurer, secretary, and president in order to simplify administration. Teachers often act as the APE secretariat when they are the only sufficiently literate persons available.

The APE's main preoccupation is maintenance of a permanent process of requesting, collecting, and disbursing resources, and organizing special fund-raising efforts when regular payments fall short. Though methods of mobilizing resources vary in their details, they always comprise two basic components. One is tuition, collected in cash or in kind from parents with students. In recent times this user-fee ranged from CFA 60 per student per month in the south to CFA 200 in the north. Second, and usually more important, is a cash or in-kind levy paid by all households regardless of whether they contain students. Called membership dues and assessed on the basis of ability to pay, this levy produced between CFA 150 and 4,000 per student per year in the north. Some southern communities also collected annual dues, from CFA 125 to 500. But in most places the collective component of finance was all or part of the Cotontchad rebate that the village association allocated to its school.

Collection rates for these charges can be high or low, depending on economic circumstances. These were usually good in the north, giving collections for tuition and dues at or near 100 percent in all places and allowing teachers to receive monthly wages between CFA 7,500 and 15,000. Things were not usually as good in many southern communities because of drought, low cotton prices, and financial difficulties at Cotontchad that delayed rebates. Some villages were able to pay teachers their target salaries of CFA 3,000 to 7,500.[5] But others, with collections down to 25 percent because many families paid considerably less than their full assessments, sometimes mustered as little as CFA 600 for salaries.

To mitigate the effects of the economic downturn, or to raise additional revenue where things were good, individual APEs experimented with various methods of financing. These included: use of alternative crops to fund schools, such as peanuts instead of millet; establishment of school fields; borrowing the bullocks of village notables to plow private fields for a fee; remunerating teachers with labor (i.e., having students and/or parents work teachers' fields); increasing the ratio of students to teachers; and joining with surrounding villages to finance common schools. There were limits to what creativity could accomplish, however. Some places, understanding that financial difficulties might result less from limited funds and more from limited knowledge about ways to mobilize and manage available resources, requested and were still waiting for technical assistance to help them make better use of what they had.

In the meantime, schools in financially strapped places remained open because teachers, for the most part natives of the area and tending their own fields or cattle, were willing to continue working for very little. Here villages carried the shortfall forward as a communal liability to be paid when the local economy improved. Confidence was high that this liability would be taken care of in the future, as it had been in the past, because the cause of revenue shortfall was inability, not unwillingness to pay. APEs make allowance for poor families, but they do not tolerate nonpayment by families with means to pay. Barring special circumstances, the children of would-be free riders cannot enroll.

Financial discipline manifested in high collection rates, willingness to undertake communal debt, and low tolerance of nonpayment stems from several factors. Important among them is the belief that schooling is a public good that benefits the whole community. One meaning of this, already noted, is that everyone benefits from having more schooled people in a village. Another meaning is that the school is usually part of a wider package of investment in community development that includes such things as wells and dispensaries. Even if families believe that they cannot benefit from schooling, the idea that they can eventually benefit from other parts of the overall community effort allows them to feel that they have a stake in the package, and therefore also in the school. This is especially true where surplus school revenues, as in the cases of two-thirds of the villages we visited, finance and manage other local services.

Notwithstanding their demonstrated willingness to pay for a service, most villages have yet to take full charge of what they pay for. Part of the reason for this is a general sentiment that the community is doing for itself what the state promised to do for it since independence. The village is helping the state to do its job. Accordingly, localities continue in a waiting mode, hoping that one day soon they will get a state teacher and financial relief. Similarly, though the APE assures that teachers are in class during designated hours and conduct themselves appropriately, it rarely deals with the content of instruction. Parents recognize that the content of the primary curriculum is insufficiently adapted to realities of rural life, and thus that what they pay for is not a good as it could be. But they can do nothing to alter the circumstance because many of them still believe that the content of public education is the exclusive domain of the state or, for those believing that content should not ignore parental wishes, because most have no effective means to communicate with or influence state actions.

Intermediary Structures

Local governments have no effective means to influence the state because the hierarchical line of authority and communication that APEs, associations, and village leaders follow is to the canton chief. Often doubling as traditional chief, the canton chief represents the state at the local level. In principle, all things that have to do with the state, such as requests for a state teacher, must pass through him on the way to other parts of the central apparatus, including the inspector. In reality, because the power of the chief has diminished in step with the growth in numbers of secondary graduates in positions to directly represent their villages to upper levels of the apparatus, most community schools operate in an institutional void.

Inspectors are supposed to visit regularly. But the MEN's budgets have rarely allowed them means to travel. Many state schools, let alone community ones, have not seen an inspector in ten years. School directors, teachers, and APEs must go to them. To maintain contact with the outside world, communities depend on irregular calls from inspectors who discover unexpected travel possibilities, directors of nearby state schools, other MEN personnel who pass through on trips elsewhere, missionaries in the vicinity, visits from village natives residing in towns, and exchanges with people from neighboring areas during market days.

Where they occur, these irregular contacts often produce tangible benefits, such as books and supplies dropped off by missionaries. They sometimes yield useful information too. We encountered cases where creation of one school prompted creation of others nearby, with APEs of established schools helping neighbors organize for this purpose. A more important benefit of these contacts, however, may be their psychological impact. The fact that outsiders have heard of a school and think it worthy of a visit does much to encourage a community in its efforts. Visits show that a village has earned respect and is honored in the world outside. Small things mean a lot in isolated places.

Some localities have been especially fortunate in this regard because they lie within the orbits of nonstate entities that to some extent fill the institutional vacuum in schooling and other matters. Especially interesting are indigenous entities that serve as intermediaries between groups of communities and important actors in the larger environment, not only the state but also donors and their nongovernment affiliates.

One example is the Steering Committee for Educational and Cultural Problems of Ouaddai (Comite de Suivi des Problemes Scolaires et Culturelles du Ouaddai—CSPSCO), a federation of APEs representing the interests of eight French and eight Arabic schools in Abeche, a northern town near the Sudanese border. Since its inception CSPSCO has engaged in several types of activity. These include production and dissemination of slate boards and Arabic books to primary schools in Abeche and surrounding areas; trips by CSPSCO officers to these areas to encourage existing APEs and to promote creation of schools in villages that do not have them; guidance and orientation of state teachers (i.e., from the south) newly assigned to the region; lobbying the European Development Fund and the government, successfully, to finance a general secondary school (CEG); raising funds to equip the school's science laboratory; and mobilizing resources to finance an Arabic CEG, a facility that did not exist in Chad before.

CSPSCO's positive achievements derive from several factors. For one thing, its officers represent Abeche's most influential socioeconomic strata, including owners of large commercial establishments, ranking clergy, school directors, professionals in government and nongovernment organizations, officials, and so on. Another thing is that the organization maintains good relations with the MEN. The inspector, for instance, serves as one of CSPSCO's counselors. Last but not least, CSPSCO has permanent representation in Ndjamena through which it maintains contact with the large number of individuals that moved there from Abeche. This allows CSPSCO to not only raise substantial sums from the emigrant population but also to have direct contact with people of influence in government and nongovernment offices in the capital.

Another example is the Association of Parents of Students and Rural Promotion of Djokou Canton (Association des Parents d'Eleves et de la Promotion Rurale du Canton Djokou—APECD). It is a federation of APEs that represents the interests of the twenty-two villages of Djokou, a southern canton bordering the Central African Republic. Its main objectives are to foster solidarity between parents living inside and outside the canton; develop community schools, medical centers, pharmacies, and cooperatives to sell necessities; promote the status of women; and implement maternal-health and agricultural-modernization programs.

The association was formed in 1979 by individuals who left the canton to pursue studies and government careers. They were among the first to graduate from the canton's only school and to achieve positions in the capital and other towns from which they could help their villages. Outside help was important because flooding isolated the canton from June to December. Health, education, agricultural, and other public services were poor as a result and people suffered when floods prevented travel to obtain essential goods and services. APECD members visited the canton to implement a strategy of action soon after its formation, but only had time to facilitate the opening of a second state school before fighting closed both schools in 1980.

The effort resumed when stability returned to the region in 1986. Initial actions focused on helping to organize village associations that, depending on priorities in the twenty-two localities, contained a health committee, an agricultural committee, and an APE. Outside the canton, APECD members pursued their roles as ambassadors by soliciting funds and services from individuals, government, and nongovernment organizations. In addition to APECD membership dues of CFA 500 per month from its fifty members, which yielded CFA 300,000 per year, this solicitation produced a total of more than CFA 18 million between 1986 and 1996.

These resources allowed APECD to finance many things, the main one being schools, the number of which grew from one in 1986 to fourteen in 1990. APECD assisted these schools in several ways. It recruited teachers and organized training for them in 1987 and 1991. It convinced the MEN to assign state instructors to four schools in 1988 and 1989. It procured equipment, books, and supplies for all schools at the start of every year. And it interceded whenever crises required outside mediation. For instance, it intervened when students went on strike to protest parents' unwillingness to pay their dues in 1988. It supported an APE demand that a village chief return a bull and plow that he appropriated from the school. It defended the right of parents to take disciplinary action when teachers acted irresponsibly, such as being absent without cause and taking commodities from APE stocks without permission.

Entities such as CSPSCO and APECD are rare. For the moment, they consist of associations of APEs in a few scattered zones. But their number seems likely to increase because they are logical extensions of the basic idea that every community needs schooled people to defend and promote its interests in the external world. One individual representing one village can do certain things for one community. A group acting in concert to represent the collective interest of many communities can do much more.

Doing more to help villages communicate with each other is especially important because, with information tending to move vertically between communities and national or regional centers rather than horizontally (i.e., if it moves at all), much learning from experience remains inaccessible to them. Earlier we noted that contacts between adjacent villages could sometimes yield productive outcomes, such as collaboration to establish a single facility for all, and APEs of existing schools that helped neighbors organize their own. Beyond these and a few larger clusters that operate within the orbits of nongovernmental organizations, the people we met seemed unaware of the ways in which a problem that they were confronting was solved somewhere else, or the way in which their own solution to a different problem might help another village.

This isolation from the flow of potentially useful information constitutes a tremendous waste of Chad's most valuable resource: APEs, village associations, and similar local entities. They have a lot to teach each other and outsiders. School fields, student labor in teachers' fields, organizing one school for several adjacent villages rather than separate schools for each, promoting the idea of schooling as a collective good for all families rather than just for those with students, diversifying the range of commodities used for school support, establishing student-teacher ratios that are optimum in different local economies, and other variations on the theme of finance that come from experience at the base, for instance, are not appropriate or feasible in all places. Nevertheless, they are practical ideas that have been tested somewhere at some time by some villages. When APEs asked us for suggestions about ways to improve finance or management, the best answers we could give, even though we visited only a very small number of villages, came from our notes about how things were done in other communities.

These same notes contained potential counsel about how to deal with teachers, the responsible as well as the irresponsible ones, how to think through the relative benefits and costs of acquiring state teachers, how to narrow the gap in enrollment between boys and girls when this was desirable, and how to treat many other items of greater or lesser importance. In a wider perspective, the notes also contained interesting ideas concerning alternative ways to place a school within the larger enterprise called community development. It could be the only activity of the enterprise, the first or the last in a sequence of projects, or one of several parallel activities taking place in different sectors at the same time. Each option had its particular advantages and disadvantages. All of them, at the very least, were food for thought.

And scarcity of such nourishment, in addition to slowing the pace at which schooling and other services spread to places that do not yet have them and to narrowing the range of available ideas that places with services can use to improve their quality, also postpones the day when state and other external actors see the merits of viewing communities as responsible partners in the provision of public services, and of helping them realize their goals.

Supportive Actions

In principle, there should be several ways to help communities such as those we describe advance faster than if left to their own devices. But the MEN and its main donor assistants have usually done little of constructive value. One reason is that they remain encumbered by belief that the state should "control" primary instruction. A study of community schools prepared by senior MEN personnel and UNESCO consultants, for instance, recommended that these schools, in order to qualify for external assistance, must satisfy the requirements of the *carte sco-laire* (distance from a state school), provide guarantees of permanence, and possess teachers with at least four years of secondary education (Esquieu and Péano 1994). To qualify for inspector visits, villages must promise to maintain buildings and books, assure salaries and operating costs, and participate in construction and repair.

Communities already do everything that the study recommends to qualify for supervision, but rarely receive this help. With regard to assistance, it is true that communities do not respect the *carte scolaire*. They know nothing about it. Even if they had a copy, one that was not hopelessly out of date and out of touch with what is on the ground, few would refuse to school children just because the action is inconsistent with a distant piece of paper. The same applies to the other thing that communities do not respect, the level of secondary education of teachers. If all schools had to have teachers with four years of secondary schooling, this would mean dismissal of over 60 percent of teachers in community schools, about 25 percent of those in private schools, more than 40 percent of community teachers in state schools, and almost 20 percent of state teachers. Where Chad might find the more than three thousand replacements needed to fill these positions is a question the study does not answer.

Another reason is that officials sometimes make unwise decisions. In 1997, for instance, MEN and World Bank officials decided that it would be a good idea, as part of a Bank-funded basic education project, to give community teachers a CFA 20,000 per month supplement, an unheard-of sum, for eighteen months. They gave little consideration to potential negative impacts that this action might have on instructor expectations, on the matter of who is in charge of community schools, or longer-term relationships between teachers and communities after the supplementary compensation fund ran out. Although the proposal met stiff opposition from MEN and donor cadres who believed in encouraging rather than undermining community initiative, the plan went forward, with one thousand teachers receiving the extra compensation between 1998 and 2001. The action, as expected, caused considerable grief.[6]

This does not mean that the MEN suffers a shortage of people qualified to devise useful actions. Most personnel that we met impressed us with their grasp of the basic issues, ability to envisage workable ways to address them, sensitivity to the sacrifices that parents make for their children, and capacity to make sensible suggestions. One such suggestion was that the MEN should make it clear that a community school is as "public" as a state school. All parents want their schools to be recognized as integral parts of the national education system because they do not wish to invest resources and children in hopeless exercises. If the only way to assure that the exercise is not a waste is to obtain a state teacher for the school (i.e., because this makes a school official), then they will never stop asking for one. Making clear to parents that their schools are as public, as official, and as recognized as others, might not only lower pressure on the MEN to supply state teachers but also encourage higher enrollment and stronger financial support of community schools.

Another suggestion was to formalize activities that MEN personnel already undertake in the field on a voluntary basis. The MEN could, for instance, subdivide Chad's forty-four inspectors into smaller units, each centered on a key state school. Directors of these schools, acting as intermediaries between distant inspectors and nearby community facilities, might then take responsibility for providing information, assistance, and encouragement to teachers and APEs in surrounding communities, most of which are within walking distance. Many directors do this already, and the schools we visited that had contact with them appreciated the relationship. If nothing else, it showed communities and their teachers that someone in the MEN respected their efforts and cared enough to visit. Formalization of this practice, as with the other things mentioned, can do much good at relatively low cost.

Indeed, low-cost actions can sometimes lead to dramatic outcomes, as shown in experiences of the Swiss Cooperation Agency, which, with the MEN's consent, has been working with northern nomads—among whom enrollment and literacy rates are almost nil—to establish schools.[7] This effort began in early 1994 with discussions between project staff, composed of one consultant and two animators, and nomads in sixteen scattered encampments about responsibility for education. Although the nomads rejected schooling, because the atmosphere of French public schools is inconsistent with Muslim and nomad values and because they teach little of practical social or economic relevance, they put high value on education. What they wanted but could never obtain from authorities was a type of school consistent with what parents wanted for their children. Staff asked why the community, like others throughout the country, had not established its own school, as an extension of formal or informal Koranic instruction already in place, for instance. The answer, invariably, was that although some people had considered the idea, no one in authority had told them that they had the right to create schools. This was something that only the state could do.

After firmly rooting the idea that parents not only had the right but also the obligation to improve education of children, staff worked with them to design an acceptable school and to establish agreements on respective roles and responsibilities between the nomads on one side and the agency on the other. In the event, each community agreed to form a school committee, outline a curriculum, provide structures and basic furnishings, recruit and pay teachers, and arrange housing and food for students sent from surrounding encampments. The agency agreed to organize and supply recurrent teacher training in collaboration with the MEN's regional offices and *medersas* (modernized Islamic schools), an endowment of books and other learning materials, and such heavy investment as might be required to assure the school's functioning through the dry season (usually repair or deepening of wells). Progress was quick after that.

No more than three hundred boys and girls in the sixteen camps touched by the project in early 1994 studied the Quran in organized ways. Most learned directly from parents and other family members. At the end of 1994, in schools that taught not only the Koran but also Arabic literacy, arithmetic, astronomy, history, geography, and other subjects, including French in some cases, there were 1,350 students, 35 percent of whom were girls. A year later the number rose to 1,500, with 40 percent girls, plus more than 150 adult women studying inside the schools and a comparable number of adult men doing the same outside.

At the end of 1996 there were thirty schools containing 2,200 students, a year later forty-three schools with 4,000, and in 2001, a hundred schools with 5,200 students, 45 percent of them girls and adult women. And financing of these schools was reaching levels that greatly exceeded original expectations. Nomads, mobilizing anywhere from CFA 500,000 to more than 1 million per community per year, paid for almost everything.

In parallel, government officials, ranging from the director-general of primary education to prefects and education inspectors, especially those who originated in or worked in areas covered by the project, became enthusiastic supporters. Though receiving nothing from the project (because it was organized as a nongovernment undertaking), they provided moral and tangible support whenever possible, including allotment of several hundred Arabic reading books that an earlier program sponsored by the World Bank could not distribute for lack of students in state schools.

This enthusiastic support, in conjunction with similar reactions to efforts by the Swiss to help southern APEs improve quality in community schools and with reflections on design errors in earlier donor-financed efforts, helped nudge MEN, World Bank, and other donor officials toward thinking concretely about establishment of a partnership in education between central and local actors. Design documents for the next Bank-supported education project, for instance, include statements recognizing APEs and emphasizing their important place in national policy dialogue and school management (World Bank 2002b). Translating statements into promises for action, project documents also call for establishment of a special-purpose entity, with APE representatives and other nongovernmental organizations on its board, that would be responsible for allocating CFA 2 billion per year in project funds to community schools.

Time will eventually tell whether these statements are sincere. Even if not, accumulation of small experiences of the kind described for nomad schools, in combination with creeping democratization at the center and what looks like an unrelenting expansion of governance at the local level, is building up a degree of interest that seems likely to yield increasingly productive relationships between state and citizens.

Allowed some suspension of disbelief, we might imagine the state and donors one day deciding to actively husband such relationships, by expanding efforts of the kinds made by CSPSCO and APECD. This might involve a sustained process of institutional development on behalf of communities so that they serve not only as local but also as national partners in the provision of a fuller range of public services. In most instances this would mean insisting that state agencies and donors do one or more of three things: (1) encourage and enable local entities to take (or take greater) charge of designing and financing their own priority services; (2) help them communicate with and learn from each other; and (3) cultivate a process of collaboration that can lead them to create regional and national federations of local institutions with capacity to lobby the center in their self-interest. With annual oil revenues of CFA 50 to 100 billion scheduled to make their fiscal presence felt after 2003 (*The Economist* 2002), the only thing that would prevent institutional development efforts such as we outline would be lack of vision and/or will.

Conclusion

Though the main focus in the foregoing is schooling, it is important to recognize that what we describe is only one dimension of a broader process that encompasses self-managed markets, water supply, agriculture, forestry, health, and other service areas where local supply has become more important than state supply. As such, it is also crucial to understand that the village associations, sectoral committees, APEs, and other entities responsible for finance and management of supply, though not officially recognized as such, function as elements of local governance. Their origins and operations satisfy the definition of formal governments and effective governance processes in most societies. On their own or with help of outsiders (e.g., National Rural Development Office animators), people in a community collectively decide to create a new organizational structure for the common good to deal with matters that they cannot address via existing mechanisms. In the process they voluntarily transfer to the new entity the right and authority to exercise direction and control over the actions of specific individuals (e.g., teachers and parents) in specific areas of communal life (e.g., schooling), as well as to require compliance of the general community in financing operations (e.g., membership dues that support schooling).

It requires only a little stretch of imagination to view an APE as the education department of a local government. This department has a financial section that, alone or in conjunction with the larger village association, collects user-fees in the form of tuition charges and school taxes in the form of dues and rebates. It incurs public debt when tax revenues are less than expenses (e.g., to teachers). It transfers surpluses to the community's treasury for use by other sectoral departments when expenses are less than revenues. And it initiates special fund-raising actions if required. The public-works section organizes construction and repair of buildings and equipment. Procurement obtains books and materials. Personnel recruits teachers, negotiates salaries, supervises performance, and if necessary sanctions or dismisses them. External relations cultivates and maintains contact with the inspector, non-government organizations, donors, alumni in towns, and chance visitors.

Adopting the view that APEs and school committees such as those we met are or at least act like branches of government yields observations that seem relevant to improving or expanding services in many countries. One is that they show the existence of willingness by communities to self-tax for the common good when it is clear that common good will result, and when they are assured that they have control of the uses to which their resources are put.

Second is that tax rates are respected by village ratepayers when they are part of the process of deciding the rates. This respect is reinforced by the sophistication of local taxation systems. These usually show a finely tuned capacity, based on a high level of knowledge of village economic circumstances, to adjust rates according to the ability to pay. When the economy falters, as in many southern villages when we visited them, everyone knows who suffers and who can or cannot pay. Tax rates and fees, as a result, tend to be progressive. The same knowledge also allows entities to assess willingness to pay. By being intolerant of this, they limit the problem of "free riders" (i.e., people that use a public service but choose not to pay for it) that bothers taxpayers in all countries. Progressive taxation and minimization of free riders help to maintain the credibility and acceptability of tax assessors and collectors.

Third is that this sophistication extends to fiscal resourcefulness, which further nurtures the respect of taxpayers. An example is the jointly financed education service arranged by adjacent villages in the north. Similar arrangements in the United States, made for like reasons, led to emergence of the "special" or "independent" school district that today serves as the unified school administration for groups of towns. Another example is the deliberate flexibility accorded to the student-teacher ratio. This is also a way that education systems adapt to economic and fiscal disaster in wealthier countries.

These observations suggest that there is considerable scope for successful devolution of tax authority to individual communities because there exist systems that communities can devise that taxpayers will view as fair. Given the tremendous intervillage differences in conditions and tax rates with respect to schooling, such systems are at the very least likely to be regarded as fairer than rates devised by outsiders, such as flat taxes and user-fees that governments and donors often propose as means to cofinance services in other parts of Africa.

Expanding this theme, we have also seen considerable intervillage variation in perceived priorities, between sectors and within them. Schooling could as readily be the most or least important item in a list of planned community actions that includes wells, dispensaries, health, agriculture, and other items. Within education, the relative importance accorded to construction, expansion, books, supplies, salaries, state teachers, training, official status, debt repayment, and the like also varies. In most instances, community rankings seemed eminently sensible. When it is hard to find, water should be ahead of education. When a village cannot enroll children because an existing facility cannot protect students and materials from the rains for two or three months, construction should take precedence.

Because it reflects understanding of immediate realities, a community's general or sectoral development plan, to paraphrase what we said about taxation, is likely to be regarded by villagers as reasonable and, therefore, is also likely to elicit the resources required to implement it. This plan may have flaws, but it will be less flawed than plans prepared by outsiders who do not understand local priorities or grasp why they are what they are. The state and donors may have good reason to insist that communities respect the *carte scolaire*, but these things have more to do with the priorities of the outsiders than the priorities of communities. This is a main reason why external plans do not reach many of their goals, especially goals related to local resource mobilization.

The implication in this instance is that there exists considerable scope for successful devolution of responsibility for planning public services. This is because communities are better equipped than outsiders to know whether an action will result in improvement of the common good and, as with taxation, are more likely to respect and support the plan if they are part of the process of designing it.

It follows that national governments and their donor assistants have much to gain by treating the local governments that villages have created for themselves as full partners in the design and implementation of all public goods and services. They also have much to gain by actions that can strengthen the community entities that already exist and stimulate their emergence where they are absent. Chad provides ample evidence that mutually beneficial cofinancing, cost sharing, and joint planning is possible. If it is possible in a country as poor and turbulent as Chad has been, then it is also possible in the many other more peaceful and better-endowed countries of Africa.

Notes

This chapter is based largely on Fass and Desloovere (1995), with updated data and other unpublished materials obtained in Chad during annual visits through 1998 and from other sources.

1. These interviews were conducted in different areas of Chad for different purposes over several years. In 1992, as part of a research project on political participation funded by the Organization for Economic Cooperation and Development (OECD) and the United States Agency for International Development (USAID), Fass met with staff and officials of the MEN, UNESCO, World Bank, and several nongovernmental organizations (NGOs) in the capital to learn about and discuss community involvement in provision of basic services. In 1993, to help evaluate the Swiss Cooperation Agency's assistance program to state primary education, Fass held meetings with APEs of fourteen communities served by public schools in several southern and northern prefectures. Although meetings were often joined by more than fifty people, in most instances the number of vocal participants ranged from five to ten. These active individuals usually included the village chief, officers of the APE, other engaged parents, and some teachers.

In 1994, under a research project on decentralization funded by the OECD's Club du Sahel, Fass and Desloovere interviewed the APEs of thirty-seven community schools in Mayo-Kebbi, Ouaddai, and Moyen-Chari prefectures. The kinds of individuals we spoke with were the same as described above. We also met with representatives of six large NGOs. In addition to CSPSCO and APECD discussed later in this chapter, these included: Africare,

Swissaid-Altaawoun, Bureau d'Etudes et de Liaison des Actions Caritatives et de Developpement (BELACD), Association Pan-Africaine pour la Promotion des Initiatives Communautaires en Afrique (APPICA), and Secours Catholique pour le Developpement (SECADEV). From 1994 through 1998, to help monitor progress of the Swiss Cooperation Agency's new program of assistance to community schools, Fass made annual visits to interview eighteen APEs in Kanem Prefecture, sixteen in Batha, and nine in Moyen Chari. Ignoring repeat visits and using seven as the average number of active participants at each meeting with APEs, we estimate that we spoke with a total of 660 individuals in ninety-four communities during 1992–1998; more than 750 if we include MEN, donor organization, and NGO staff and officials.

2. This section on the political history of Chad draws from Britannica Online (1994, 1995, 1997, 1998a, 1998b); Chapelle (1986); Foltz (1995); and Miles (1995).

3. Enrollment for 1975 is from World Bank (2002a). Enrollment for 2002 is our estimate, based on extrapolation of data in World Bank 2002a and 2002b.

4. Women rarely participate in these meetings or serve as members of the group. Their preferences, as in most other aspects of public life in the village and nation, are transmitted behind the scenes, through husbands who usually do not or cannot ignore the opinions of wives.

5. The marked difference in salary scales, CFA 7,500 to 15,000 in the north and CFA 3,000 to 7,500 in the south, mainly reflects the difference in additional earning possibilities. Most community teachers in the south have land to work nearby, and so view teaching as one of several sources of income. For their counterparts in the north, salary is usually the only source of income. Accordingly, communities in the north must pay more to attract and retain instructors.

6. MEN and World Bank officials seem to have recognized their mistake. The document that describes the next Bank-funded education project indicates that an important lesson learned from the experience is that

> the partnership between the State and the communities should be based on the principle that the State would provide training and supplemental compensation to the [community teachers] without modifying the hiring and management arrangements in place, so that the strong accountability ties between the [teachers] and the communities employing them would be preserved. Moreover, donors should refrain from funding the State's part of the [teachers'] compensation, which should come entirely from the State's regular budget resources to ensure the continuity and sustainability of this compensation system. (World Bank 2002b:12)

7. This work with nomad communities is one of two project components. The other component, operating in the south, seeks to increase the relevance of basic education offered in existing community schools in order to raise attendance, reduce dropout (especially of girls), and bring about other improvements. This component has proven highly successful as well.

8

Uganda:
Multiple Levels of Local Governance

James S. Wunsch and Dan Ottemoeller

The Local Councils of Uganda

This chapter's focus is the local council (LC) system of Uganda. Originally, these organizations were called resistance councils because they were created as a political and logistical support system for the National Resistance Movement (NRM) and its military wing, the National Resistance Army, which conducted a guerrilla war against the government of Milton Obote in the early 1980s. Following the NRM's ascension to state power in January 1986, resistance councils were organized as a five-stage pyramid of committees based on directly elected village committees. Originally they were to culminate in a national-level legislative body through a system of indirect elections, though that never occurred. With the promulgation of a new national constitution in 1995, the name and duties of the system changed; the system was renamed the local council system and the national representative functions of the system were replaced by a directly elected parliament. However, at district and lower levels, the pyramid outline of committees remains in place, albeit without the practice of indirect elections.

From its inception, this system of councils was charged with a wide range of responsibilities that implied meaningful devolution of political and administrative functions across a wide range of government activities. The original resistance councils were also supposed to democratize the NRM state through indirect elections to a national parliamentary body, the National Resistance Council. In practice, the impact of the system was limited to the local level (up to districts), and the potential of the resistance councils to control government ministries or provide democratic control of the state was never realized. Ill-defined relations with a parallel administrative system, a domineering central government, and a lack of resources combined to blunt the system's ability to improve vertical relations between state and society (Brett 1994).

The promulgation of the 1993 decentralization statute, the Local Governments (resistance councils) Statute (Republic of Uganda 1993), significantly reinforced the political authority of the LCs. The current system is composed of five levels. These range from the village (LC1), to the parish (LC2), to the subcounty (LC3), to the county (LC4), and the district (LC5). However, only subcounties and districts have major budgetary, programmatic, and personnel functions. The parish and county have essentially minor administrative roles, while the village performs judicial, security, and grassroots planning roles. Urban areas are similarly organized, though there they are referred to as "wards," "divisions," and the like. According to the law, upper-level LCs (subcounty and district) would have effective control over the activities of all government ministries and personnel in their areas with respect to subnational issues. Perhaps the most important provision of the 1993 statute dictated that subcounty-level LCs would retain a minimum of 50 percent of tax revenue collected within their areas. The 1993 statute was superseded by the Local Governments Act of 1997 (Republic of Uganda 1997). This most recent legislation preserves and clarifies the 1993 decentralization law and places even more emphasis on local-level (i.e., subdistrict) governments as it provides for retention of 65 percent of revenue collected by subdistrict-level LCs.

Field research conducted by a number of authors (Brett 1994; Burkey 1991; Ddungu 1989, 1994; Karlström 1996; Makara 1993; Ottemoeller 1996; Tideman 1994, 1995; Wunsch 2001b) indicates that the LC system has established a positive record with regard to purely local (i.e., horizontal) judicial and security functions at the village (LC1) level. In addition, the same research indicates that the LC1 councils achieved this success because they replaced a discredited system of local administration based on appointed chiefs. Less research has been done at the LC3 and LC5 levels; still, the work done there indicates that a foundation has been laid for local governance, but that they have had some difficulty in performing their diverse budgeting, taxing, and administrative duties (Livingstone and Charleton 1998, 2001; USAID 2001a; Jeppson 2001; Makara 2000; Muwanga 2001; Wunsch 2001b).

The commitment of the government of Uganda to decentralization and local governance is colored by the experiences and priorities of its president, Yoweri Museveni. Museveni has maintained a serious commitment to participatory democracy since his period in the bush, organizing the movement that eventually drove Obote into exile. Indeed, many observers credit Museveni with establishing and encouraging a stable and reasonably effective government at the center with many attributes key to liberal democracy, as well as organizing and supporting a substantial decentralization reform (Therkildsen 2002; Furley 2000; Kasfir 1998). Even if, as some suggest, the multistage LC system was intended originally primarily only to legitimize continued NRM rule, it clearly has grown far beyond that, and in the process ended the abuses of chiefly power that developed around the Obote and Idi Amin regimes (Burkey 1991; Ddungu 1989) and greatly enhanced local participation in governance (Muwanga 2001).

However, at the same time, Museveni has demonstrated that he places a high priority on governmental stability and his continued occupancy of the presidency (Ottaway 1998). Thus, he has maintained no-party elections in Uganda, a continued dominant role for the NRM (though the existence of the NRM beyond Museveni has been questioned by some [Kasfir 1998]), and intrusion by the national government into local governance when it acts at cross-purposes with national policy goals (Carbone 2001; Haynes 2001; Furley and Katalikawe 1997). N. M. S. Muwanga's insightful study of education shows one example of this. Museveni and the NRM's commitment to mass education as a way to address regional and other inequalities led it to reassert central dominance in education in 1996. This preempted local participation through the LC system in an area where parents had developed a lengthy tradition of school leadership during the state disintegration of the Obote and Amin era (Muwanga 2001). Anders Jeppson also notes the same tension and pattern over LC budgeting decisions in health programs (2001).

While these are merely two more manifestations of the all-too-common center's propensity to intervene in "local" issues in Africa, it is remarkable here because it occurs even in a regime where there is significant evidence of commitment at the very top to participatory and local governance. Furthermore, and as J. D. Barkan notes, such patterns may also grow out of the continuation of neopatrimonial relationships and dynamics well into "transitional" democratic regimes (Barkan 2000). Since state resources are critical to sustaining neopatrimonial relationships, one might reasonably expect personnel at the center to resist strongly the transfer of those resources to others. As this chapter will discuss, among other things, this is a problem for localities in Uganda. Of course, there is no guarantee as well that neopatrimonial actors at the local level will not capture resources once they are transferred to that level (Hirata 2001).

Taking Decentralization
Beyond the Standard Analytical Variables

In recent years, the tendency of African central governments to abuse their power, along with the failure of centralized systems to deliver socioeconomic development, has increased attention to decentralization as an institutional means to check the power of central governments. More broadly, the worldwide revival of classic liberal theories of politics and economics has sparked interest in decentralization. In line with liberal prescriptions for African political economy, governments are seeking ways to make democratic processes more direct and accessible to their citizens, while at the same time governments are also seeking to decrease the role of central government in planned development (Crook 1994; Kasfir 1983; Olowu and Smoke 1992). Democratic decentralization—that is, the transfer of authority, decision, and management responsibilities from central governments to lower levels of government, as well as accountability to local residents leading to local governance—is one way to achieve these goals.

However, renewed interest in decentralization has not led to many new insights or approaches to the study of decentralization. In the early 1980s, authors referred to the following list of factors as predictors of decentralization success: levels of political commitment (especially state-level support), administrative skills, financial resources, appropriate program design, and adequate infrastructure (Rondinelli, Nellis, and Cheema 1984:46–69). More recently, analyses of decentralization in Ghana (Ayee 1993, 1996, 1997b), Senegal (Vengroff 1993), and Anglophone Africa (Tordoff 1994) provide parallel lists of lessons. Contemporary authors tend to weight the political aspects of decentralization (especially as decentralization is linked to democratization) more heavily than did the development administration theorists of the late 1970s and early 1980s. However, most often, the contemporary literature simply reiterates the lessons identified by earlier analysts (Rondinelli, Nellis, and Cheema 1984; Conyers 1983), while it reports a disappointing record of success for decentralization in Africa. Recent literature on decentralization is often very useful for its insights into state-level politics (Barkan and Chege 1989), but the literature is notable for its lack of recommendations about how political and economic impediments to decentralization in Africa can be overcome. Most treatments of decentralization appear to be caught in the structural cul-de-sac familiar to students of African politics, namely that plans for invigorating local government tend to founder in political environments marked by three crucial factors: (1) the political insecurity of those who hold state power; (2) the economic poverty of both state and social actors; and (3) the lack of administrative and technical skills in both state and society.

Understanding these structural problems of governance in Africa is key to understanding decentralization in Africa. Still, it is important that analysts seek to learn any new lessons they can from recent decentralization efforts as they may offer new insights into prerequisites and strategies for its success. To this end, this chapter focuses on several lessons that can be gained from the Ugandan experience with decentralization through the LC system. The chapter finds that the LC system has experienced varying successes and problems among its five levels. At the lowest, or village, level, it has had some successes as a grassroots political and administrative institution, albeit only with reference to variables that receive little attention in studies of decentralization. Most observers find that the LC system at the lowest level is successful because of its functional responsibility for local judicial processes as well as its responsibility for local security. Both of these are effectively public goods. In addition, the success of the lower levels of the LC system can be traced to comparisons between the LCs and the system of local administration based on appointed chiefs that preceded the LC system. However, the higher levels of the LC system have experienced some difficulties in effectively performing their complex political and administrative tasks, problems that relate to more conventional variables. Nonetheless, they have some successes to point toward. The relative successes and problems of these levels suggest that renewed attention ought to be paid to involving the grassroots directly in its own governance.

Function and History: A "Horizontal" Approach to Decentralization at the Village Level

Village-Level Governance in Uganda: The LC1 Level

Most analysts to date have maintained a focus on the standard variables associated with decentralization identified above. Standard analyses are also marked by their interest in the "vertical" aspects of decentralization, that is, attention to linkages between lower and higher levels of government. Emphasis on vertical linkages is easily justified. African states tend to be weakly linked to their societies and communication between states and societies meant to ensure efficient utilization of political and developmental resources is an important goal for decentralization. In addition, the democratic impulse that often lies behind decentralization (Ayee 1997b; Crook 1994; Davis, Hulme, and Woodhouse 1994) is inherently vertical in nature. Democracy implies control of government by the people, and the hitherto superior-inferior relationship between state and society is vertically arranged. However, the LC1 level of governance in Uganda offers analysts a chance to see how genuine proximity to people and the possibility of utilitizing existing social capital might affect the emergence of local governance.

Average citizens may embrace decentralization because it appears to offer stronger vertical avenues of access to state resources, but the simple truth is that available resources—both economic and political resources—cannot satisfy grassroots demands. African politicians are likely to be too insecure to cede significant political power to grassroots forums, while demands for physical inputs easily outstrip the resources of the state. Decentralization may incrementally expand political capital in vertical relationships, and it may inspire some successful self-help projects. However, rural Africans are likely to be frustrated when decentralized government bodies prove incapable of exerting real power at higher levels of government while they soak up economic resources in recurrent expenditures, leaving little for development activities. For instance, Richard Crook reports that two district governments in Ghana spent 85 percent of their budgets on recurrent expenditures (Crook 1994:359). Thus, most decentralization programs founder when it becomes clear that efforts to improve vertical relationships between state and society are, at best, only a partial solution to the political and developmental problems that face grassroots populations.

In contrast to the vertical emphasis of most analyses of decentralization, this section of the chapter suggests that we take a closer look at the local (i.e., horizontal) context of decentralized government. This will focus on how decentralized governments relate to the day-to-day concerns of local people (function) and people's experience with local government (history). With regard to functional aspects, key questions are: Do local people feel that decentralized bodies have a positive effect on their lives, and do local people feel that participation in decentralized bodies is meaningful? People embrace governments that serve their needs. Exposure to locally relevant government can help create a record of legitimacy and accountability among local people that can strengthen a decentralized government's ability to assume broader political and developmental responsibilities. However, if decentralized bodies are principally concerned with allocating scarce state-provided development resources, or if decentralized bodies are designed primarily to extract new taxes from local people, then it seems likely that these bodies will either have little impact on most people's lives, or they will be seen as a new layer of intrusive government. Control of government functions that are not heavily dependent on taxation and resource allocation, such as local dispute settlement and rural security—extending to protection from an abusive or intrusive state—may increase people's participation in and support for decentralized organizations.

It should be noted that this section's focus on local functions is not novel. Other analysts, including some cited in this chapter (Ayee 1993, 1996; Olowu 1990a; Wunsch and Olowu 1990b) also draw attention to such factors. The importance of local functions is also frequently noted in studies of development administration where many authors embrace the notion that "small is beautiful" or that development should be based on local institutions (Uphoff 1986). Thus, the importance of function asserted by this chapter is not a fundamental critique of existing analyses. Indeed, it is very likely, given the distance between the village and the center, that other intermediary levels of governance will also be necessary to take on more costly and technically complex functions, ones with larger economies of scale, and to deal with externalities. However, the village may be a critical "leg" for those to build on.

Attention to history is crucial because a government's legitimacy is a product of people's experience with that government. Studies of decentralization often include summaries of the history of local government and of previous attempts to decentralize power. However, these historical summaries do not seriously engage the possibility that local concerns and traditions should be important factors for the design of decentralization. In most cases, local government history is treated as a "blank slate" on which politicians and administrative theorists are free to experiment. Attention to history is also important because it helps overcome the tendency to appraise technical aspects of administration in isolation from people's experience with local government.

Local Functions of the Village Councils

Uganda's LC1s, or village councils, are an example of how a decentralized system can achieve legitimacy by addressing local issues. As noted previously, the design of the original resistance councils was ambitious, as the system was supposed to provide political leadership at all levels of society. In practice however, the system assumed real control over a very limited but very important set of local issues. Because of recent attention to financial decentralization, the system is poised to assume a more direct role in government and administration. However, to date the success of the system has largely revolved around two issue areas—security and conflict resolution.

Survey data helps to underline the importance of these issues, while also giving a sense of how successfully the LC system, in particular the LC1 or village-level council, has reached the grassroots of Ugandan government and administration.[1] As Table 8.1 demonstrates, virtually all the respondents in the survey recognized the LC1 as an important venue for local problem solving. Table 8.2 elaborates on the data in

Table 8.1 Solving Village Problems

Question: "If people in the village have a problem they cannot solve by themselves, where do they go to solve the problem? If there is more than one place to solve problems please tell me which is the most important, and which are less important."

Response	N	%
LC alone or mentioned first	366	85.1
Police, chief, or other mentioned first, or no difference between LCs and other authorities	64	14.9
Total	430	100

Table 8.2 Local Councils and Local Conditions

Question: "How has the LC made life better?"

Response	N	%
Peace and security	107	35.5
Problem solving	65	21.6
Development	28	9.3
Close to the people	19	6.3
Problem solving and peace	15	5.0
Better, no reason	10	3.3
Civic education	9	3.0
No harassment	8	2.7
Freedom	8	2.7
Brings unity, cooperation	7	2.3
Free speech	5	1.7
Participation avenue	5	1.7
Community information	4	1.3
Other	11	3.7
Total	301	100.1

Table 8.1 by giving an overview of reasons why respondents gave positive evaluations to the LC.

Evident in Table 8.2 is the fact that the LC1s' ability to deal with peace and security issues, along with local problem solving, accounts for more than 60 percent of the reasons respondents gave to explain why the LCs had improved their lives. The impact of these two issues is central to the understanding of the LC1 level.

LC1s are charged with providing security in their areas. In some places, this extends to the formation of local defense units (LDUs). Drawn from local populations, the LDUs are a kind of "informal police force selected, supervised and paid by the LCs but trained by the army" (Tideman 1995:140). In urban areas, LC1s often hire private guards who patrol the LC after dark. The nine-member LC1 committee, and especially the LC's secretary for security, becomes in effect a police force easily accessible to local residents. This security function is extremely important to rural peoples who seldom have direct access to police protection.

The LCs have also empowered the people by making the LC1s the courts of original jurisdiction for virtually all petty and noncapital crime in Uganda. Through the LC1s people have the authority to deal with local legal disputes without involving the formal legal system. Previously, most cases now tried by LC1 courts came under the jurisdiction of local chiefs. It is difficult to generalize about the justice system based on the chiefs because so much depended on the quality of the local chief. If the local chief was considered to be a legitimate authority, it is likely that the local justice system functioned effectively. However, if the local chief was corrupt or considered illegitimate for some reason, then local justice was probably distorted. In contrast to the appointed chiefs, the LC1 committees that hear cases are elected. The committee's elective status assures that the LC1 courts have the potential to be more accountable to the people than were the appointed chiefs. Administration of justice through the LCs may then be more legitimate and responsive to local needs, though accountability through elections does present its own problems and is not a simple panacea.

LC1 courts guarantee that local people will be judged before their peers in a setting where they will understand the proceedings and where punishments are likely to match community standards (Tideman 1995). In contrast, adjudication in the formal legal system takes place before government-employed magistrates, legal proceedings are conducted in the language of the colonial era and cluttered with formal-legal jargon, and the rules used often bear little relation to local people's conceptions of justice. One of the most interesting features of the law governing LC1 courts is the fact that lawyers are forbidden from appearing before most LC1 courts. Among rural Ugandans, this is a popular feature of the LC1 justice system since lawyers seem to them capable of bending court decisions in favor of the rich and educated. In addition, the formal legal system is relatively easy to corrupt since a single judge or a police official can be bribed. Bribery of an LC1 court is far more difficult both because the courts are made up of nine individuals and because it is difficult to keep secrets in intimate village settings. If a village-level LC committee accepts a bribe, sooner or later someone in the village will find out about the miscarriage of justice. Moreover, in the formal judicial system, hearings and trials are often conducted in venues that require expensive and time-consuming travel. In LC courts, however, legal proceedings always originate in village settings that are easily accessible to litigants.

Not surprisingly, the LC1 system's judicial powers have been attacked by the legal establishment. Legal professionals suggest that LC1 courts can distort the law through ignorance and lack of attention to legal procedure. But the fact remains that the LC1 justice system touches a strong chord of legitimacy among the common people, and even the legal community has increasingly accepted the fact that LC1 courts have a role to play in Uganda's legal system. A typical statement concerning the popularity of LC1 judicial functions is offered by John-Jean Barya and J. Oloka-Onyango, both members of Uganda's Makerere University Faculty of Law: "There is no doubt that LC Courts are popular and that their establishment (even if from above by the state) is almost universally welcome . . . where disputes are among peasants and where the law is not overly class-specific, the courts appear to be proper avenues of the dispensation of popular justice—quick, cheap and easily understood" (Barya and Oloka-Onyango 1994:79).

Of course, it is also possible to define the LC1 system's "popular justice" as a fragmenting influence with possible detrimental effects for achieving social equality. Indeed, it is important to note that the concept of popular justice is extremely complex since, while it appeals to the notion that justice should be dispensed in a manner that is accessible and comprehensible to the common man, it also makes few formal allowances for minority rights or the fine points of legal process (Barya and Oloka-Onyango 1994). In rural Africa, popular justice may be preferred over definitions of justice codified in written law, but popular justice suffers in its association with vigilantism, the phenomenon of mob rule, and inequities associated with patriarchal traditions. The popularity of LC1 courts could hamstring the promulgation of national legal standards with poorly defined local legal traditions. This potential outcome is especially dangerous with regard to issues surrounding land tenure. The potential for conflict between the LC1 court system and the formal legal system is evident as wealthy, often nonresident landowners prefer to present land tenure cases to the formal legal system, while tenant farmers engaged in disputes with landlords prefer to utilize LC1 courts (Tideman 1995:143). Also, to the degree that the local norms protect existing power relationships, LC courts may be insensitive to the problems of historically disenfranchised groups, such as women and ethnic minorities. As in any justice system, there are potential problems of conflict of interest and abuse of power by elites. To keep these findings in perspective, it is important to recall that these can occur at national, regional, and local levels. None is immune from them.

Whatever the potential pitfalls of the LC1 judicial system, it appears that judicial functions are among the most popular of the system's activities. Much of this popularity can be interpreted as a product of the LC1 system's success in redefining state-society boundaries in rural areas. Justice systems are among the most important points of contact between rural peoples and government. The LC1s' security responsibilities, coupled with the LC1s' judicial powers, makes the LC1s the people's first line of defense against insecurity; whether that insecurity is caused by thieves and brigands, or the coercive powers of the government in the form of all-powerful local chiefs, or at the hands of miscreants from the army.

Perhaps the most astonishing achievement of the LC1 system has been its ability to empower local peoples in their relations with the military. In the words of a lecturer in political science at Makerere University in Uganda, Sabiti Makara: "Most people would agree that a fundamental change has taken place in the Ugandan polity since 1986. It is almost a miracle that [LCs] can apprehend an army officer whom they find staying illegally in their area for questioning. In the past, the army was untouchable" (Makara 1993:134).

Security and judicial functions lie at the core of any description of the LC1 system. Legislative and vertical linkage functions assigned to the lowest-level LC1s have tended to atrophy, leaving security and judicial functions at the center of LC1s' activities. As Expedit Ddungu remarks: "Most of the [LC] meetings [become] problem solving gatherings; such that if there is no case to solve, and no big official from government who is to visit the area, councils do not meet" (Ddungu

1994:41). But even if the LC1s' success has been limited to local security and problem solving, this represents a significant victory for rural
peoples in their struggle to control their lives.

The judicial and security functions that form the core of lower-level
LC activities guarantee that average citizens have a stake in the system.
These functions are remarkable because they flourish without state-
level support. They appear to be examples that match Joseph Ayee's
dictum that "the assignment of functions to sub-national governments
must match their financial and manpower capacities" (Ayee 1996:49).
Ayee also alludes to the historical importance of judicial functions in
traditional African governance when he points out that local government laws in the colonial period in Ghana created a division between
"native authorities (made up of chiefs and their councilors) who were
responsible for law and order and who dispensed traditional justice, and
district commissioners (colonial agents), exercising both the authority
and initiative for local development using central government funds"
(Ayee 1993:115). Ayee suggests that the failure to incorporate traditional judicial-administrative functions into newly designed decentralized
systems may be one of the reasons why decentralization has been difficult to implement in Ghana.

To be sure, local governments will not become efficient development agencies or legitimate democratic institutions simply because
these functions are included in their responsibilities. But judicial and
security matters are examples of functions that might be assigned to
decentralized governments not only because they make few demands on
resources, but also because they hold the possibility of meaningful
involvement of local people in decentralized government. Indeed, success in handling such functions may serve to invigorate other functions
assigned to local-level bodies. An analytical model for the flexible
assignment of responsibilities to various levels of governance was
developed by James Wunsch (1991a).

The History of the Local Councils and Village Governance

History can inform studies of local governance by offering clues to the
adaptability and staying power of institutional arrangements. As part of
a range of criteria for measuring institutionalization, Samuel
Huntington has suggested that true institutions should demonstrate the
ability to adapt to changing circumstances (Huntington 1968:13–23).
The Ugandan local council system has evolved through a turbulent history that suggests it has acquired a degree of institutional status that

enhances prospects for successful local governance through the LC system. But the most important point to be drawn from a historical analysis of the LC system concerns comparison of the LC1s with the former system of local government that was based on chiefs appointed by the central government.

In fact, it is difficult to overstate the importance of the change from a system of local government based on appointed administrators to a system based on elected committees. The largely homogeneous local communities, at least in rural areas, that elect LC1 committees include high degrees of interpersonal knowledge and understanding of local issues. The "face to face" democracy practiced at the lowest levels of the LC system assures that elected LC1 committees are more politically legitimate than the appointed chiefs. Thus, the LC system takes maximum advantage of the legitimacy of the village-level democracy that many observers have noted in Africa (Bayart 1986; Decalo 1992; Owusu 1992; Wunsch and Olowu 1990b).

In Uganda, local government based on chiefs was begun during the colonial era and continued after independence. In the colonial era, administrative, judicial, and policymaking powers were fused in the office of the chief. Many argued that this fusion of responsibility granted the chiefs excessive power (Republic of Uganda 1987). Even today, appointed chiefs play administrative roles in Ugandan local government, but the chiefs' judicial and policymaking functions have been transferred to the LC1s. In the early days of colonial administration, the British indirectly encouraged chiefs to engage in corrupt and extractive practices because the appointed chiefs were given very little by way of official compensation at a time when they were no longer effectively accountable to their subjects. To compensate for the lack of salaries, chiefs were often given a virtual free hand to plunder their districts. In addition, following the precolonial traditions on which the chief system was based, appointed chiefs often considered it their right to demand tribute from their subjects. Due to their close ties to the colonial administration and their tendency to abuse their offices for personal gain, chiefs often became symbols of colonial oppression. Following independence, continuation of local government based on chiefs meant that chiefs were often involved with the intrusive and arbitrary power exerted by the central governments of Obote and Amin.

The legitimacy of the chief system varied according to the personal qualities of chiefs, but it is clear that local government based on the chiefs came to symbolize an abusive state for many Ugandans. Evident in the work of virtually all early analyses of the LC system is the notion that the LCs, particularly LC1s, had broken the village level of an oppressive state apparatus (Burkey 1991; Ddungu 1989; Mamdani 1988; Tideman 1994, 1995). Representative of these authors is the following passage from Ddungu: "[The LCs] promised to be more radical than anything else hitherto witnessed in post independent Africa. . . . The institution of the [LCs] was the first attempt to crack the regime of dictatorship introduced by the colonial power into the village society in Uganda. This was the regime which had created out of the traditional chiefship an absolute institution, without any check on balance from countervailing institutions" (1989:1).

Thus, the LC1 system replaced a discredited system of local government based on appointed chiefs with a system of local government based on elected committees. To be sure, LC1 committees are often dominated by the same local elites that have dominated lower levels of governance in the past, as one often finds even in advanced industrial democracies. But it seems clear that the authoritarian powers of the appointed chiefs have been decisively checked by the advent of the LCs.

Local Governance in Uganda Beyond the Grassroots: The LC3 and LC5 Levels

As noted above, the village, or LC1, level of governance has developed important judicial and security functions that seem to have resulted in widespread support. Above it, however, are where most administrative and fiscal resources are lodged, as well as where most interaction with the center occurs. Two of those, the subcounty (LC3) and district (LC5), are authorized to hire and fire personnel, make budgets, pass bylaws, administer programs, and raise revenues. Two levels, the parish (LC2) and county (LC4), have primarily minor administrative responsibilities, and are not reviewed here. This multilevel design could mean the grassroots have an opportunity to participate, while different economies of scale of the various activities could be facilitated by lodging them at appropriate levels. By 2001, two cycles of local elections had been held, giving popular representatives time to establish ties with the people, and for both them and civil servants to begin learning their respective roles under a democratic decentralized system.

The scale of transition involved in fulfilling the potential for genuine local governance at these levels should not be underestimated. Legal reform, no matter how sweeping, is only the first step to building working relationships among key actors and effective systems of governance in the field. This task is particularly large when those relationships and systems require substantial alteration in the control of field personnel exercised by still-powerful ministries in Kampala; the development of a large number of new, locally based political institutions (elected councils); the development of working relationships between new and already established actors (councils and elected chairs versus district-level civil servants); and new systems to make and implement complex decisions (local planning, budgeting, and financial management). The "legs" that the first section of this chapter suggested might exist at the village level need to be linked with the superior levels if each is to reach its potential. Finally, all these transitions are particularly challenging in a less-developed country where scarce resources inspire intense competition.

The purpose of this section is to analyze the successes and problems the superior levels of Ugandan local government have experienced in this transition. Specifically, it will focus on fiscal transfers from the center and the weakness of local revenue base, the effectiveness of local councils, and the effectiveness of the planning and budgeting processes and delivery of services to the grassroots. In exploring these topics, it will draw on six weeks of fieldwork completed in Uganda in 1994, during which one of the authors of this chapter and his colleagues visited six districts and numerous subcounties. Key actors at each level were interviewed and key documents were examined. While none of the chapter's observations should be seen as conclusive, they are certainly suggestive of issues worthy of further study.[2]

In general, this section finds that important progress toward a viable democratic, decentralized system has been made in Uganda. However, there are serious obstacles to achieving the constitutional and legislative provisions of local governance at the LC3 and LC5 levels, and in linking them to the LC1 level. Until these are addressed, the potential of local governance to provide an opportunity for Uganda's citizens to set and achieve local priorities will be seriously constrained.

Central Fiscal Transfers, the Local Revenue Base, and Local Governance

The fiscal system for local government in Uganda is based almost entirely on revenue transfers from Kampala. While locally generated revenue records are unreliable and difficult to assess, our field research indicated that rarely more than 5 percent of district budgets are based on local revenues. The remainder comes from one of some twenty-six revenue transfer systems. These can be usefully organized into four categories, as shown in Table 8.3.

Table 8.3   Transfers from Central Government to Local Government

	1997–1998		1998–1999		1999–2000		2000–2001	
Grants	Uganda Grants (billions)	%	Uganda Grants (billions)	%	Uganda Grants (billions)	%	Uganda Grants (billions)	%
Unconditional grants	54.3	24	64.4	23	66.8	17	79.1	15
Conditional grants– recurrent	168.4	75	202.1	71	275.2	71	321.3	63
Conditional grants– development	2.2	1	18.8	7	45.0	12	107.8	21
Equalization	0.0	0	0.0	0	2.0	0.5	4.0	0.8
Total	224.9	100	285.2	100	389.0	100	512.2	100

Source: A. Batkin, *Fiscal Decentralization in Uganda: The Way Forward* (Kampala: Government of Uganda and Donor Sub-Group on Decentralization, January 2001).

In reality, "unconditional grants" (UGs) are entirely consumed by essentially fixed administrative costs: maintaining the district-level personnel apparatus prescribed by the 1997 Local Government Act. The remainder of the budget (84 percent), less the small amount of "equalization grants" allocated to the poorest districts, are "conditional grants" (CGs) outside the control of the district council.

In effect, this leaves districts with only revenues raised locally as discretionary funds. As noted above, these usually only add approximately 5 percent to the district budget. Since these funds are collected by the subcounties (LC3 level), transferred by it to the districts, and based largely on the unpopular and narrowly based "graduated tax," these are also not particularly reliable revenue streams. Collections are erratic, varying both with the agricultural cycle and with the good or poor fortune of each year. Transfers are also often uncertain, with some LC3s simply not passing upward the funds they owe the district (LC5 level). Not surprisingly, in general the poorer the district is, the less revenue it receives from this tax.

The only exception to these patterns is the centrally based District Development Project (DDP), now expanded into the Local Government Development Project (LGDP). These programs are funded by the World Bank, and offer funds local governments can allocate to all service delivery functions (except security) noted in the LG Act, Schedule II, Part 2, as well as up to 15 percent for investment planning and monitoring. These funds, however, are only available to districts that have met specified performance requirements, including development-planning capacity, financial management capacity, technical capability, and 10 percent cofinancing.

Districts are evaluated annually by the Ministry of Local Government on these criteria, and newly eligible ones are added. Also, ones whose performance has improved receive additional monies, while ones that have remained static or degraded in these areas receive no increment or can be penalized by a 20 percent reduction in the grant.

A total of USh 3.9 billion (3.9 billion Uganda shillings; approximately U.S.$2.2 million in 2000) in the DDP/LGDP programs were transferred to districts and subcounties in 1999–2000. Since five districts were included that year, this averaged some U.S.$440,000 per district, including those funds allocated to the LC3 level. Sixty-five percent of these funds are to go to the LC3, LC2, and LC1 levels, while the districts retain 35 percent. Thus, the average district in this program would have available for its budget approximately U.S.$150,000. Subcounties varied greatly, but a typical grant was around U.S.$4,000.

In percentage terms, DDP/LGDP transfers increased the district budgets by around 15–20 percent, and the subcounty budgets by between 10 and 15 percent. While these are not particularly large increments considering the entire budget of each level, since they are broadly discretionary and are added after the district or subcounty has covered its fixed administrative costs, they represent a substantial addition to the choices local leaders have. Nonetheless, many districts in Uganda are still not in this program, and even the amounts available to the districts that are in it pale in comparison to their vast needs.

Among the districts studied, actual budgets ranged from approximately U.S.$500,000 to nearly U.S.$1 million. Education is regularly the largest cost item in the district, running between 60 and 70 percent of the budget. Second are the administrative costs, including the council and the various boards, at between 15 and 25 percent. Health runs between 8 and 13 percent, while works varies from 5 to 8 percent. Production (agriculture, veterinary services, and fisheries) varies from 1 to 5 percent, while gender programs and community services bottom out at less than 1 percent.

Subcounty, or LC3, budgets are virtually entirely dependent on local revenues. While a few civil servants are paid by the district (administrative chief, subaccountant, sector officers such as health, agriculture, education personnel, etc.), the bulk of the LC3-level operating and service-delivery expenses (approximately 90 percent) are dependent on their share of the graduated tax. Subcounties surveyed for this research varied in actual expenditures in 1999–2000 from

USh 24 million to 110 million (U.S.$13,300–U.S.$66,600). Typically, around 30–40 percent of subcounty expenditures are for the council and the central administration, though in some subcounties and urban divisions this reached 65 percent. Most of the remainder is nearly equally divided among financial transfers (to LC2 and LC1 levels), education and sports, and works and technical services. Of the latter two, typically nearly all is spent on salaries, with only a fraction of a percent for operational expenses.

The subcounty, or LC3 level, is not "driven" by national grants, but limited by its dependence on erratic and regressive local revenue such as the graduated tax. Frequently, councils budgeted more than 400 percent of what they would typically collect in such revenues. Their fixed administrative and salary costs consumed most of their revenues, leaving little for local choices. The only important exception to these constraints at each level is DDP/LGDP funds, as discussed above. These introduce only relatively small amounts of money (around U.S.$4,000 per subcounty), but do offer some flexibility the local governance units would otherwise never have. Both this field research and the Batkin study of fiscal transfers observed distinctly better planning, budgeting, fiscal management, council performance, and broader participation in districts that had qualified for and received these grants (Batkin 2001).

Overall, then, one finds both district and subcounties spending a significant amount of revenue on administrative costs. Districts are virtually entirely dependent on transfers from the center, which are either conditional grants and driven by national ministry decisions, or unconditional grants consumed by fixed administrative costs. Only a small amount, ranging in our fieldwork from 4 to 9 percent, of district revenues came from local taxes, and therefore were open to district discretion.

The consequence of this for decentralization and local governance is that localities are, in fact, still unable to set and meet local priorities. In this regard, Uganda has experienced more a move to deconcentration than to devolution or democratic decentralization. For example, and as will be discussed below regarding local planning and budgeting, these time- and personnel-consuming processes really have little impact on the allocation of resources. Local plans and budgets are largely, though indirectly, dictated by national ministries, with locally controlled resources affecting a few decisions at the margins. It logically follows that the efforts invested in working on local councils as well as getting elected to them, are relatively irrelevant. While local dwellers may or may not see this now, it seems likely that they will figure it out eventually.

As well as making much of local governance meaningless and

wasting many resources in relatively pointless exercises of planning and budgeting, the dominance of CGs also buries local governments in mountains of paperwork and ever-changing requirements to comply with reporting demands. Much staff time is invested in both the CGs and UGs, but delivers no services to any citizens. Interestingly enough, recent reports on the fiscal transfer systems find that the ministries in Kampala, for the most part, lack the staff to analyze the reports and, for the most part, do not do so (Batkin 2001).

All of this is not to argue that the center should have no role in local decisions and services. General guidelines on monies allocated to broad sectors, standard setting, quality control, and inspection all are needed and appropriate for local governance in Uganda, as seen in Chapter 5. But the current pattern of preemptive micromanagement is a dead end for the emergence of local governance.

Effectiveness of Local Government Councils

If decentralization is to be democratic and local governance is to emerge, locally accountable institutions must be established that make key decisions: setting local priorities, allocating resources, and supervising implementation of these decisions. To provide representation for large numbers of diverse people, such institutions are normally made up of multiple persons. To clarify accountability and avoid conflicts of interest, such institutions are normally separated from those that actively implement policies and programs. Thus any assessment of democratic decentralization finds its success closely linked to that of locally elected legislative bodies, normally called councils.

Newly established councils face substantial challenges in building community confidence in and support for them, making decisions that effectively utilize available resources for local priorities, and holding executives accountable. These challenges include gathering sufficient information about local conditions, needs, priorities, and personnel, as well as alternative public policies and programs, so that they can make informed decisions. They include developing an understanding of their role and of internal processes and procedures that expedite informed decisions, and building enough cohesion among the members that they can work together. They also include developing and sustaining ties to local communities and constituencies to encourage both the flow of information and support for council decisions, ones that will always leave some wants unsatisfied. Finally, they require councils to achieve enough institutional development to resist dominance by the executive and by civil-service personnel.

Uganda's key elected and juridical councils are at the district and subcounty levels. As they have been in place at most only four years as of this research (recently formed districts have much "younger" councils), it is unlikely one would find councils to have fully mastered these challenges. Indeed, the fieldwork that underlies this chapter found many problems in these areas, though there was substantial variation among councils. In general, however, councils were weak in gathering and processing information, developing internal cohesion, making decisions independently of executive direction, and developing ties with constituents. These problems grew, in turn, from weaknesses in their committee systems, infrequency of meetings, their personnel's low educational levels, the dynamics of the budgeting and revenue systems, and the weakness and political disengagement of local civil-society organizations. These weaknesses were found at both district and subcounty levels, though they are substantially worse at the subcounties.

Perhaps the single greatest cause of council weakness in Uganda is the weakness of their committees. While one of six district councils studied had committees that met regularly, gathered information from the executive branch, and made autonomous decisions and recommendations regarding planning priorities and budgeting, the others did not. Many committees met only quarterly and their members readily confessed they had only a limited understanding of the subject areas they were responsible for, e.g., the documents given them by the executive or civil servants, and tended to accept whatever recommendations were made to them by the district or subcounty chair and his/her cabinet. In budgeting, committees tended to approve far more programs and projects than funds could sustain. Again, respondents readily admitted that this was done so they could avoid "difficult decisions," where they might cause internal conflict or alienate a local community that wanted a certain project.

What this did, in effect, was pass actual budgeting authority to the executive, which decided which of and when the many projects and programs authorized by the council would be actually funded, as the revenues gradually trickled in throughout the year. Most councils had no further involvement in this process, much to the chagrin of some councillors interviewed. The few councils that were involved in those spending decisions were notable in that they met more frequently than the norm (bimonthly instead of quarterly), and had committees that also met more frequently and could articulate more clearly what their responsibilities were.

The weaknesses of committees seemed to be associated with several factors:

- Length of council life: more recently established councils were notably weaker in their committees.
- Weakness in educational levels of committee members: committee members illiterate in English were at a substantial disadvantage in these roles, and were aware of this; similarly, civil servants looked upon such persons with little respect, and were usually not helpful to them in explaining their programs and relevant issues; such councillors had less self-confidence in dealing with the executive body.
- Infrequency of meetings.
- Incomplete understanding of the role of committees.
- The paucity of resources actually available to the councils, which led some councillors to become cynical about the significance of their efforts, and others to avoid difficult decisions in allocating resources; either perception or action made committees less likely to make serious decisions.

Councils were also weakened by internal fragmentation and factionalism. This had a variety of bases in our field sites. In some cases councillors reported "bickering" over what the council's role was to be vis-à-vis local programs ("micromanaging" or policymaking?). Also, in many instances factionalism developed over which councillors would be elevated to cabinet status (political head of one of the sectors such as finance, health, education, public works, etc.). Such promotion was desired as it gave that councillor a salary, office, access to a vehicle, and potentially much greater influence over planning, budgeting, and implementing decisions. This factionalism also tended to follow divisions between a personal faction linked to the chair and those who were outside it. Finally, religion and ethnicity were also mentioned as sources of factionalism in councils. At least implicitly, all these divisions followed the issue of how resources were distributed, including key positions (such as to cabinet), projects, and programs. This factionalism appeared to make the councils easy targets for executive manipulation, and probably explained why most respondents suggested few of the executive's planning and budgeting recommendations were changed by the councils, and why executive dominance over spending choices during the budget year was also usually unchallenged.

Finally, most respondents reported that local civil-society organizations were weak, narrowly based, and generally politically inactive. This meant that councillors' passivity was unchallenged by those who might otherwise make demands on them. It also meant that a potential political resource for councils that might help them challenge dominant executives was never brought to the table. Similarly, council-constituent relations were underdeveloped. Few councillors spoke of meeting regularly with constituents, or of trying to mobilize constituents to pressure the executive. Councils did note they tried to be sure their constituencies got a "share" of development projects. Still, this was an underdeveloped relationship.

Certainly, underlying all these dynamics is the dominance over local decisions by the central government ministries in Kampala, as already discussed. As a result, in a real sense the stakes of the local political game are relatively low. Planning and budgeting *are* largely preempted by the center, so it may not make sense to invest much of oneself in an unpaid duty (committee work) that has in any case little potential to affect the flow of resources to the public. With this in mind, the frequent accusations that councillors were primarily focused on private goods for themselves instead of the community's general concerns (usually, public goods), may be both correct and understandable. Unfortunately, such attitudes and orientations keep councillors easy prey for executive manipulation and retard development of public confidence in and support for councils as institutions.

The Planning and Budgeting
Process and Local Service Delivery

Planning and budgeting are key processes at any level of government. When well executed, they allow for:

- Control by and accountability to elected officials of governmental institutions.
- Broad input by the public in the allocation of resources.
- Rational decisionmaking to assess and respond to priority needs and to meet longer-term objectives.
- Efficient management of resources during the budget year.
- Cross-sectoral coordination to maximize the impact of resources and project/program interdependencies to be taken into account in plans and their implementation.

Uganda's local government statutes and regulations outline a lengthy and detailed process by which an annual plan is generated at both the LC3 and LC5 levels, and a comparable process by which budgets for these two levels are also generated. However, there are a number of aspects to district and subcounty planning and budgeting that work to impede performing the above functions.

A major problem in the planning-budgeting process is the lack of linkage and articulation among its several processes and components. These would include the approval of the coming year's activities as outlined by the three-year rolling District Development Plan (DDP), presenting and responding to the Budget Framework Paper (BFP), doing the subcounty planning process, and doing internal planning for the key sectors active at the district level (health, education, roads, water, and production). For the system to work well and meet the above goals, the four should be closely interlinked. Instead, each goes on virtually autonomously of the others.

For example, the annual plan is discussed and approved by the council in June, but the BFP, which should grow out of the plan, is required in March. At the same time, the LC3 planning process is occurring, but has no input to the district's plans for spending conditional grants, which occurs largely within the sector offices. Indeed, LC3 plans were poorly integrated into all district-level activities, and vice versa. District planners review LC3 investment project proposals, and pick up a few for the annual plan. The rest are rolled into future years of the three-year plan for an uncertain fate. As for district-funded activities, many LC3s reported they knew nothing of district-funded investments in their subcounties, such as schools and clinics, until construction had actually begun. Perhaps, not surprisingly, LC3 personnel frequently felt that what was provided was not a local priority, was badly designed, etc. As for the sector-specific plans, it is a rare occurrence when a sector/CG plan is changed to fit local priorities, but other researchers report frequent changes in *approved* district plans to meet line ministry requirements (Batkin 2001). Line ministry staff commonly work directly with local government departments, bypassing both district political and administrative leadership. While their work plans are included in the final district annual plan, district planning officers report the information is given begrudgingly, often late, and not as an input for a conversation about the coming year, but simply to inform them of the figures to "plug" into the annual plan. Indeed, several district administrative and political leaders complained that the District Technical Planning Committee, composed of the sector heads, did not perform its role of integrating programs among the various sectors. Instead, the department heads treated it as "a staff meeting to air complaints and other issues that concerned them."

In effect, there was a parallel planning process occurring at the national ministries, and in some measure their district offices, that largely supplanted and displaced locally based planning. As discussed regarding budgetary transfers and local revenue base, few shillings are allocated according to local priorities. Several district planners reported that they attempt to "pick-up subcounty proposals" in their final version of the district plan. However, that is driven by chance coincidence between LC3 desires, the requirements of the national CGs that drive most of the projects funded, and services delivered by district governments.

A second general problem lies in the effectiveness of district planning in assessing and following grassroots priorities. Planning is, in fact, intended to be driven by the grassroots. The planning process should begin with a general meeting at the LC1, or village level. There, where every adult is a voting member, the council is to meet, discuss problems and needs, and develop a set of project proposals to pass to the parish development committee. The latter is made up of the parish (LC2) administrative chief (an employee of the LC3 level) and two representatives from each village. They select a number of projects to recommend and then pass them to the subcounty council (LC3 level). The subcounty council, in turn, is to select from the several parishes a number of projects that it feels able to fund. The remainder is forwarded to the district (LC5), which selects some for its plan.

In reality, there are several problems in this process. First, in many cases respondents reported that the village meetings frequently did not occur, or were attended by only a fraction of those eligible. Thus, the initial (and only true) grassroots input to the process is often compromised. Second, if one judges the quality of the plans produced at the LC3 level, there is little if any needs assessment going into planning, and no discernable strategic or cross-sectoral thinking occurring at all. LC1 input into these plans is very weak. Plans are merely "wish lists" of diverse projects desired by local dwellers and their representatives that, given the level of local poverty and need, are indeed lengthy. But, without needs-assessment and strategic thinking, it is difficult to set any priority to the various proposals, nor was this done. Furthermore, it is unlikely there will be any synergy among them. Finally, costing was rudimentary at best.

Many problems also trouble local government budgeting in Uganda. At the LC3 level, budgeting should logically flow from the projects selected, along with the salary and program needs of LC3 civil servants (some of whom are paid by the LC5 level), and the operational costs of the LC3 political and administrative personnel (salaries, sitting allowances, etc.). In fact, LC3 budgets consistently wildly overestimate expected local tax revenues and miscellaneous income (donor and NGO grants), and thus are almost meaningless documents. In effect, administrative and personnel salaries are paid first, and if there are monies remaining, a few LC3 projects and operational expenses for programs are funded. In all but one subcounty, the latter decisions were made by the administrative chief and the subcounty accountant, without any participation by the council or elected chair of the subcounty. Budgeting thus was an ineffective tool to maintain control by and accountability to local elected officials at the subcounty level, and seems unlikely to provide for efficient management of resources as well.

Budgeting at the district (LC5) level is a more formal and involved process. It includes an annual budget conference, to which key LC3 officials, key civil servants, all the district's civil-society organizations and other interested parties are invited to come and plead their case. From there it goes to a conference of senior civil servants who bring a proposed framework budget to the district council, which makes changes it sees fit, and returns it to the civil servants. They in turn revise it and submit it to the council for final approval. Final changes and amendments occur there, and the budget is approved.

There are some positive aspects to this process, including the budget conference, the involvement of the council committees in reviewing the proposed framework and final budgets, and the "back-and-forth" between the council and the civil servants. Certainly, this is an immense improvement over a budget written in Kampala, or one by locally based civil servants accountable only to their sectoral supervisors. Nonetheless, there are still problems with district-level budgeting.

In some districts, the annual budget conference simply was not called, ostensibly because of cost consideration. In most districts, committee effectiveness is an issue, as already discussed. Committee members admitted they had difficulty understanding the budgetary documents they were presented. In reality, few changes or amendments came from the committees. The same applies to the general council session on the budget. While many respondents described the debates as "heated" over the budget, it was always approved at the end of the two-day session allocated to it, and with "few changes or amendments," in the words of most councillors interviewed. Councillors were concerned, to be sure, that each of their constituencies was getting its "fair" allocation of resources, but that seemed to be their primary concern. LC1 desires were never mentioned as a significant input into these processes. Underlying this dynamic, again, is the dominance of CGs in the budgetary process. In fact, the CGs cannot be changed by the councils, so the vast majority of the budget, approximately 95 percent, is beyond debate by the annual budget conference.

Inspection of budget documents shows several patterns. First, departments blessed with large CG allocations do have substantial resources. Second, district councils are generous in funding their own direct and indirect needs: salaries, sitting allowances, vehicles, etc., are provided for. Third, the salary and operational expenses of non-CG-funded departments are parsimonious to the point of near starvation.

The last pattern was repeated at the LC3 level as well. Often referred to as "facilitation," these allocations funded the field expenses of those personnel who actually delivered services to the grassroots. While "headquarters" functions were well provided for, field costs were the least budgeted and, when revenues ran short, the first cut. Although total district budgets were not as far out of line with their actual revenues as subcounty budgets, once one removes the CGs from them, there was still a substantial discrepancy between budget and revenue. This meant that civil servants funded by local revenues were never sure what they could do during a year, when monies would become available, or when projects and programs would be interrupted.

As a result of these factors, planning and budgeting at district and subcounty governments failed to achieve any of the goals listed above. Local accountability and political control were weakened by the dominance of CGs and the, in effect, parallel planning and budgeting process that rendered moot most local planning. Local accountability and political control were also weakened by the ineffectiveness of council committees at both levels (LC3 and LC5), and by the tendency of councils seriously to overbudget. This meant local elected representatives lost an opportunity to set priorities and to discipline decisionmaking by administrative personnel. Instead, the real or operating budget was in effect determined by the latter.

Planning, as a tool to think strategically and set priorities, fell short for several reasons. The parallel track that planning followed in the nationally driven sector offices meant that most priorities in the plan were set by individuals with little or no local knowledge. Similarly, the possibility of cross-sector integration was lost as most planning was completed within sectors, independent of any contact with officials from other sectors or the district as a whole. Finally, the educational and technical background of most parish and LC3 elected and administrative personnel generally did not prepare them to think or organize decisions in this way.

All these factors, along with a shortfall in meetings at the grassroots, conspired to diminish any effective input from the grassroots in either process. Finally, the practice of overbudgeting made it difficult for service personnel at all levels to efficiently allocate their time or resources. Poorly funded for programs to begin with, they rarely knew when or how much money would be available for them to deliver services. While their salaries were fairly reliable, the resources to convert their time into delivered services were not.

In reality, the district is overwhelmingly the most powerful actor among the five levels of local government. Its budget dwarfs the others, most technically skilled personnel are employed by it, its physical facilities and resources vastly exceed those of any others, and what small latitude in planning and budgeting are left to local governments by the national CGs is dominated by the district. In effect, the subcounties pay a few personnel salaries, the impact of which are reduced by the absence of operational funds, and fund a few very small capital investments. The village, at which grassroots democracy was to be the base of the planning process, is so far down the line from what few decisions are actually made at the subcounty or district level, and has so few resources or personnel, that it is effectively marginalized.

In essence, then, what decentralization has occurred in Uganda has been a transfer of resources and some control to the districts. While districts vary widely in population, with several exceeding a half-million, they are hardly arenas of grassroots democracy. Since districts are subdivided into multiple subcounties, the latter might provide a greater chance for actual popular participation in governance. However, they currently have little effective power as their resources are so limited. LC1 participation, as suggested in the first section of this chapter, is stronger but has little control over or input on use of resources at the higher LC levels.

Conclusion

While this chapter has reported on the challenges that still face decentralization in Uganda, in reality much has been achieved. A complex local government structure is largely in place. Elected councils are operating at the two key levels of decisionmaking, elected and civil-service personnel have made substantial strides in learning their roles in decentralized governance, a local civil society is forming, local elections have been held, and local officials have begun to learn how to operate complex planning and budgeting systems. Many local officials have begun to yearn for more autonomy from the center to pursue local priorities, and most elected, appointed, and civil-society representatives, as well as rank-and-file local residents, were adamant in our conversations that decentralization's opportunities far outweighed its burdens and disadvantages. At every group interview, people asserted that decentralization had made them "free to speak our minds" for the first time, as well as offering some advantages in administrative efficiency and local prioritization. This emphasis on "freedom" as a key value parallels the findings of Richard Marcus, Kenneth Mease, and Dan Ottemoeller (2001), as well as Vicki Clarke (2001) in Ghana.

The LC1 system has become an effective element of local governance. Through the LC1 system, rural Ugandans are exposed to locally meaningful democracy, and they have been given an institutional framework for local collective action. At minimum, the LC1 system acts as a training ground for the practice of electoral democracy and an incubator for the notion of autonomy from the state, both hopeful observations for the future of local governance in Uganda. How well it is linked into LC3 and LC5 deliberations, however, is open to question.

Notwithstanding the potential for complex interaction between elements of local governance systems, this chapter's analysis of decentralization through the Ugandan LC system has identified potential for institutional innovation, particularly at the grassroots. The functionally and historically defined success of the LC system indicates that the centralized "hegemonial state" is being challenged in contemporary Uganda. In addition, the LC system's role in the debate about the future of multiparty politics in Uganda is an example of how contending bases for legitimacy arise in systems with multiple levels simultaneously offering citizens real opportunities to participate in their own governance.

There are still many problems involved in developing councils that are successful in fulfilling their critical responsibilities as the elected mechanisms of local accountability. Particularly at LC3 and LC5 levels, problems remain in effectively engaging councils in local decisionmaking and in revising planning and budgeting systems so they work to reflect local needs and priorities, efficiently managing resources, and ensuring accountability to elected officials. So far, executive dominance is a problem. Finally, a major underlying problem exists in relaxing the tight control exerted by the center over the grants that fund local governance. The DDP/LGDP program offers one strategy that might balance legitimate concerns about local capacity to handle funds effectively, as well as maintain broad parameters to guide the proportion of resources allocated among the key service sectors (health, education, etc.). If the currently favorable climate at the center for democratic governance can be sustained and consolidated in a multiparty and (eventually) post-Museveni era; if the central ministries can be persuaded gradually to relax their currently tight control over the LC system; if council personnel and management systems (planning, budgeting) can continue to improve; if the currently favorable macroeconomic and democratic conditions continue; and if the linkages between the LC1 and LC3/LC5 levels can be strengthened, Uganda's decentralization will continue to progress and be a leading example to the rest of Africa.

Notes

1. Survey research for this chapter was conducted in Uganda from May through September 1994 with support from the National Science Foundation (grant no. INT-9311512). The random-sample survey data are based on 436 interviews conducted in nine rural grassroots-level administrative units and three urban grassroots-level units (Ottemoeller 1996).

2. Sites visited include Apac, Kabale, Luwero, Mbarara, Nakasongola, and Tororo. Documents were examined at each site, while one-on-one interviews were conducted with nearly one hundred local elected and civil senior personnel, including planners, district chairs, council members, financial personnel, and leaders of civil-society organizations. In addition, open fora were held at each district and each subdistrict where civil servants, councillors, and local residents were encouraged to attend and respond to numerous questions about local governance. Several hundred people participated in these. Where appropriate, follow-up interviews were conducted with selected participants at these fora.

9

Kenya:
Erosion and Reform from the Center

Paul Smoke

K enya has a rich history of local governance, both from ethnic-
group traditions and the system set up during the British colonial
era, when local governments were fairly autonomous and had significant revenue sources. However, after independence (1963), when
Kenya's economy and population growth accelerated, demands were so
heavy that some local governments could not deliver key services adequately. This situation, combined with the central government's desire
for political consolidation to minimize ethnic power conflicts that
increased in the postcolonial era, prompted the government to weaken
local authorities. Key services (health, education, major roads) were
recentralized, and the local graduated personal tax (GPT) was taken
over by the center. Grants were established to compensate local governments for their revenue losses, but they were gradually phased out.
Control over local governments expanded, with few spending, revenue,
or employment decisions permitted without scrutiny by the Ministry of
Local Government (MLG).

In spite of their generally diminished status during the past three
decades, some local governments in Kenya have continued to provide
basic services, such as water, local roads, solid-waste collection, prepri-
mary schools, etc. They have also maintained significant sources of revenue, particularly property rates, and continue to be governed by largely
elected local councils. Kenya has long been among the most fiscally
independent local government systems in Africa and, more generally, in
the developing world. But the local governments have increasingly
developed a reputation for corruption and poor service delivery, which
is fostered by some elements in the central government and has been
used to maintain restrictions on local powers. Local governments, on
the other hand, believe many of their problems result from heavy cen-

tral control. There is some truth in this claim, but the MLG has weak capacity, so many aspects of "control" are largely perfunctory nuisances rather than insurmountable obstacles to improved local performance.

In any case, a stalemate developed over the years. Central officials complained about local government incompetence and corruption, but seemed unwilling or unable to do anything about it. Local officials blamed their problems on central government meddling in their affairs and argued that they could not make significant progress until they received more freedom and resources. In this contentious environment, there was little positive reform undertaken by anyone at any level of government. Recognizing the social and economic impacts of the problem-ridden system, some international donors began to provide large loans and grants for local development in the 1980s.[1]

Unfortunately, these large donor-funded projects were initially more concerned with quickly building infrastructure than solving the institutional structure and capacity problems of the local government system. This was accepted by the central government, which wanted improved infrastructure but was not particularly concerned with strengthening local governments. To the extent that these projects tried to empower local authorities, supporting provisions were heavily influenced by, if not outright forced, through strict loan conditionalities, raising questions about the level of national government commitment and the prospects for sustainability.

In recent years, there has been encouraging central and local movement to revive the local government system. A new decentralization policy that holds promise for genuine reform is emerging. In this chapter, I examine recent attempts to strengthen local governments and the forces underlying them. Before considering new reforms and probable future directions, I provide additional detail on the history and structure of the Kenyan system and its weaknesses.

Evolution of the Local Government System

Decentralization has been a controversial political issue since Kenya's colonial days, when there were separate forms of local government for natives and settlers (Oyugi 1983; Akivaga, Kulundu-Bitonye, and Opi 1985; Bubba and Lamba 1991; Smoke 1993, 1994). The Kenya African National Union (KANU), which has dominated Kenyan politics for decades and was for many years in the postindependence period (until 1992) the only legal political party, developed a highly centralized system. Kenya's original constitution provided for strong provincial governments;[2] however, under the leadership of the country's first president, Jomo Kenyatta, KANU was successful in a controversial bid to reform the constitution and eliminate provincial autonomy.

Local authorities were not immediately affected by the dismantling of provincial government, but as Kenyatta consolidated power in the late 1960s, he restricted local powers, probably to prevent minority ethnic groups from building local power bases, but officially for other reasons. First, national leaders argued that central control was required to promote unity in the ethnically diverse country. Second, rapid growth of local service demands in the 1960s created massive financial pressures and performance problems that were used to justify greater central intervention. Third, central control was further legitimized by consensus among early development experts that central planning would lead to more rapid development.

In 1966, a commission charged by Kenyatta with considering the future of local authorities called for sweeping reforms to strengthen them. In response, the government issued Sessional Paper No. 12 (1967), which accepted most commission recommendations. Instead of implementing them, however, parliament passed the Transfer of Functions Act (1969), which abolished most grants to local authorities and transferred substantial service responsibility and the main local revenue source, the GPT, to central government.[3] Rural councils, whose aggregate expenditures fell by 85 percent from 1969 to 1970, were particularly affected (Oyugi 1983:134). This deliberate weakening of local authorities was declared temporary, but no revitalization plan was ever drawn up.

Since the 1970s, the need to strengthen local authorities has been highlighted by national development plans, special commission reports, and an International Monetary Fund (IMF) study requested by Kenya (Government of Kenya 1971, 1973, 1980, 1982, 1986, 1989; Bahl and Mant 1976). The recommendations of these efforts were largely ignored, and local government performance continued to deteriorate. Pushed by economic, fiscal, and political factors discussed below, the government recently began to accept a number of modest changes and to work more closely with a number of donors to develop programs to strengthen local governments. In 1995, President Daniel arap Moi constituted a Commission of Inquiry on Local Government Reform, widely known as the Omamo Commission, which recommended a number of major reforms.[4] During 2002, work began on drafting a new constitution that is expected to define a new role for local governments.

Present Role of Local Governments in Kenya

Semiautonomous local authorities in the British tradition exist parallel to a deconcentrated central government administration similar to the French prefect system. Provincial commissioners under the Office of the President govern provinces, all of which except Nairobi are divided into districts administered by district commissioners (DCs) and several lower tiers. In 1983, President Moi transferred much responsibility for centrally funded projects from central ministries to districts under District Focus for Rural Development, which was portrayed as decentralization, but widely seen as an attempt to extend central control in the districts after the August 1982 coup attempt.[5] The DCs coordinate this strategy through district development committees (DDCs), which include local members of parliament, district officers of national ministries, and local officials. The exact relationship between districts and local governments is not specified and varies, but all district development projects, including those of local authorities, are subject to DDC review (as discussed in Chapter 2).

The legal basis of the local authority system was set by the Local Government Act of 1963.[6] This act details local authority organization, sets forth the powers and responsibilities of the four types of councils, and firmly establishes their strict control by the minister for local government. Municipal councils cover large urban areas and normally provide a wide variety of services. Town councils are in smaller urban areas and have less responsibility. The county councils, in almost every case geographically identical to districts, normally provide only a few basic services in areas not governed by municipal or town councils. Finally, the urban councils, which cover emerging centers preparing for transition to town councils, are under the legal jurisdiction of the county council in which they are located.[7] There are currently 174 local governments in Kenya.

Seven of the original municipal councils are required to provide health care, education, and local roads, but only minor services, such as the burial of destitute persons, are formally required of all local authorities. Most functions listed in the Local Government Act are permissive rather than mandatory, i.e., the councils may elect to provide these services, subject to MLG authorization.[8] Several acts of parliament empower local authorities to raise revenue from various sources.[9] No source is reserved exclusively for any particular type of council, and no source is automatically available, as the MLG must approve bases and rates. Councils must adopt bylaws to legalize any revenue source sanctioned for their use, and these must be approved by the attorney general.

Performance of the Local Government System

Although local governments have a much smaller fiscal role than the central government, typically accounting for only 4–5 percent of total public spending, municipal councils provide many public services. Many rural authorities also have responsibility for a few services, such as farm access roads, water, and veterinary services, which meet basic needs and support economic growth. Thus the question of the effectiveness of local authorities is of considerable importance. As noted above, a number of weaknesses have long been evident in the structure and performance of the system, some of which are being addressed by reforms explained below.

Service Provision

Service provision decisions should be based on local needs and capacity, as well as the comparative advantage of other potential providers; however, there are few guidelines in this regard. Attempts in the 1970s to define and standardize service functions of different types and sizes of settlements were largely ignored.[10] As a result, the service portfolios of local authorities are highly diverse, particularly among rural councils and small towns.[11] Although diversity is not undesirable per se, the fact that it is often based on arbitrary and inconsistent central decisions rather than local self-selection or well-defined criteria creates problems with some services. The present assignment of health to certain municipal councils, for example, is based on historical accident rather than a determination that councils are financially or administratively capable of providing the service.

Other problem areas include education, water, and veterinary services. All could be provided locally, but may require central intervention to alleviate inequities and/or to compensate for externalities. Education is currently centralized, while water and veterinary services are provided by ministries in some areas and by local authorities in others. The government, however, does not consistently follow rational guidelines in making assignment decisions. As a result, some capable councils are subsidized (by having a service delivered for them at no cost), while others unable to deliver adequate services receive no assistance. In some areas, both central and local agencies provide services; in other areas, neither does.

The MLG, which oversees the councils, often generates local service provision problems. In addition to arbitrary decisions on service assignment, annual local authority budget and employment requests that must be reviewed by MLG have been subject to few rational guidelines and decisionmaking rules. As a result, legitimate expenditure levels are sometimes cut arbitrarily, making it difficult to meet local service demands. The MLG also has a major impact on local capital expenditures, about 75 percent of which have historically been financed by the now dormant Local Government Loans Authority (LGLA). This agency has long had a reputation for politicized fund allocation, highly inadequate loan recovery,[12] failure to repay its own substantial debts to the treasury, and an inability to provide sufficient capital for basic local infrastructure development (Government of Kenya 1986; World Bank 1992a; Davey 1997; Duke Center for International Development 2002).

Although MLG is the primary link between the central and local governments, there are important relationships between local authorities and various sectoral ministries, such as public works, which are necessary because local technical capacity is limited. Coordination among councils, these ministries, and the MLG is often plagued by lack of appropriate and committed staff, inadequately designed procedures, and interministerial competition. Many development projects suffer long delays or never begin because of these problems.

Other service provision bottlenecks are related to local government relationships with district administration. Some council officials are reluctant to cooperate with the DDCs because they feel threatened by a perceived loss of autonomy under District Focus or view DDCs as little more than a new level of bureaucracy. In a few cases, substantial conflict has emerged, usually due to rivalry between elected local councillors and local members of parliament. Some DDCs have held up projects for years, even where a council had proven the need and capacity to undertake them. This is a point of concern because nonelected district technocrats dominate the DDCs, with only a few locally elected representatives among fifty or more DDC members. Contrary to claims of national politicians, such membership is unlikely to facilitate genuine local participation.[13]

Service provision is also hindered by poor local institutional performance. Many local personnel suffer from the typical lack of training and experience. Low pay and weak incentives are widespread, and unsuitable procedures result from both local and central actions. Deficient record-keeping practices, for example, partly reflect local inertia, but the accounting system long officially required by the MLG is based on practices with higher standards than those to which Kenya's central government holds itself. In many local authorities, budget estimates submitted to the MLG are virtually meaningless. Budgeted expenditures are not based on cost-effective service standards and are rarely used as expenditure control ceilings (Smoke 1994; Duke Center for International Development 2002). Cash-flow management is also complicated because most revenues are collected during a several-month period, while expenditures are ongoing.

Finally, many councils suffer from extensive political manipulation of expenditure decisions. Resulting projects may not be inherently undesirable, but the funds could often be used more productively. Although such situations exist in industrialized countries, Kenya's weak local institutional development and poor management practices have greatly reduced accountability.

Revenue Generation

Although no sources of revenue are reserved exclusively for specific types of local authorities, there are wide variations in revenue generation patterns.[14] For example, given diverse ecological conditions in Kenya, location is a prime determinant of activities that generate public revenues. Fertile highland areas depend on agriculture-related taxes, while livestock revenues, such as stock auction and slaughter fees, are important in more arid areas. Type of council is another key factor. Municipal councils historically derived revenue largely from water charges, land rates, house rents, and market, slaughter, and bus park fees. Town councils relied less on rates and infrastructure revenues and more on land rents and fees from less capital-intensive services, such as markets and bus parks. Both municipal and town councils often relied heavily on the local authority service charge (LASC), an approximation of the abolished GPT readopted in 1988 and abolished again in 2000. County councils have few productive sources of revenue, except for those that levy "cess" on high-value crops or levy agricultural land rates.[15] Most rely heavily on market fees and licenses, some have bus parks and slaughterhouses, and a few collect game reserve fees.

Because few services are assigned by the central government, and most sources of revenue are allowed to all councils provided the proper clearances are obtained, a good correspondence between service provision and sources of income should be a realistic goal, particularly in urban areas. In practice, revenue bases are inconsistently defined, intrinsically unstable, and poorly administered, and it is common for councils to collect less than half of their target revenues, even for easily identifiable sources such as land rates and house rents.

A key revenue problem for local authorities is the poor buoyancy of their revenue bases, which results largely from weak administration. Councils are permitted to impose interim rate increases between periodic land revaluations, for example, but this rarely occurs. The recently abolished LASC was structured in a way that undermined buoyancy and was complicated to administer (Duke Center for International Development 2002). Other local taxes, such as market fees, are normally per unit rather than ad valorem, so that yield growth lags behind overall trading volume. This problem is exacerbated by the failure of many councils to raise specific fees regularly.

While the responsiveness of local taxes to economic growth is limited by administrative factors, yields can also fall dramatically during downturns due to the nature of the local economy. This is evident in councils with heavy direct reliance on agricultural taxes, but even more stable taxes can also be affected where agriculture and subsistence lifestyles predominate and formal-sector savings are limited. If income is significantly reduced as agricultural production declines under such conditions, people may be unable to pay any local taxes. This asymmetric revenue elasticity creates serious local fiscal problems. In good times, expenditure requirements increase faster than revenues, so that many local governments face growing deficits even when the economy is flourishing. During economic crises, revenue yields can plummet and budget deficits soar.[16]

Nonuniform tax treatment of economic activities is another widespread local revenue problem. In some municipal councils, there has been some coverage of much of the local economic base through a system of land rates, licenses, and fees. In some urban centers, however, land rates are applied only in selected areas, and similar inconsistencies are evident in rural councils. Many with agricultural land rates or cess, tax lightly in trading centers, while those with no productive rural taxes rely heavily on urban sources such as market fees and licenses.

Even when similar resource bases exist for a particular type of council, levels of taxes, fees, and charges can vary dramatically and unsystematically across local authorities. Although recent reforms have helped in some respects, it has long been common, for example, for two comparable councils to charge very different fees for the same license or service without apparent justification on the basis of population, wealth, or costs of service provision. Such inter- and intrajurisdictional differences in local tax bases and rates can affect the composition and location of economic activities,[17] as well as create vertical and horizontal inequities across and within local authorities. Moreover, lack of a solid basis for setting revenue rates means that services with cost recovery potential often operate at a loss (Smoke 1994; Duke Center for International Development 2002).

As with service provision, local governments depend on central agencies that hinder revenue generation. The MLG has often been arbitrary and late in making decisions about the institution or modification of local revenue sources, largely due to inadequate staffing and procedures. The diverse revenue-yield patterns noted above result to a great extent from wide disparities in permission granted to use or raise key sources. The MLG has also failed to deal effectively with the poorest councils. The small annual MLG grants to "needy" councils were historically distributed entirely at the minister's discretion rather than according to objective criteria of need. Until recently, no other intergovernmental transfer or tax-sharing program existed.

Other ministries are supposed to provide an ongoing service related to local revenue generation, but are unable or unwilling to do so. Because most councils cannot afford a full-time land valuer, for example, they rely on the Ministry of Lands, which revalues on average every ten years instead of at the statutorily required five-year interval. Sometimes there are long delays in a one-time service, such as attorney general approval of local bylaws to legalize revenue collection. Where residents are aware of such delays, they can refuse to pay the tax in question.[18]

Central government agencies have also created local fiscal problems in two ways. The first problem is some "competition" between central and local government revenue sources. For example, until recent reforms, centrally imposed business license fees competed with similar local fees. A second concern is that central government agencies and parastatals often failed to pay local authority taxes and fees.[19] Ministries rarely budgeted enough money for their district offices to pay user-fees and mandated local contributions in lieu of land rates (CILOR),[20] and CILOR payments were long channeled through the MLG, which usually kept a significant portion for its own purposes. In addition, local officers cannot easily take enforcement steps against government agencies, e.g., turn off the water supplies of schools and hospitals. In some cases in which a council has tried to take a debtor to court, the MLG has intervened on the grounds that it is undesirable to involve government institutions in litigation.[21]

Lack of legal enforcement authority is a common problem, even in councils with proper bylaws and adequate staff. For example, the Rating Act allows councils to collect rents directly from tenants of plots in arrears on land rates; however, this can be politically difficult, and councils have little recourse if such measures fail. They cannot independently fine delinquent taxpayers or confiscate the property of defaulters. They must rely on the centrally managed Kenya police, who have no formal obligation to assist them, and the delay-plagued national court system.

The local institutional weaknesses discussed with respect to service provision are equally detrimental to revenue generation. Inaccurate financial records make it difficult to determine revenue targets and prepare forward estimates. Poor revenue control creates opportunities for misuse of council funds. Even if local managers are aware of abuses, they may be reluctant to take action because the employees involved have political connections, the centralized procedures for hiring and firing are so cumbersome, or they themselves are involved.

Finally, local political pressure reduces local ability to collect revenue. This problem stems from the universal unpopularity of taxes and the need for councillors who wish to be reelected or aspire to national office to be popular. As a result, councillors intervene to prevent water from being turned off for water bill default, to block eviction of tenants in arrears on house rent, etc. They are also reluctant to raise taxes regularly even if councils run persistent deficits, not only because of reelection concerns, but also because many councillors are directly affected by higher taxes.

The Overall Situation

The result of this wide variety of problems and constraints is that many Kenyan local authorities have long been struggling to make ends meet, and service levels have deteriorated to unacceptable levels (Smoke 1987; Bubba and Lamba 1991; Smoke 1994; Harvard Institute for International Development 1997; Duke Center for International Development 2002). A significant number of councils consistently run deficits and cannot repay their heavy debts. Revenue-expenditure linkages are weak, access to capital for development expenditures is limited, infrastructure maintenance is inadequate, and many service demands cannot be met.

The dimensions of this increasingly dysfunctional system are varied and complex. On the one hand, the system appears overcentralized. Key ministries, particularly the MLG, exercise various controls, but often in arbitrary and superficial ways that fail to improve and often impede local performance. Other central agencies have formal responsibilities to local governments, including support services and payment of fees, but compliance is poor. There are few incentives and no coordination mechanisms to force central agencies to meet such responsibilities, sometimes leading to jurisdictional battles and sending conflicting signals to the local governments.

On the other hand, local governments' accountability to their constituents is also weak. This occurs partly because some council members are still centrally appointed, but more importantly because local officials in the longtime one-party state grew used to looking to the central government for direction. Equally important, local residents have grown unaccustomed to holding local leaders responsible for anything, contributing to growing local political apathy.

Thus, the central government long tended to ignore or impede local governments. Local government officials stumbled along trying to juggle the inconsistent bureaucratic demands of the center and to meet their own personal objectives. There are certainly some local officials who try to undertake productive activities, but many pay too little attention to their constituents. Local citizens are frustrated with their local governments, but they do not try to do much about the lack of responsiveness, sometimes accepting the excuse that the central government ties the hands of local officials. The end result is a system substantially devoid of clear direction and genuine accountability, with frustrated actors at all levels almost resigned to living with the unnecessarily substandard performance of local authorities.

The reasons for the increasing deterioration of local authorities, many of which were treated in the earlier discussion of the evolution of local government, are largely political. The environment that developed after Kenya's independence in 1963 and that was reinforced by the 1982 coup attempt, led to attempts to recentralize that undermined the link between the more autonomous pre-independence local authorities and their constituents. The erosion of that link intensified over time with continued central neglect and poor local performance, reinforcing the popular perception of local government incompetence, and the central government view of local authorities as problematic entities to be controlled rather than productive entities to be supported.

Why was something not done earlier to try to turn this situation around? During much of Kenya's postindependence period, the economy grew and funds from donors to support local services were plentiful. Many services provided for the key engine of growth, agriculture, were primarily central responsibilities. The central government was in a relatively strong budgetary position, and it could afford to pay back international loans for local infrastructure, even if local governments did not. In fact, it may have been politically expedient for the central government to do so, particularly after intergovernmental transfer programs were discontinued and the government had no other mechanism until recently to subsidize local authorities. Perhaps most important, genuine democracy was limited under the one-party state, which gave priority to deconcentrated entities of the center over elected local authorities as the mechanism for delivering services and building political support. Since the early 1990s, however, the situation has been changing, and steps have been taken to move the system in a more positive direction.

The New Reform Efforts

It would be unrealistic to believe that the numerous problems outlined above or their underlying causes can be solved simultaneously or rapidly. In recent years, however, a variety of economic, fiscal, and political factors have generated efforts for reform. A few international donors have worked closely with the government to move slowly and carefully in developing a reform process, defining broad reform measures, and designing a strategy for initiating change.

The Impetus for Reform

Several emerging conditions have provided potential opportunities for local government reform in Kenya. First, genuine opposition political parties emerged during the early 1990s. For some years the opposition remained too fragmented to pose an immediate threat to the ruling party's national dominance, as evidenced by the December 1997 elections that returned President Moi to power. Allegations of corruption, regional/ethnic bias in fund allocation, human-rights abuses, and the generally poor service delivery, however, placed the Moi government in a much more defensive position than it had ever faced since assuming power. The opposition also gained control of some local government councils (including the Nairobi City Council), and its members were increasingly bold about challenging the government. In December 2002, the opposition presidential candidate, Mwai Kibaki, defeated Moi's handpicked KANU successor, Uhuru Kenyatta, raising some hopes for improved governance—and perhaps stronger decentralization—in Kenya.

Second, the international community has gotten much tougher on Kenya in recent years. The IMF froze its budgetary support program to Kenya in 1998 to protest the lack of political and institutional reform, the first time the IMF had taken disciplinary action on such grounds. This and actions of other international organizations increased pressure on the Moi government to institute reforms in spite of its electoral victory. Combined with political competition, the new level of international scrutiny and criticism forced the government to be more concerned about its image.

Third, the effectiveness of local service delivery systems in Kenya has been declining. During the 1980s, economic growth accelerated urbanization and generated a rise in real disposable incomes. These trends led to a substantial increase in demand for public services in cities and towns, exacerbating already serious backlogs in infrastructure investment and maintenance. Even though much of the responsibility for these services is local, the deteriorating performance reflects significantly on the central government because it so heavily regulates and controls local governments. Gradually the government has been recognizing that this situation has serious consequences in terms of hindering economic growth and generating the political dissatisfaction that inevitably comes with the failure of the overall government system to provide basic services.

Fourth, rapidly changing central fiscal conditions in Kenya in recent years have more sharply focused attention on the budgetary implications of local governments. Although there was no significant intergovernmental transfer program for years, local governments, as noted above, have imposed a national fiscal burden. Most donor loans for local infrastructure passed on to local governments were never repaid, even by fiscally strong councils and even for projects that should be self-financing. Debt service obligations not met from direct returns to local investments must be covered by general revenues from the central budget. The structural-adjustment program imposed on Kenya by the IMF and the World Bank is not tolerant of this type of fiscal behavior.

Fifth, there has been considerable negative publicity in the media regarding problems associated with the poor performance of local authorities in Kenya. National scandals have also undermined the credibility of the central government, weakening the legitimacy of the center in calling the local authorities corrupt.

Finally, there seems to be an emerging recognition among some central politicians and bureaucrats that more effective local governments need not pose a substantial threat to them. On the contrary, central measures to strengthen the local governments could help to correct a growing service delivery problem that widely affects the quality of life. Such efforts, if effective, could improve the environment for economic development and reflect favorably on the central government. In this respect, Kenya may be learning from the ambitious decentralization programs of two neighbors, Uganda and Ethiopia, which are trying to increase the legitimacy of central governments by giving more powers to lower tiers.[22]

The Broad Substance of Reform

Although the reform program is still in a relatively early stage, recent documents and actions illustrate the broad dimensions of the proposed local government reform program, which are largely targeted at the problems discussed above. I will summarize the general directions here, later turning to a more detailed summary of recent concrete achievements.

First, the government has expressed its intention to consider the service assignment issues discussed above. The goal is not only to clarify local service responsibilities, but also to define sector-specific programs for further decentralizing and/or improving service delivery performance.

Second, there has been a new willingness to consider changes to the Local Government Act in order to reduce unnecessary central government control over local authority activities and to allow decentralization of routine activities within the MLG. Efforts have been made to examine reform of the act, and the MLG has begun a process of internal decentralization, most notably with the devolution of the annual process of reviewing local authority budgets to the provincial level. More generally, the government is trying to transform the main role of the MLG from control and regulation to technical assistance and enhancing performance. Local authorities will continue to require some supervision until their capacity is proven. There does, however, seem to be an emerging support for the idea that local councils meeting certain standards in service delivery and revenue generation could be granted more autonomy and resources, while those with poorer performance should be targeted for higher levels of monitoring and technical assistance.[23]

Third, in order to increase local government accountability, the government is considering revising provisions in the Local Government Act that allow some councillors to be appointed. There is also a movement to develop, through the MLG and relevant sectoral ministries, performance standards by which citizens can judge technical aspects of councillor performance. In addition, reform efforts are under way to develop broad-based community participation mechanisms.

Fourth, with respect to intergovernmental fiscal relations, the Ministry of Finance has taken steps to ensure that payments owed by central agencies to local governments are made in a timely manner.[24]

Steps were also taken to harmonize problematic central and local sources of revenue,[25] and an objectively defined system of intergovernmental transfers has been reestablished.[26]

Fifth, clear steps are being taken by the government to deal with the local infrastructure investment crisis. The mutual debt situation among local governments, central government agencies, and parastatals is being better documented, and options for resolving it in a fair and pragmatic way are being considered (Kelly and Ramakrishnan 1997; Duke Center for International Development 2002). Although politically contentious, it has also been made clear that local authorities will be required to repay loans from LGLA or the agency that replaces it, thus establishing better fiscal responsibility. In addition, there are plans to eventually restructure the LGLA to ensure more efficient use of funds and to introduce greater fiscal discipline (Davey 1997).

Sixth, the government has instituted a number of measures to enhance local authority revenue generation, including the reform of agricultural cess and the introduction of the local authority service charge. Some of the earlier efforts were too hastily defined and the LASC was replaced with a transfer system in 2000, but the actions demonstrated an attempt to take concrete steps. Other resource mobilization reforms have been instituted more recently in selected councils, including improvement of the land rate system and the development of better collection mechanisms.

Seventh, broad reforms to enhance local authority management have been undertaken. The MLG has instituted clearer guidelines for local authority department and committee organization. In addition, better procedures and incentives for budgeting, financial management, and internal auditing have been or will be designed to improve the utilization of local resources.

Finally, the government has recognized a need for reforms in local authority employment policy. These include new local government employment regulations, a system of employee evaluation and incentives to enhance performance, and intensification of efforts to train council staff through innovative training programs (Delay 1997). These efforts are not at an advanced stage, but they will be incorporated into the national civil-service reform program under development.

The Strategy for Implementation

Obviously not all of these proposed activities can be undertaken at the same time or in all local authorities. On the contrary, a clear, gradual, pragmatic strategy is required. The problems detailed earlier have pushed both the Kenyan government and the interested donors to begin experimenting with a new approach. The development of a strategy was initiated by the Small Towns Development Project (STDP), an MLG-based project for local capacity building jointly funded by the Kenyan and German governments. The STDP has involved experimentation with around twenty local authorities, mostly smaller towns, since the late 1980s (Eigel 1995).

Under this project there have been some broad common reform goals among the local authorities participating in the program, but the exact steps each local authority took and the pace at which they took them differed. The project used a mobile team of experts to work individually with each participating local government to design a unique package of reforms that best met their needs and capacity to advance. In addition, the mobile technical assistance team worked periodically with local governments to implement the negotiated reform program gradually, and, as necessary, to modify it. Citizen participation mechanisms were required as part of the process, and some task-specific training was provided for local officials. Local governments that met the goals they agreed to were rewarded in various ways, such as greater access to funding and reduced MLG interference in their decisions. The performance of most of the participating local governments—in terms of adoption of new procedures, revenue collection, and service delivery—has improved considerably.

It is important to note that the STDP project slowly developed over a period of more than five years in very close consultation with MLG officials, and it has been in operation for more than a decade. Thus, the project gradually developed very strong credibility with Kenyan counterparts. This was an extremely important factor in helping to get project ideas on limited, gradual, negotiated, individually tailored reforms accepted by government officials and policymakers. It is also important to note that the STDP did not start from scratch—it built on other, more modest donor efforts, primarily a U.S. Agency for International Development (USAID) market towns project that started in the early 1980s. By the mid-1980s, when the STDP came on the scene, USAID had already begun to focus more on financial and managerial capacity building than on simply producing infrastructure projects.

The STDP has also had other benefits. First, virtually all of the technical-assistance personnel have been local rather than foreign consultants, further raising the acceptance and affordability of the initiative. Second, STDP efforts generated information that has assisted MLG to create procedural manuals and training materials for local governments. These have helped to get central and local officials to accept the use of standards in making revenue and expenditure decisions. Third, the STDP supported the Association of Local Government Authorities of Kenya (ALGAK) to play a more active role in organizing local governments and lobbying the center. Fourth, the continual presence of the STDP over a period of years raised the visibility of local governments among central officials and the general public and demonstrated that, with adequate assistance and incentives, they can improve their long-poor performance.

The Kenyan government, with support from the World Bank and the British Department for International Development, has recently been implementing a broader program of reform—the Kenya Local Government Reform Program (KLGRP)—largely based on successful experiences of the STDP and lessons learned from past donor efforts. The KLGRP started as the Municipal Finance Project in the early 1990s, but was soon substantially broadened to reflect the need for critical legal, institutional, and technical reforms at both the central and local levels. While there is broad recognition that the MLG is the appropriate lead institution, KLGRP is managed interministerially to improve overall coordination.

Following the lead of STDP, the KLGRP is being built gradually and systematically in a series of manageable, mutually reinforcing steps. Most KLGRP staff members are regular government employees who have continued to perform many of their regular duties. This creates a situation in which KLGRP is not seen as separate from government activities, but an integral and mutually reinforcing part of them. In addition, most of the KLGRP consultants are from local firms.

KLGRP involves three major phases, each of which has several components.[27] The first phase in 1996–1998 solidified agreement on basic reforms and instituted preliminary steps toward implementing them. The key tasks included defining in an operationally specific way reforms on basic local authority organization and financial management. In addition, there were comprehensive recommendations on intergovernmental fiscal relations, including tax harmonization, transfers, mutual indebtedness, and LGLA reform. Finally the first phase developed procedures to identify priority infrastructure needs of the local authorities and the technical and financial resources at their disposal to meet these needs. This involved further development of broad-based participatory stakeholder assessment mechanisms. The information and procedures developed in this phase are intended to provide a better basis for more advanced reforms to be required in Phases II and III.

The second phase of KLGRP is advancing the process of implementing basic reforms defined in Phase I and laying the groundwork for the third phase. Phase II includes substantial policy and operational reforms, including basic organizational and financial management reforms, improvement of local resource mobilization, and development of a participatory planning system linked to local budgets.

The anticipated third phase of KLGRP would involve the development and implementation of a substantial institutional and physical infrastructure program for local authorities. Building on Phase II, this would be done through a tiered process that requires progressively more substantial institutional and financial reforms at both central and local levels. Funding for basic infrastructure would be provided after minimal reform requirements were met. As a precondition to additional funding, an increasingly comprehensive set of reforms would have to be satisfactorily undertaken.

Design and Implementation of Basic
Organizational and Financial Management Reforms

During Phase II, KLGRP has expanded some of the organizational reforms relating to local government committees and relationships between councillors and professional staff originally begun under the STDP. In addition, the MLG began testing and enhancing simplified financial management systems piloted by STDP and enhanced during Phase I in several local authorities during fiscal year 1998–1999. Building on the introduction of a computerized Business Registration Information Management System and a Rates Administration Management System in the towns of Mavoko and Nyeri, KLGRP has developed a plan to refine and implement a broader Integrated Financial Management System (IFMS). The IFMS system is expected to be fully operational in Mavoko, Nyeri, Karatina, and Kirinyaga in 2003, and it will then be modified as necessary and replicated in other local authorities.

Design and Implementation of
Key Intergovernmental Fiscal Reforms

Intergovernmental fiscal reforms on a number of fronts have advanced remarkably well during the course of the past few years. First, the MLG has been working with the Ministry of Finance to ensure that adequate funds are available to meet the central government's annual CILOR obligation to the local authorities. The level of contributions has been increasing annually. Perhaps the most important achievement is that payments have been issued directly from the Ministry of Finance to the councils, removing the problem of these funds being channeled through and diverted by the MLG.

Second, the Local Authority Transfer Fund (LATF) Act was passed by parliament in December 1998.[28] The law stipulates that the LATF will be capitalized with 5 percent of all tax collected under the Income Tax Act. Although the allocations for fiscal year 1999–2000 were only 2 percent of the income tax (1 billion Kenya shillings [KSh]), the allocation has increased steadily to KSh 3 billion in the 2001–2002 budget.[29] A special LATF account was established in the Ministry of Finance, and a broad-based LATF advisory committee headed by the private sector was established to manage it. The formula is currently based largely on population, but this will change when more objective measures of service needs can be developed. Perhaps the most significant feature of the LATF is the fact that the disbursement is substantially contingent on local authorities meeting certain requirements and undertaking certain reforms. Sixty percent of a local government's LATF allocation is released when a proper budget is approved, but the other 40 percent requires other actions, such as improved financial statements, debt reduction plans, and revenue and service enhancement plans. In its first year of operation, about sixty-two local authorities lost about KSh 35 million for failure to meet requirements, indicating the resolve of the government. Using an intergovernmental transfer system to encourage adoption of broader reforms in this way is relatively unique. LATF also requires reports to enhance transparency and accountability. LATF allocations and disbursements are published in newspapers, and local authorities must submit detailed financial reports that are widely distributed to members of parliament, permanent secretaries of government ministries, and other local authorities.

Third, the government has begun to help local governments with resources specifically devoted to key services through its efforts in the transportation sector. The Finance Act of 1997 allocated a portion of the Road Maintenance Levy (RML) Fund (financed by a national fuel tax) specifically for financing local road maintenance. In addition, the government established a special advisory committee (chaired by the MLG) to advise the Ministry of Finance on objective and transparent RML fund allocation to local authorities. Since the enactment of the Finance Act of 1997, the government has allocated substantial funds for the local road network. The central government recently backtracked on the role of local authorities in road provision, but the experience provides a model for funding sectoral expenditures.

Fourth, in the area of central-local tax harmonization, the 1998 Finance Act introduced changes to the Local Government Act to allow the introduction of the "single business permit" at the local level, removing most central government fees and consolidating multiple local fees into a single fee. Guidelines issued by the MLG include criteria for determining fee levels, thus helping to reduce the problem of arbitrary and inequitable treatment of businesses within and across local governments.[30] It should be noted that the introduction of the LATF also supports central-local tax harmonization, as it has replaced the contentious, administratively difficult, and politically unpopular LASC discussed above.

Fifth, with respect to local governments' own sources of revenue, the government is sensibly focusing its initial efforts on property rates, the uniquely local source with the greatest unmet potential (Kelly 1996a). The reform strategy is designed to enhance the equity and revenue yield of the current property rates system. The introduction of improved property rates administrative systems, which initially involved the updating of fiscal cadastres and appropriately simple computer-assisted mass appraisal systems, has been piloted successfully, but collection has been slower to improve. To deal with this situation, the MLG has adopted a collection-led strategy as part of the development of the previously discussed IFMS, which incorporates all aspects of revenue mobilization and administration. The IFMS is expected to be fully operational in four local authorities in 2003, at which point the fiscal cadastre and mass valuation reforms will be introduced and the overall system extended to other local authorities.

Design and Implementation of Local Planning Procedures

Based on STDP experiences and early KLGRP experimentation, MLG has been further improving the local planning system. Perhaps the most important efforts in this area are those designed to increase citizen participation in governance, to enhance local authority accountability and transparency, and to improve the delivery of local services. Small "microprojects" have been used as a vehicle to bring about the adoption of new procedures for consulting citizens and delivering services. Stakeholder groups (SGs) were created at the local level in the three pilot local governments, Nyeri, Mavoku, and Maragua. These SGs incorporate a broad spectrum of local actors—business leaders, NGO leaders, etc.—into bodies that assist local councils to select, prepare, implement, and operate a variety of local public-investment projects, through public-private partnerships when appropriate. In addition to playing this oversight role, the SGs are the bridge to the community in other ways. For example, SGs negotiate with local people to accept responsibility for paying increased taxes or charges to meet the cost-sharing requirements of the new projects. They also play the role of community monitoring of completed projects. Getting people to participate in these planning efforts has not been a problem, but it remains to be seen whether the efforts will be sustained through the operation and maintenance stages.

Based in part on successful experiences with the microprojects, the MLG launched in 2001 the Local Authorities Service Delivery Action Plan (LASDAP), which is a participatory three-year rolling plan directly linked to the local authority budget. The LASDAP is determined through a participatory process based on the mechanisms that have been evolving over the past few years. Local authorities are expected to develop an LASDAP and a revenue enhancement plan (which should indicate the volume of local resources they plan to mobilize next year), and they receive an indication of their LATF allocation. Using this information, local authorities should be able to develop a realistic, consolidated budget. The LASDAP and budget data, both of which will be computerized, are compared and analyzed to monitor and tailor the LASDAP process. If these efforts are successful, Kenya will finally have a local planning system that is not heavily controlled by the central government, involves greater citizen consultation, and is adequately linked to the local government budgeting process.

Conclusion

Nobody familiar with the difficulties of intergovernmental reform could pronounce Kenya's local government system to be reformed and healthy yet, nor anywhere close to providing a genuine system of "local governance." Much remains to be done, and it will take many years to build a more broadly effective system. Nevertheless, it seems possible that Kenya is finally moving in the right direction after many years of rhetoric and minimal action. Even the long-critical press has expressed some hope for optimism, and key central government players that once all but ignored local governments, such as the Ministry of Finance, are pushing reforms and raising popular expectations. It is inconceivable that these things could have happened in Kenya even a few years ago. If the ALGAK becomes more active and if citizens learn over time to demand responsiveness from their local councils, it will gradually become increasingly difficult for the central government to reverse the ongoing reforms and for local governments to fail to meet the growing expectations of their constituents. As this book goes to press, Kenya is in the process of developing a new constitution that is expected to propose radical and progressive reforms to the local government system.

It must be recognized that local government reform with the goal of sustained, effective local governance involves moving forward in environments in which all of the major actors involved must make substantial changes in their accustomed behavior. Central government agencies are typically used to making many major decisions unilaterally, often in an uncoordinated way, and controlling local units extensively. Even officials who appear to be outspoken decentralization advocates may have a very cautious attitude about the degree of responsibility that local governments can and should be allowed to handle. In addition, local governments themselves may be quite comfortable with being heavily subsidized by and answerable to central governments, and they are not used to feeling particularly accountable to local residents. Finally, local constituents are often alienated from their local governments. They are accustomed neither to paying for services nor to expecting much responsiveness from local leaders. The mind-sets and patterns of behavior that have developed under such circumstances will require substantial time to change in a fundamental way. Perhaps the most important question a local government reform program needs to consider is how to begin moving forward.

Does Kenya's ongoing experience suggest any lessons for other African countries attempting to develop decentralization and/or local government reform programs? As the program is still relatively young, and the contextual situation differs among African nations, generalization is difficult, and perhaps dangerous. Most countries, however, face some of the same obstacles to decentralization that Kenya has begun to overcome, and most countries are also subject to many of the same pressures that spurred Kenya to move forward, albeit slowly. Thus, a few very broad observations may be offered for consideration.

Perhaps the most important step required is to adopt a carefully designed, pragmatic, and strategic implementation approach, as is partially emerging in the Kenya case.[31] There are several main issues here. First, it is critical to guard against doing too much too quickly, and the steps that are taken need to be phased in a logical way. It makes sense to first undertake those reforms that have the greatest possibility of succeeding in a relatively short time frame. Second, it can be very useful to differentiate among local governments rather than treating them all uniformly. Some are likely to be relatively capable and can manage greater responsibility effectively, while others will require heavier control and more substantial technical assistance. Third, central government agencies and other relevant actors, such as local government associations, must have an incentive to work cooperatively in a mutually supportive, coordinated way in bringing about reforms. Fourth, it is necessary to build the capacity and commitment of local governments to act more efficiently and responsibly. Such efforts, however, should be pragmatic and focused, and they should be phased in with performance incentives. Fifth, a great challenge for decentralization reformers is to increase the participation of local people and help them to learn how to hold their local governments accountable for meeting their service needs. Without increased local input and accountability, decentralization is a meaningless exercise. Finally, international development assistance and donor agencies should play a more low-key and consultative role in supporting decentralization reforms than they often have in the past. Heavy-handed donor conditionalities can get a central government to "commit" to reforms, but they are unlikely to be realized in the expected way if there is not reasonably solid consensus among the key players.

Undertaking an approach that incorporates these types of strategic elements in its design should raise the prospects for initial success with decentralization and local government reforms, thus creating a base for momentum in the future. Perhaps the key to bringing about continued reform in Kenya is the ability of policy analysts to continue making progress in their struggle to convince senior politicians and bureaucrats that stronger local authorities need not undermine the central government. On the contrary, stronger local authorities are an integral part of the broader multilevel system of government. Their success will increase the overall satisfaction of citizens and help to provide an improved environment for local economic and social development. If people perceive that national efforts help to strengthen local authorities, this can only reflect positively on the central government. Kenya has begun to understand and embrace this perspective. Changing attitudes and the victory of the opposition in the 2002 presidential elections suggest that the prospects for effective local government reform are more encouraging than at any time since Kenya's independence. Other African countries should take notice and derive what lessons they can from Kenya's move toward a more responsive and effective system of local government.

Notes

This chapter is based on the author's extensive research and policy-advising activities in Kenya since the mid-1980s, including a four-year period of residency. Specific documents and other resources drawn on are cited throughout the chapter, and a broader review of the author's research and policy work can be found in Smoke 1993 and 1994.

1. These included the U.S. Agency for International Development, the World Bank, and the British Overseas Development Administration (now the Department for International Development).

2. The Kenya African Democratic Union, a coalition of minority tribes, was the main advocate for regional government during independence negotiations.

3. Seven colonial-era municipalities retained their major service functions and were preferentially subject to a gradual phasing out of the GPT.

4. See Government of Kenya 1997. Although this commission was broadly consultative and made sweeping recommendations, it has not been as influential as expected. Some recommendations were followed, but the findings were rarely discussed publicly, and the commission did not tackle some of the worst problems of local governments.

5. For more details on District Focus and district planning, see Government of Kenya 1987, Makhokha 1985, Cohen and Hook 1987.

6. The Local Government Act has been amended many times, but not to strengthen local governments in any major way.

7. There has been a proliferation of new and upgraded local governments in recent years, often for political reasons. Some new and upgraded councils are not fiscally viable, leading to concerns about their ability to perform.

8. The act allows certain types of services to be undertaken only if conditions of relevant laws and/or overseeing sectoral ministries are met.

9. These include the Local Government Act, Rating Act, Valuation for Rating Act, and Regional Assembly Act.

10. One particularly detailed attempt is outlined in Government of Kenya 1978.

11. See Smoke 1994, Evans and Lewis 1996, and Duke Center for International Development 2002 for a detailed discussion of service provision issues.

12. Available evidence from past detailed research indicates, for example, that in 1989, only 8 percent of payments due from councils were received by LGLA, which paid only 2 percent of what it owed to the National Treasury. Recent data (Duke Center for International Development 2002:68) indicate that outstanding total local government debt as of July 1, 2001, was about KSh 10 billion, approximately the level of total local government recurrent revenues. However, this does not include long-term external loans from Nairobi City Council that in fiscal year 2000–2001 amounted to about 15 billion KSh. It is thus estimated that the total local government outstanding debt is about 25 billion KSh. (See note 29 for details on the Kenya shilling–U.S. dollar exchange rate.)

13. District Focus guidelines indicate that it is an attempt at administrative deconcentration rather than devolution. J. D. Barkan and Michael Chege (1989) argue that two political goals were at least as important as administrative reform objectives in designing District Focus: (1) to restructure clientelistic relationships inherited by Moi from Kenyatta by undermining the power of provincial commissioners and neutralizing incumbent ministers of parliament

with followings beyond their own constituencies; and (2) to redirect development resources to regions that had not been favored by the Kenyatta government. In this view, the main function of District Focus is to consolidate central government power.

14. Smoke (1987) examines local revenue patterns during the 1980s. More recent treatments include Smoke 1994, Harvard Institute for International Development 1997, Kelly and Devas 1996, Devas 1996, and Duke Center for International Development 2002.

15. Cess is an ad valorem agricultural production tax, which has historically varied across both crops and districts. The government standardized cess nationally in 1988 at a rate of 1 percent on a fixed set of crops.

16. There is no systematic time series analysis available, but the potential instability of local revenue yields is demonstrated by performance during the 1984 drought. Agricultural production fell by 3.7 percent from 1983, and GDP increased by only 0.9 percent, the lowest postindependence gain. In spite of the downturn, central recurrent revenues rose by 10.4 percent between 1983 and 1984, from 924 to 1020 million pounds. In contrast, municipal revenues fell from 53 to 47 million pounds (11.1 percent). Other councils were even more affected, with income plummeting from 13 to 8 million pounds (36.2 percent). Local revenues rose in 1985 as the country recovered from the drought, but by far less than central revenues.

17. Although efficiency effects are difficult to measure, it is unlikely that they are serious in Kenya because of constraints on mobility, the low levels of most local taxes and charges both in absolute terms and relative to other production costs, and the need for many producers to locate in specific areas because of the nature of their business.

18. Turkana County Council, for example, once waited more than two years for trade license bylaw approval.

19. Officials in sixteen of twenty-six councils studied by Smoke (1987) cited government agency arrears as their most significant revenue problem. Later investigations (Harvard Institute for International Development 1997) confirmed this problem.

20. The Rating Act exempts government properties from local land rates, but requires compensatory contributions in lieu of rates (CILOR). MLG estimates suggest that, prior to the recent introduction of reforms, less than half of the total amount owed was provided for in the central government budget, and substantial portions were diverted by the MLG. For a discussion of CILOR, see Kelly 1996b and Duke Center for International Development 2002.

21. For example, the MLG once forbid Kisii Municipal Council to sue Gusii County Council to recover unpaid land rates accounting for a third of their rate revenues, and Karatina Town Council was prevented from suing Kenya Railways.

22. Good references on Ugandan decentralization include: Bahl 1997, World Bank Public Expenditure Reviews 1994–1999, and Government of Uganda 2001. Good references on Ethiopian decentralization include: Cohen 1996, World Bank Public Expenditure Reviews 1994–2000, and World Bank 1999b.

23. In order for such differentiation to occur, a system for evaluating local capacity and performance will have to be developed. Information collected for

this system would also allow the MLG to develop guidelines for creating and upgrading local authorities, adjusting service and revenue assignment, and measuring performance. For a discussion of local government rating issues and the case of Indonesia, see Smoke and Lewis 1996.

24. The 1997–1998 budget speech by the minister of finance announced the first large increase in the allocation for contributions in lieu of property taxes (CILOR) to local governments. These contributions have since continued to grow. R. Kelly (1996b) provides an analysis of CILOR.

25. Reforms to the Trade Licensing Act that would harmonize central and local business taxes were initially announced in the 1997–1998 budget speech.

26. Options for instituting an intergovernmental transfer system were outlined by R. Crane (1997).

27. The summary of KLGRP achievements presented here is largely taken from internal documents and memos prepared by KLGRP staff in the Ministry of Local Government. In addition, Roy Kelly of the Duke Center kindly provided information on KLGRP activities for international development.

28. Government of Kenya, Law No. 8 of 1998.

29. As of February 2003, the U.S. dollar was worth approximately 80 Kenya shillings. The currency has fluctuated in recent years, but has generally been declining since 1995, when the exchange rate was closer to 40:1.

30. Ministry of Local Government, Circular No.11 of 1998.

31. Recent attempts to consider more broadly the strategic design and implementation of decentralization programs (in some cases with an emphasis on fiscal aspects) include: Dillinger (1995); Bird and Vaillancourt (1998); Litvack, Ahmad, and Bird (1998); Cohen and Peterson (1999); Bahl (2000); Smoke (1999, 2000, 2001); and Bahl and Smoke (forthcoming).

10

Conclusions:
What Have We Learned?

The purpose of this book is to explore under what conditions decentralization reforms in Africa develop into effective local governance. In Chapter 1, the authors presented a working model of the political and institutional prerequisites for local governance to emerge. This model was developed deductively (from Simonian assumptions about human capacities and politics), with reference to literature on local governance, and inductively from the authors' previous fieldwork (Wunsch 1999; Olowu 1999c). Throughout the book, elements from the model are used to organize the topics the case studies cover, while important contextual factors such as those discussed in Chapter 1 are also included as they apply to the cases.

To be sure, the various case studies grew out of research undertaken before this model was developed. Thus, at times the data reported are uneven in their coverage of each aspect of the model. Table 10.1 is a summary of the cases along these features. While the measurements are only ordinal and must be understood to include much variance within each of them, nonetheless, the pattern revealed is supportive of the volume's working model and working hypothesis.

A major question from Chapter 1 remains: What explains the variance in the critical "prerequisite" variables among these cases? The explanations for that could be conceptualized as key intervening factors between the legal and procedural reforms undertaken at the center, and the emergence of the four keys prerequisite to local governance in the periphery. This is represented in Figure 10.1. The remainder of this chapter will explore this question.

To do this, we will briefly revisit each case study, review the critical successes and failures in local governance, and explore what intervening factors seem associated with those patterns. From that we will

Table 10.1   Key Local Prerequisite Variables and Effective Local Governance

Variable	Chad	Botswana	Uganda	South Africa	Ghana	Nigeria	Kenya
Local autonomy and authority	Medium to high[a]	Medium	Low	Medium	Low	Medium	Very low
Resources available to local units of governance	Low to medium	High	Medium	Medium	Medium	Medium to low[b]	Low
Effective local institutions of collective choice (i.e., local councils)	High	Medium	Medium to low	Medium to low	Low	Low	Very low
Effective, open, and accountable local political process	High	High	Medium	Low	Medium to low	Low	Very low
Effective local governance	Medium to high	Medium	Medium	Medium to low	Low	Low	Very low

Notes: a. During the period of effective state withdrawal from rural Chad, localities had virtually no de jure authority to act, but had virtually unconstrained de facto autonomy.

b. When central government grants actually arrived, they could be substantial. They were, however, erratic, unpredictable, frequently late, and at times preempted by central government allocations to certain areas, such as to pay local teachers' salaries (Olowu et al. 2000).

inductively generate a model of four critical intervening factors that influence the development of the local "prerequisite" variables, which in turn affect the emergence of local governance (Tashakkori and Teddlie 1998; Tilly 1984).

Lessons from the Case Studies

Chapters 4 through 9 developed and illustrated issues discussed in Chapters 1–3. While each of the cases demonstrate policy, legislative, and/or constitutional changes by the center that are favorable to decentralization and local governance, we find that the record in their imple-

**Figure 10.1   From Democratic Decentralization
to Effective Local Governance**

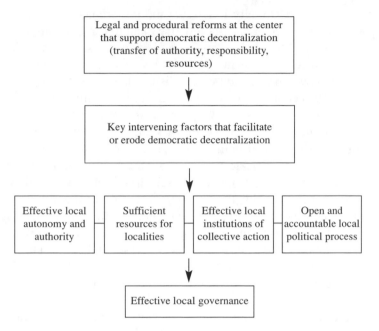

mentation is mixed, and each case offers its own unique insights on the questions raised in Chapter 1. This section will review and develop the insights these chapters offered on these questions, and explore what factors appear to explain the varying performance in local governance.

Chapter 4, the comparative analysis of decentralization and local governance in southern Africa, applies several aspects of the framework discussed in Chapter 1. Evaluating local governance in Botswana and as it operated in one province of South Africa in 1995–1996, it explores the extent to which devolution of authority and of resources, existence of local mechanisms of accountability, and local institutions of collective action are associated with effective performance by local governments. The last, the independent variable, the chapter subdivided into "process" (budgeting, planning, personnel systems, auditing) and "outcomes" (service delivery).

Although the chapter only reports qualitative data, the two country cases seem to support our working hypothesis: all qualities are necessary for effective local governance. Although one must tread carefully with only two cases, the chapter suggests that effective mechanisms of local accountability and of collective choice are associated with higher levels of service delivery. This should be seen as a hypothesis for further study.

Chapter 4 also strongly illustrates the importance of a stable and supportive national political framework, including particularly support for democracy and the rule of law, in achieving and sustaining effective local governance. This seems particularly clear in Botswana, where emerging partisan competition at the district level is offering a mechanism for some accountability. Clearly, the national climate in Botswana, with its tolerance of a two-party system with some real competition, is important for this to occur. However, in South Africa, the scale and pace of change in the national political context, while offering promise for the future, had yet to "trickle down" into effective accountability mechanisms at the local level, or manifest itself in clear policy directions and actions at the center at this time. This and the end of the old party system, while the ANC was still only developing in these local governance units, meant local government was in some measure on "autopilot," and local accountability was thus weak in our case study in South Africa. Nonetheless, the peaceful acceptance of a democratic constitutional compromise and the effective articulation of civil and criminal laws and courts across the two regimes helped give local governance a stable and predictable framework within which to work. Accordingly, local politics were peaceful, and a transition to an ANC mayor and ANC majority council went smoothly in our case study.

Contextual factors such as the great poverty and harsh environments of each state also affect effective decentralization. Simply put, in neither state can local units of governance hope, for the foreseeable future, to come up with the resources to satisfy their immense needs. In South Africa, the severe asymmetry of wealth between black and white communities adds a potential source of conflict to this dilemma. As a result, local governments in each state must look to their centers for resources to respond to local needs and, in South Africa, for help in managing the asymmetry in wealth and influence. This condition will almost certainly slow the development of effective local governance regimes. Indeed, in Botswana, both elected and professional personnel complained intensely about "micromanagement" from the center, which of course controls the revenue that localities desperately need.

Local institutional design issues are not as clear in these two cases. Council organization in South Africa was in great flux at the time of this research. However, it appeared to suffer from overly large councils, weak elected executives, and poorly trained new councillors. In Botswana several local councils were organized along partisan grounds, and seemed to have developed rules and procedures that were effective in discharging their business. Principal-agent issues were potentially serious in South Africa, with bureaucrats there on autopilot, and the councils preoccupied with adjusting to the significant changes majority rule brought to them. Other scholars have noted similar patterns elsewhere in South African local governance (Pycroft 1999, 2000). In Botswana, councils had developed committees and enough cohesion that they were wrestling with central ministries for control over their administrative personnel. So far, however, the central ministries were still in command of local affairs through their effective control of local operational and capital budgets.

The long history of decentralization in Botswana suggests time, patience, and tenacious support by the center are all necessary if effective local governance is to emerge. This, of course, can occur only in states that escape or control the turbulence often typical of African political economic and social environments. Histories of decentralization in Botswana report many of the same patterns of poor management, corruption, poor local service delivery, incompetent personnel, etc., in the 1970s, as are criticisms frequently leveled at recent African decentralization efforts today. Its progress since then suggests that patience, persistence, and consistent policies are each part of the recipe for effective local governance.

Joseph Ayee, in Chapter 6, analyzes in perceptive detail the problems decentralization has experienced in Ghana. On the one hand, there were impressive policy pronouncements by the former president of Ghana and other major leaders, as well as seemingly impressive decrees, legislation, financing mechanisms, and on-the-ground local institutions. However, on the other hand one finds local government leaders deeply discouraged about their inability to set and achieve local priorities, and local councils ineffective in supervising the local executive and his/her subordinates.

Ayee finds three general problems underlie these outcomes. First is the dilemma of incomplete or flawed reform and the recentralization that grew from it. Specifically, key actors at the districts, the district chief executive (DCE) and a proportion of assembly members are appointed by the president. This means the center not only retains significant authority, but the prestige and power of the president's office lies behind their representatives. The most important of them, the DCE, is in a position through his chairmanship of the district executive committee and supervisory role over local civil servants, to dominate local decisionmaking. Second, in numerous areas such as budget, personnel decisions, and bylaws, central ministries retain the right to review and negate any actions by district assemblies. Finally, even though day-today personnel management is nominally devolved to districts, the vast majority of civil servants and their parent ministries have refused to acknowledge this, and proceed to ignore local officials. Key in this was the failure of ministries to disaggregate their budgets and allow districts to control that portion which is expended in their areas.

A second general problem of decentralization reflected in the Ghanaian experience is the problem of overcoming several of the collective action problems discussed in Chapter 1 and reviewed in Chapter 4 as aspects of problems of accountability. District assemblies, for example, remain fragmented and ineffective bodies in the face of the concentrated power held by the DCE. Committees do not function effectively, and the one figure who might have been able to concentrate enough resources to integrate the diverse assembly members, the assembly chairman, is excluded from the executive committee by statute. While there were strong constituency pressures for each to get its "share" of the district budget, this figure was in no position to manipulate rewards for cooperative behavior. Instead, the DCE could easily dominate the assembly via his control of resources and ability to reward and punish cooperative and uncooperative council members. As a result, councils have not functioned as bodies and have been ineffective in asserting local priorities and balancing his power. Another result is serious principal-agent issues between the council and administrative and service personnel, with the latter largely escaping any council direction or oversight.

Another example of a collective action problem lies in the weakness of local accountability mechanisms. As Chapter 1 discusses, public opinion is usually fragmented, largely uninformed, and often focused on particularistic and individually oriented goods. Thus accountability is frequently ineffective regarding generalized community concerns, and instead responds to small groups with relatively intense and focused demands and concerns, to well-resourced individuals, or (when there are few resources to pass out) to no one in particular because no one is paying much attention. While it is not clear which of these patterns is dominant in the picture Ayee presents, it is clear that broadly based accountability is absent. For this reason, he discusses the pros and cons of introducing partisan politics to local government.

Ayee's chapter also illustrates the critical role that the national political framework plays. Ambiguous commitment by the center to decentralization allowed numerous ministries to drag their heels for many years in implementing the administrative changes required to make national pronouncements into realities. Furthermore, the ambiguous commitment of central government to democracy, and to a rule of law that would protect those who challenged local elements of the dominant national party, impeded development of a viable local political process. These and other factors Ayee discusses gave evidence to localities that the center, in spite of its rhetoric and legal reforms, valued *control* far more than decentralization, and would marginalize anyone who challenged that.

The severe scarcity typical of Africa raised the stakes of local governance in Ghana. Central ministries were loath to let go of their budgetary and personnel resource–control powers, while local executives were loath to let elected personnel control the resources they had controlled for many years. Rawlings and his party leaders were not about to let local governments loose when there were elections coming. Each of these factors meant that people of wealth and power were reluctant to cede influence to others, who happened to lack both. Scarcity, of course, conditions all that local governments can and, more often, cannot do. Like Botswana and South Africa, in Ghana it keeps them vulnerable to central government control. Richard Crook and James Manor (1998) report, as well, that it led to a severe shortfall in local government performance (vis-à-vis local expectations) that substantially reduced popular support for it in the late 1990s.

Overall, Ghana presents a picture of missed opportunity. Deliberate or inadvertent design flaws by the center have prevented effective authority and adequate resources from flowing to districts. The evidence suggests that the primary goal of key actors at the center was *preventing* the emergence of any genuine local governance in Ghana. Most key policies took back with one hand what was seemingly given by the other. As a result, localities had neither authority nor resources. The problems Ayee finds are thus not surprising. Additionally, local institutional design problems and the difficulty of overcoming basic collective-action problems seem to have prevented the emergence of effective accountability mechanisms for local populations. Still, much has been done to lay the foundation for local governance in Ghana, should the recently established national government choose to pursue it.

In Chapter 5, on local governance and primary health care in Nigeria, one sees the difficulty of achieving effective local governance even when substantial elements of the national government are in favor of it, legal reform supporting devolution has been completed, and the economic and political stakes associated with it are relatively low. This has been because of a number of factors, including: a turbulent national economic and political context that repeatedly disrupted the decentralization process as a whole, as well as the timing, size, and buying power of national grants for localities; the turbulence associated with the continuously changing number of states and local government units that repeatedly diluted personnel cadres and disrupted personal and institutional relationships; and the lack of clarity of roles and weak capacity of the national, "zonal," state, and local governments. It also included institutional and policy design issues such as intergovernmental procedures regarding the nature and terms of the grants from the center: that they were automatic, which provided no incentive for raising local revenues and therefore little incentive for localities to spend money wisely or become particularly concerned about local corruption. Further problems were personnel issues such as the compression of salary differentials and overall inflation of the currency, which rendered salaries unlivable. These problems meant there were few incentives for strong personal effort, either from service delivery personnel or supervisors. Other problems included a faulty primary health care (PHC) organizational structure that made it ambiguous as to whom lower personnel were responsible, for what supervisors were responsible, and thus made local principal-agent issues impossible to manage; and weak councils that were dominated by the "mayor" in the strong-mayor/council system in place in Nigeria.

Additional problems for effective local governance in the PHC sector grew from the absence of any viable local political parties or attentive publics and the lack of incentives for local dwellers to participate in the "health committees." The large average size of Nigerian local authorities (about 200,000 persons) meant that the collective-action problems associated with popular political organization were immense, and popular identification with local government units was very low. Nigeria's poverty made these collective-action problems even more difficult to resolve, as few people had the time or resources to invest in such activities. The poverty and size of the LGs also weakened the role that local civil-society organizations might be expected to play, as LGs are generally much larger in area than these organizations were. Local institutional design issues added to these problems: the dominance of the local authority chair through a strong-mayor system that made it difficult for local councils to influence his preferences in budget, personnel, and the like. This was reinforced by a second institutional design problem, the preemption of a council committee system to check the executive by an executive-controlled "cabinet" system, where salaries and other perks of office gave the council chair effective control over the cabinet members. This led to weak performance by local authorities, who unfortunately were neither challenged nor assisted by the states or federal ministries. The latter also were weak in resources and as institutions. Finally, the large size of the electoral constituencies meant that close ties between representatives and electorate were unlikely, given the poverty, social heterogeneity, and transportation costs of Nigeria.

In summary, local governance in the largely decentralized PHC system was made ineffective because of *poor institutional design* (local governments, the primary health care managerial system); a *disruptive political context* (national political and economic conditions), including an unsupportive policy context (national revenue-sharing policy that discouraged local resource mobilization, repeated establishment of new states and local government units); *unsupportive local political environment* (absence of local attentive publics or political parties and LG size that put it at a larger scale than most local organizations operate); and *institutional and personnel weaknesses in intergovernmental relations* (weak state ability to assist and challenge LG-PHC and weak LG-PHC personnel). With all these problems, it is no wonder governance in this sector faced difficulties. As in many cases, success in establishing local governance here lies in learning from policy and institutional mistakes; in long-term thinking, planning, and action to remedy personnel and institutional weaknesses; and in a bit of good luck, not the least of which might be a stable national political and economic context. One of the most important lessons of this case study is how many things must be made to work well, even after fairly serious devolution reforms have been made, if local governance is to succeed.

All of the above underscore the long-term nature of institution building for local governance. They also highlight the need to be careful in rushing to judgment concerning failure or success of local government building experiments. For instance, in spite of the failure of many local governments and communities in Nigeria, important lessons were learned of the ingredients for success in a few local government areas that got the institutional factors right. Local political and administrative leadership, as well as local governance processes, were found to be crucial ingredients for success in these local governments. Finally, and perhaps needless to say, the Nigerian case underscores the need for a consistent national political and institutional framework, so local populations and leaders can have the time to learn how to operate their institutions, fix the problems solvable there, and discover the ones that require changes by supervisory levels of government. There are signs that the context provided by the new democratic experiment in the country might help to restore the Nigerian local governance initiative in many if not most of the thirty-six states.

Simon Fass and Gerrit M. Desloovere, in Chapter 7, offer a case study of local governance as it emerged out of the grassroots in Chad in the 1980s and 1990s. Since the central government was seriously weakened by the civil war, most services it provided outside the capital collapsed. However, in many areas village dwellers saw a need for local schools. They organized themselves, raised funds through locally designed and managed taxation systems, engaged personnel, constructed and maintained buildings, and developed linkages to other communities doing the same thing: to exchange experiences and ideas and to lobby the center for technical assistance, formal recognition as accredited schools, and additional funding. Furthermore, many local communities branched out into other service areas, such as health, water, and roads. In 1998, such communities provided one-third of the nation's schools. In many other communities all the teachers, except the school director, were also funded in the same way. If this is not viable local governance, the authors of this chapter do not know what would be!

How did Chad's village dwellers accomplish this significant feat? Fass and Desloovere suggest it was via a combination of circumstances that one cannot expect to replicate precisely elsewhere, but nonetheless ones that are quite informative on how Africans have solved many of the problems and challenges discussed in Chapters 1, 2, and 3. These circumstances provide suggestions on how problems seen in our other case studies might be resolved.

As the chapter's authors well demonstrate, the first thirty years of independence for Chad were ones of continuing political turmoil. In this context, the central state proved itself seriously inadequate to most localities as a source for services. This was juxtaposed against a growing awareness in villages, particularly those in the south engaged in cotton production, of the need for literacy and numeracy, even if only to assure they were not cheated in the sale of this cash crop. Villagers also saw how villages with schooled people were able to organize village associations to create and manage marketing and storage cooperatives, wells, dispensaries, etc. Villages with enough educated people also earned rebates from the national cotton parastatal (Cotontchad) by performing weighing and classifying functions. Similar results occurred in the north when fighting forced rural dwellers into urban areas, where they saw the value of literacy in French, as well as in the Arabic that was already taught to many via their Koranic studies. Thus there was a local *demand* for education. Second, while the Ministry of Education (MEN) had always provided teachers, salaries, and school management, local associations of parents of students (APEs) had always been responsible for constructing and equipping school buildings, and maintaining them over the years. Thus localities had some experience in working together to provide some aspects of local education. When the civil war spread to the capital in 1979–1980, many educated residents fled. These individuals became a primary source of key personnel, the teachers. Finally, there was some existing institutional infrastructure in the traditions of local councils at the villages. The major problems the villagers faced, therefore, were replacing the finance lost from the center, and managing the schools in an orderly and effective fashion so that educational goals were reached.

The chapter offers rather undeniable evidence that local governance is clearly possible, and in some situations already operating in Africa. It makes a strong argument that such arrangements will grow out of a community's desire and need for a specific good or service if it cannot be provided by the market and on an individualistic basis, and if there is sufficient local social capital for the community to organize and act to provide it. In Chad there was no private entity that could provide the education that parents saw as necessary for their children. It required a broadly based effort to initiate and pay for this. The desire of individual parents for education for their own children in Chad was reinforced because many local people had seen that education had important spillover benefits for the community in general: assuring farmers fair prices, enabling the community to operate a cooperative and receive rebates from Cotontchad, and in some cases evidence that literacy in French would help the community defend itself from outsiders who had taken advantage of it in the past. Because of this mix of private and collective benefits, unobtainable from markets or from the central government, many people found it necessary and rational to invest their time and money developing what was essentially a local governance structure to provide and sustain education over a period of time.

Providing for this demand was eased by the experience many people had sharing management duties of now-closed state schools, a tradition of community support for such schools, and the presence of capable people willing to teach in the community-based schools for relatively low and sometimes irregular salaries. Finally, in some cases associations of community notables, "sons" and "daughters" of the community, or the cotton cooperatives, raised money from members or used operating surpluses to pay for the "step" cost of getting the school operating. The existence of traditional councils in many areas (made up of the eldest males from each household) offered a locally legitimate way of selecting a committee to operate schools and to assess general dues (taxes) to operate the schools. Finally, the authors note these taxes were assessed according to ability to pay, collected flexibly, and complemented by per-student tuition charges paid by students or their families. No doubt, the small size of these communities facilitated social pressure that reinforced local dwellers' sense of obligation to pay.

As noted in Chapter 1, and demonstrated by several of these case studies, fragmentation in legislative bodies is a major impediment to local governance. Achieving majority agreement is always difficult, given the fragmentation of most communities, the frequent absence of majorities behind any single proposal, the historic tendency of local government in Africa to redirect public goods to private use, and the frequent weakness of leaders of such bodies in building coalitions. However, in the case of education in Chad, there was a strong and general community desire for this good and the existence and willingness of preexisting community associations or cooperatives to pay down the initial cost of the good and lead public opinion. These might have been what made it possible for traditional councils, unofficial but legitimate bodies, to establish effective school management committees. This overcame many of the collective-action problems associated with effective decisionmaking by legislative bodies. Using local knowledge, these provided effective assessment and collection of dues from the community, and thus avoided free-rider issues in funding and delivering public services. And while the role of the MEN was not large, there was ongoing contact between it and many of these schools, as well as unofficial assistance from head teachers in some nearby official schools. This helped sustain quality and consistency with official school standards and curriculum, something Fass and Desloovere note was important to many village residents who did not want "second-rate" education for their children. As we note in the next section, the social capital documented for Chad exists in many other African countries, but only a few countries succeed at connecting it to the local government system.

Other interesting observations of this chapter include the stubborn adherence by the center to controlling models of service delivery. Even well after the MEN lost all control of local schooling to community schools, it continued to issue regulations and pronouncements (the required distance between schools, minimum education levels for teachers, unrealistic salary requirements) that were impossible for local schools to meet, and which were entirely ignored. The lack of information and realism of the center was rivaled only by its unwillingness to accept the loss of control, and perhaps of the power that entails. This of course reflects the powerful impact that the tradition of central control and the presumption of central "tutelage" still have long after the reality has totally changed, as well, perhaps, as a strong desire to reestablish the bureaucratic dimensions of the neopatrimonial state. Also interesting were the information networking, creative cross-community arrangements, and dynamism of what were in effect emerging local "systems" of schools. They traded ideas, merged to operate a single school when it made sense, and the like. This shows the ability of such local governance systems to learn, adapt, and change over time in spite of poverty, national turbulence, and other challenging contextual factors. Also, the management committees' proximity to their employees and control over their wages appeared to work to resolve both social and physical distance problems of principal-agency.

Few public goods will likely marshal the general support of the population as well as education apparently has done with Chad's rural people. But it is the rare area that lacks a strong desire for some effective public good such as malaria control, roads, public markets, dispensaries, potable water, education, and the like. One strategy to build local governance is to use that desire plus existing local institutional infrastructure to get local governance going in the area, and then build on that experience by adding other activities, as has since happened in many villages in Chad. Meanwhile, central government can offer valuable technical assistance to such locally based efforts. Thus local governance can be built.

Dan Ottemoeller and James Wunsch, in Chapter 8, review the achievements of the local council (LC) system in Uganda. Ottemoeller focuses on the lowest level, the village (or LC1), while Wunsch considers the higher levels, the subcounty (LC3) and district (LC5) levels. In Ottemoeller's research, he found that village residents would turn first to the LC1 council to resolve any local problems, needs, or disputes they had. When asked how the LC1 council had improved their lives, nearly 60 percent said it had improved local peace and security or been effective in solving local problems.

Ottemoeller believes these results, rather than an emphasis on "development" (i.e., completing projects or delivering services) reflects the village council's relative advantage in local information and legitimacy. It also reflects a system that is more accountable to local dwellers than the former appointed-chief system. The chiefs, he feels, were prone often to use their extra-village sources of power to abuse local dwellers. In any case, if they performed poorly, local residents had few means to correct or replace them, both under the colonial and the authoritarian governments of Idi Amin and Milton Obote. The LC system allows for dispute settlement by the elected local council, and for security provision by a local defense unit.

The greater success Ottemoeller finds at the LC1 level reflects the importance of providing services that are not funding-driven and are "public goods," in order to build the legitimacy of and support for local governance. Such services (here, dispute resolution, small-scale problem solving, and security) depend more on accurate time and place information, good leadership, and appropriate delegation of authority than on large outlays of money. As "public goods" they are not divisible nor can they be "captured" and exploited by local elites. And, while local election of local leadership is no guarantee that it will always remain, it does offer a learning process whereby local dwellers can see that this leadership matters, and who might be better at these tasks than others. Indeed, in his fieldwork, Wunsch found village-level leaders well informed on local governance and local issues, and comfortable vigorously participating in conversations about local problems and governance in meetings at the subcounty level. All these factors depend on the existence of social capital.

Ottemoeller's research also suggests, though only implicitly, that some of the collective-action problems discussed in Chapter 1 might be resolved by making key units of local governance rather small. There, the decision and organization costs typical of larger and more diverse population groups are smaller, feedback is more immediate when there is poorer performance, and there are fewer resources that elites can use to manipulate public preferences. Principal-agent issues are reduced as well by the fact that the principals (the community) and agents (councils) live cheek-by-jowl with one another.

Wunsch finds three general problems hurt performance at the LC3 and LC5 levels: financial strings from the center and the poverty and resource weakness at the localities; weak development of district legislative bodies; and overly heavy planning and budgeting demands by the center. The problem of financial micromanagement by the center reflects the value of the resources allocated by the central ministries, both economically and politically. Professional careers and political patronage are linked to these, and forcing those who hold them to relinquish them requires more political resources than most localities have. Of course, the generalized local poverty weakens the districts' ability to raise enough resources on their own to assert programmatic autonomy. Furthermore, the inability of local councils to develop effective mechanisms to operate as institutions means individual councillors are either ripe for co-optation by local executives, or are simply ineffective. In this regard, local councils have failed to solve the principal-agent problem that faces many legislative bodies trying to manage executive and administrative professionals. The frequently ineffective local planning and budgeting systems are probably also related to a combination of principal-agent problems and the center's intention to continue its control over local resources. In this regard, the problems of Uganda strongly parallel those Ayee found in Ghana. Finally, the weakness and fragmentation of local civil-society organizations at the district level suggests that crucial collective-action problems among the public also remain unresolved. High costs of communication and transportation, deep local poverty, and a realistic skepticism over the scale of resources that LCs control, no doubt all contribute to the weakness of local collective-action institutions.

Having said all of this, it should be strongly reemphasized that local governance has come a long way in Uganda. Elections have been held, a complex, multitiered local governance system is in place, along with councils, executives, and civil servants who are employed by the local governments. Meetings occur, budgets are prepared, (some) funds are collected, plans are generated, and citizens repeatedly reported to the authors that this system is a *vast* improvement over the former ones. If there are problems, many of them grow out of the scale of the task the government of Uganda has set for itself, and the pace it has pursued in implementing it. These are not surprising "teething" problems, reinforced by the reluctance of the center to let go of the resources that have been nominally shifted to the districts. Not incidentally, donors have played a large role in helping strengthen district governments, as well as in encouraging a more supportive national legal and policy framework (USAID, Department for International Development in the UK, World Bank). A positive development in Uganda is also the work of the national association of local governments, which lobbies the national government for greater autonomy, stronger control over sector ministry budgets, and other legal and procedural changes that will strengthen local governments.

In all this, one must recognize the impact of the central government framework provided during the Museveni era. While not perfect, it has avoided the social, economic, and political turbulence characteristic of Uganda from independence until the mid-1980s. It has also provided generally consistent support for decentralization, and supported some of the necessary policy and organizational changes through the decentralization secretariat in the president's office. The fact that Uganda has a strong base in trained human resources and a somewhat better economic base than many other African states must also be credited for these successes.

In summary, this chapter helps make the case that bringing at least some services to the lowest "natural" community level, the village, may avoid some problems of central recapture (as the stakes there are usually too small to be worthwhile) and collective action (as the small size and face-to-face interactions typical there help make these easier to resolve). How such arrangements can be integrated, however, into effective provision of more complex and costly services (such as health care and secondary education) as well as linked to area-wide services (such as roads, flood control, disease management), and to solve principal-agent problems, institutional issues within local councils, and local collective-action problems, calls for more research and analysis. Can these smaller arrangements be "nested" into the larger ones? What other strategies can build on the first to help provide the second? Can altered revenue strategies by the center help bring about broader autonomy for localities? Can local governments develop enough of a political base that they are able to be significant political players at the center?

Chapter 9, by Paul Smoke, discusses the postcolonial weakness of Kenyan local government, some of the causes of it, and recent proposals and programs to redress that weakness. Observing that Kenyan local government had actually been rather capable in the colonial and early independence eras, he traces its rapid reduction in authority and resources during the 1960s, and illustrates the erosion of local accountability experienced under the one-party rule by KANU. Leading these declines, he argues, was the priority the government of Kenya placed on central control over local government. For example, while local governments had authority over a number of revenue sources, actually utilizing any of them or changing tax rates required central government approval. This was very slow in coming, and often arrived impossibly late for effective management of the fiscal year. Or, while local governments had authority to pass bylaws, all had to be approved by the center. Complicating local governance was the absence of any systematic allocation of revenue authority, national grants, authority to provide certain services, and the like among the local governments. Some might receive certain assistance, others not; some certain authority, and again others not. Not only were local governments of the same classification treated differently, there was no criteria to explain *why* they were so treated. All these point again to the important impact the central government has on local governance by central ministries.

Central government also used the district development committees, made up of central government personnel (members of parliament, civil servants, local appointees, and one or two elected local authority council members), to control approval of all district-level projects. Smoke notes that some local authorities had projects delayed, unaccountably, for several years. Central government ministries, such as the Ministry of Local Government, were notoriously slow and at times appeared incompetent in dealing with local authorities. Over time, Smoke notes, local populations progressively lost confidence in their local authorities. At the same time, central government retained control of major donor loans for infrastructure and agricultural development, which it allocated as it saw fit, leaving local governments out of the process. Furthermore, local councils were weak and badly fragmented. The picture this presents is one of a centrally led and systematic erosion of their local authorities: their powers, resources, and local legitimacy. The encouragement of fragmentation *among* the local governments (whether intended or not) helped make it unlikely they might work together to change their situation, as each was so different in powers and resources from the others.

In Chapter 1 we referred to the powerful contextual element that the African state provides. Founded on ambiguous authority, and faced with a fragmented elite from diverse ethnic groups, each seeking resources from a state that had relatively little to offer, Kenya developed a top-down/patron-client and neopatrimonial system to help elites stay in power. The state allocated resources among key leaders of key groups, and when these were well managed, they kept the peace, and elites safely in power. The problem with this system is the scale of resources needed to keep it operating and the corruption it encourages. Over time, first with Jomo Kenyatta and later on with Daniel arap Moi, Kenya became the quintessential patronage-based state. With Moi however, there has been greater conflict as resources became more limited, and as he either was less adept at this strategy or chose to pursue a more conflict-oriented approach. In such a patronage-based state, there are good "political" reasons to make and keep local authorities weak: one maximizes the resources one controls while making it more difficult for anyone else to control or generate new resources through any collective action. As a result, most people have only the center to look for as a "patron."

The second part of Smoke's chapter argues that recently the Kenyan state has begun to move beyond this failed strategy. Because of the combination of economic problems that weakened the state and pressures that led to competitive elections, Smoke believes there is a new interest in Kenya in strengthening effective local governance. The diverse reforms he reviews are important both for what they include and what they leave out. The majority of the reforms deal with providing a greater and more stable revenue flow to local authorities; systematizing the activities they are allowed to engage in; making the criteria of central government ministries' decisions clearer and more rational; speeding up those decisions; developing clearer and more efficient procedures for local revenue, expenditure, and auditing systems; and improving training of local personnel. Finally, a very tentative step toward enhancing local accountability is mentioned regarding a few local projects.

What is left out of these reforms is any substantial increase in local accountability or powers. Localities are still dependent for national grants for most of their activities, subject to national review and over-ride in most of their actions, and still subject to the centrally dominated district development committee for most nonrecurrent investments. There is the possibility that the reforms in progress will simply enhance the ability of the government of Kenya to manage local affairs through a more efficient deconcentrated system. This would be a more legal-rational system where there would be less confusion, less delay, pehaps even less waste and corruption. But, it would still be controlled from the center, and would still not be "local governance." However, even if this pessimistic view were correct, such reforms would nonetheless help form a sounder foundation for real decentralization and local gover-nance sometime in the future. For example, a number of civil-society organizations, notably the Association of Local Government Authorities of Kenya (ALGAK) and other civic groups are currently working in concert with bilateral and multilateral donors to open the political space for the involvement of other institutional actors in the Kenyan local government reform program.[1] A rational and predictable set of rules, as noted elsewhere this book, is a primary prerequisite for local dwellers to begin investing in local institutions such as councils, civil society, and the more broadly based popular organizations that are necessary for local governance. As our other chapters have shown, however, even when space is made for such institutions, many collective-action prob-lems need to be resolved before they can operate effectively, as well as many details such as effective intergovernmental relations, personnel issues, and the like.

Overview and Analysis

These seven country cases offer four broad lessons on building local governance. While there are no doubt other important factors, these case studies suggest that four factors are crucial ingredients for effec-tive local governance, particularly in the circumstances (see Chapter 1) in which African local governments operate. These are: (1) a supportive national political context; (2) effective systems of intergovernmental relations that support the allocation and utilization of fiscal and human resources; (3) a strong local demand for public goods along with substantial levels of local social capital; and (4) successful resolution of a number of local-level institutional design questions. Weakness on any of these variables can impede achievement of one or more of the four factors identified in Chapter 1 as necessary for local governance to emerge. These factors can be seen at work across most of the case studies, as can be seen in Table 10.2.

Clearly a powerful variable in explaining the emergence of local governance is a *supportive national political context*. While it is not sufficient to achieve effective local governance without resolving the other three issues, a supportive national context is absolutely critical. Rule of law and obedience to that law by the central government, general political and institutional stability, openness to democratic contestation and the existence of related political freedoms, a favorable legal structure for local entities to operate within, and a stable and supportive

Table 10.2   Analysis of Crucial Factors for Effective Local Governance

Variable	Chad	Botswana	Uganda	South Africa	Ghana	Nigeria	Kenya
Supportive national political context	Medium[a] (by default)	High to medium	Medium	Low to medium	Low to medium	Low	Very lo
Effective systems of intergovernmental relations	Very low	Medium	Medium	Medium	Medium	Medium to low	Low
Demand for public goods and social capital at local governance level	High	Medium	Medium	Medium	Medium to low	Medium to low	Insufficient data
Well-designed local governance institutions	High	Medium	Medium	Low	Low	Low	Very low
Effective local governance	Medium to high	Medium	Medium	Medium to low	Low	Low	Very low

Note: a. During the period of central-government withdrawal from Chad's rural areas, local governance received little to no central assistance. However, local governance also experienced little to no central interference in its affairs.

economic context are all essential. In Africa today, these factors are far more a product of politics than of the presence or absence of laws. For example, in Botswana, though certainly an imperfect democracy, political leaders have generally offered a benign environment in which a viable local politics could develop. Freedom of speech, media, and organization, along with contestation at the national level, seem to have encouraged political competition at the local level, and encouraged thereby some level of accountability. Local councils have representatives of more than one party, debate budgets and project priorities, and compete for local power. Several, including Gaborone (the national capital), are under the control of the opposition party. A relatively stable political framework in Botswana has encouraged the development of a cadre of professionals skilled in managing local governments and in navigating its intergovernmental relations. As a result, local governments there are actually beginning to manage resources, deliver services, and respond to local needs.

In contrast to Botswana one can consider the oppressive, turbulent, and at times violent national political contexts of Kenya and Nigeria. In the midst of governments determined to stay in power at any cost, including suppressing domestic democratic-reform movements and stimulating ethnic violence, local governance has suffered. Local elections have reflected local factionalism rather than any sort of institutionalized party-led politics. Losers have sought to drive victors from office through court cases rather than accepting election results and/or institutionalizing any form of "loyal" local opposition. Perhaps reflecting the climate set by the center, victors have frequently seen local office as a source of rents and other corruption. Rare are the local leaders who seriously work to develop their areas or improve local services. Local leaders supporting or opposing the center are each intolerant of their opposition, perhaps because it is seen as threatening, respectively, either their hold on the center or their efforts to topple it. As a result, perhaps, popular participation between elections is very weak, and there seems to be little or no accountability in local governance.

Somewhere in between these two extremes seems to lie Uganda. In Uganda there seems to be fairly stable national political support for local governance, though to be sure there have been moments when that has been questionable. Rule of law seems also to have been generally consolidated by the Yoweri Museveni government. In this context, a cadre of local officials is also emerging there that has a sense of how the local governance system is supposed to operate, and that is beginning consciously to push for further national legal reforms to make local governance more effective. In the absence of functioning national democratic institutions, all this would be impossible. Still, the weakness of Uganda's democratic processes seems reflected in the weak linkages that appear to exist at localities between the public and officials, and the relative dominance that local executives seem to have over the rest of local government. Also unresolved is a fiscal structure that seems to sustain national ministerial domination. Ghana is another case where limited democracy at the center seems to have led to limited accountability at localities. There, even though several cycles of local elections have occurred, the continued dominance by the national ruling party through its control of the local executives has eroded the effectiveness of local elections and postelection linkage mechanisms in providing local accountability for local governments. The extent to which rule of law has been consolidated also has affected local governance through the frequency of official corruption and the occasional abuse of political office. However, the general consistency of Ghana's decentralization polices over the past decade has facilitated the institutions of local governance there, albeit with much weakness. The recent peaceful turnover of government in Ghana may well be a positive sign for local governance there.

South Africa's new government's strong commitment to rule of law and its new constitutional structure have certainly helped consolidate democratic reforms at the local level. Still, the recency of its own democratic consolidation at the center left local governments disengaged from the new majority, and with weak linkage mechanisms between the new political elite and the general population. The dramatic challenges facing the new majority government, the uncertainty and scale of policy issues facing it, and the rapid pace of change have impeded the operational effectiveness of local governments. So have the many unsettled questions over the role of local and regional governments and the level of resources to be made available by the center. However, as long as the center remains fundamentally committed to viable local governance, the rule of law, and the new dispensation holds, the fundamental outlook for local governance in South Africa is good.

One of the outcomes of political instability and ineffectiveness at the center is often a turbulent economic framework for local governance to struggle with. Contrast the stability of Botswana with the budgetary turbulence of Kenya. In one setting, local officials are generally able to plan and complete projects; attract, employ, and retain able personnel; and respond to local needs. In the other, they can do none of these. In between these two extremes are Ghana, Uganda, and Nigeria

Policy and procedural instability at the center make it difficult for local governance to develop. For example, in Kenya, the extent to which Kenyan ministries made erratic and unpredictable decisions, were inconsistent in criteria for their policies, and did not acknowledge their fiscal obligations to local governments made it difficult for local governments to organize themselves to function effectively and efficiently. Among other things, this eroded thereby the credibility of Kenyan local governments to their constituents. The instability of, and arbitrary changes in, the framework set by the Nigerian federal military government had a similar effect on Nigerian local government authorities. The constant establishment of new local authorities and of new states repeatedly disrupted local institutions and personnel networks. The frequent and extra-legal changes in Nigeria's central government in the 1990s also meant local authorities were subjected to great personnel, policy, and institutional turbulence.

Beyond these political factors, it is also clear that in most of these states there are still issues to be resolved in the laws establishing and regulating decentralization. It is clear that some of Ghana's and Kenya's problems dealt with incomplete and/or ineffective legal reforms, though sorting out the political versus the truly legal issues is always difficult. Botswana's and Uganda's reforms were more consistent with genuine autonomy, more fully developed regarding civil-service and governmental procedures, and more stable. Nigeria's reforms were seemingly grand in scale but had critical flaws in their funding mechanisms, in the absence of a supportive and regulative role for superior levels of governance and, as noted, in the repeated and arbitrary changes made by the various federal military governments. South Africa's system is in flux at the time of this research. Botswana's local governance system has effectively decentralized many functions and powers, but now faces issues of local impatience with a continued, strong, central, directive role in local priority setting. Still, Botswana's consistency and level of decentralization has been enough to develop the base for an effective local governance system. These problems indicate that decentralization and local governance are dynamic processes that require ongoing attention. The continued existence of these problems in large measure stems from a political context in which national leadership is unwilling or unable to address obvious and easily addressed legal issues. Overall, a favorable national political context would include central commitment to clarity and stability in the roles, powers, and resources of local government; to adequacy in its funding; to effective local control over local-level personnel; to a continuing and effective supervisory and regulative role for the national government; and to effective restructuring of the national civil-service codes and routine governmental procedures so that local entities have the authority to take these actions and national entities have the obligation to support them.

The cases and other research also point to the crucial importance of the second factor cited above, *effective systems of intergovernmental relations*, which provide resources for decentralized organs. For example, regarding finance, while many African central governments have finally been won to the idea that decentralization requires the transfer of substantial powers and financial resources to democratically elected local governments, they have not yet embraced the need to build *local* sources of finance for local governments. They have used a combination of mechanisms (laws, constitutions, specialized institutional arrangements) to transfer powers and funds, as explained in Chapter 3. At times, wide powers have been transferred to local governments, either purposively as a part of central government policy backed by law, or by default, with local communities or nongovernmental bodies taking the initiative when central agents have failed. Substantial financial resources have also been transferred to local governments, especially in the form of general revenue sharing (Nigeria, Uganda, South Africa, Mali) and as specific grants (Uganda, Tanzania, and several Francophone countries). But the authority and capacity to raise substantive funds at the local level has not been well developed. Indeed, the pattern is such that many countries' local governments have become so heavily dependent on such transfers that they discourage efforts at reforming the systems of local government revenue generation, which has remained in a perilous state in most countries in the region. The evidence for this can be found in all the case chapters except Chad, and is also well documented by other scholars (Ikhide 1995; Livingston and Charlton 1998, 2001).

While there are those who hold the view that extreme poverty in many of Africa's rural communities makes local taxation either impossible or unadvisable, such assertions contradict the reality of the diversity of Africa's social and economic landscape and the extremes of income inequality among the continent's people (Guyer 1992; Prudhomme 2001; Fjeldstad 2001). It is indeed the case that most people are poor, but the major weakness of African local taxation systems is that they are very regressive: they are completely dependent on taxing people with fixed (public-sector) or low incomes, often much to the benefit of the rich and those who enjoy high incomes outside of the public sector. There are very few mechanisms for taxing these categories of citizens, many of whom are quite prosperous and conduct their businesses outside of the formal sector. In Nigeria, for instance, local governments tax only incomes *below* 600 naira (approximately U.S.$5) per annum. Similarly, in Uganda rural taxes penalize the poor at the expense of the rich and no serious efforts have been made to tackle their many abuses, aside from the regressiveness of the graduated income tax. The last remains a potentially important revenue source for local governments in that country (Livingston and Charlton 1998). Some countries have made progress with respect to rating urban property, even though the prospects are bleak without central government and/or external assistance (World Bank 1993; Bahl and Linn 1994). Progress has also been recorded with respect to the value-added tax (VAT) in many countries (Bahl and Linn 1992). In Nigeria, local governments are entitled to 30 percent of all VATs, which is a considerable amount (IMF 2001). Most countries have not been able to derive much from user charges, often because of the difficulty in effectively exempting the poor while collecting something from those with the ability to pay. This was the major weakness of the Bamako Initiative of revolving loans to finance basic health care in the West Africa subregion by ministers of health and a consortium of international agencies—the World Bank, World Health Organization, and UNICEF (WHO 2001). The chapter on Chad provides one conspicuous exception to that pattern, though it is as a result of a local rather than national initiative.

The transfer and continued support of human resources and their management to local government is in fact more crucial than finance, for human resources are the active agents of all organizational life. The human-resource problem has also been difficult to resolve by many countries for several mutually reinforcing reasons, and their local governments remain weak. First, local government pay structures differ from central ones, usually to the disadvantage of local personnel. A second issue is that many central governments have not allowed local governments to recruit and manage their own staff. Where this has been attempted, as in Nigeria in 1993, difficulties were experienced and the arrangement was reversed after only six months, as the local staff complained of victimization by local government councillors (Gboyega 1998). In Uganda, the local civil-service system has conferred greater authority on local governments, but this has also sapped the morale of local employees who see no opportunity for advancement, and feel cut off from their professional peers.

In other countries, such as Ghana, senior local government has remained staffed by central government employees, even though the decentralization laws promised to transfer them to local governments. Another problem is that many staffers consider working in local governments a demotion, even when monetary emoluments are harmonized, because many local communities lack basic infrastructures such as schools, electricity, water, etc. (Dovlo 1998). Botswana's attempt to manage this, with its national-local government service corps, has been relatively successful, but nonetheless has experienced still other problems as noted in Chapter 4. Finally, in much of Africa, the farther away a person worked from his/her local community, the greater the social esteem that person received. Because of the stubborn persistence of a colonial mentality in which all good things are seen as coming from outside, working in one's home (local) government unit is frequently resisted (Dovlo 1998). These problems have often meant that decentralization, when not coordinated with human-resource policy, undermined rather than enhanced the goals of improved service delivery or empowerment (WHO 2001; ILO 2001). As Chapter 5 demonstrated in Nigeria, the isolation of local government personnel from their professional supervisors at the state level badly eroded local morale and services.

Many of these problems have persisted because most African governments do not have effective human-resource management policies, even at the central government level. If local governance is a goal, many related issues are raised: how to distribute scarce skills among regions and localities without losing quality service; how to compensate for service in hardship regions; how to change long-established education programs that assume centralized service delivery of services such as health care and education; how to change cultural beliefs concerning serving in local governments; how to maintain technical competence and quality many miles away from senior leadership; and how to balance professional norms with local accountability (Egger, Lipson, and Adams 2000).

There is the need to build new relationships among professional cadres and administrative personnel on the one hand, and between these two and the politicians at the local government level on the other. Dramatic reorientations among these personnel are unavoidable, as the ministries of local governments and interior, which have long controlled local governments and all their personnel, are gradually weaned into more supportive roles. Of course, central "abandonment" of local personnel, as seen in the PHC projects in Nigeria (Chapter 5), is not an option either, as personnel rights, professional standards, and effective administrative practices must be sustained. Nor, however, is continued tight control from the center, as in Ghana (Chapter 6), a viable solution if one's goal is effective local governance. Given all these challenges, getting all this "right" is not simple. A number of strategies have been tried. In Nigeria, the ministries of local government were abolished and replaced with bureaus in the (regional) governors' offices. In Uganda, a decentralization secretariat with wide powers and based in the president's office worked closely with the Ministry of Local Government to bring about this transition. This model is being promoted across the continent by two municipal development programs, one in French West Africa and the other in eastern and southern Africa (Olowu 2001a). In Uganda, however, the morale of local technical personnel was dismal. They felt they no longer had a career track upward and that they had been abandoned by the senior members of their technical fields. In Ghana, local technical and administrative personnel dealt with the threat of decentralization largely by ignoring the reforms. Neither of these reactions provides a satisfactory solution.

A final aspect of the human-resource problem is that many local governments are designed in such a way that all are forced to adopt a uniform personnel structure. They are required to hire the same type, number, and quality of staff as other local governments, and all (wealthy-urban, poor-rural) are obligated to pay the same wages. In many cases, as in Ghana, Nigeria, Ethiopia, and Uganda, the salaries of such staff are paid by the central government, using specific grants. The result is that local governments are not in a position to make decisions concerning which staff they should hire and which they do not need; what services they might contract for with other local governments, central agencies, or nongovernmental organizations; or even effectively to use personnel paid by another level of government. Local government leaders complained much about this in Botswana (Chapter 4).

The third broad set of lessons suggests the importance of a *strong local demand for public goods* for the development of local governance and the *existence of local social capital*.[2] There are four aspects to this: (1) that there is a general demand for public goods that can and may be provided locally; (2) that local governments have the powers to regulate and encourage, rather than only producing private goods (divisible and individual goods); (3) that the locality bears a significant share of the cost of local public goods; and (4) that local units of government conform to historical local communities as much as possible. Why? The success of local governance in Chad and at the village level in Uganda, on the one hand, and the diverse problems faced by the local governments virtually everywhere else among our cases on the other, are the primary evidence for this section. Consider Chad and its villages' education programs. In spite of lacking virtually every favorable contextual element as discussed above, Fass and Desloovere find much evidence of effective local governance in Chad. How can that be?

In Chad, education was valued because of the collective benefit it would have for the village as a whole. There were very few, if any, lucrative benefits for educated individuals in the politically and economically turbulent landscape of Chad in this era. Similarly, individuals simply could not purchase education for their children: there were no schools available nor was anyone or any small group well-off enough to educate only their children. If education was to be had, it had to be collectively provided and managed. When this reality was combined with the advantage local communities apparently felt education would bring to them as a whole, there was a powerful incentive to build mechanisms of local governance to provide it. Building on available local social capital and local institutional infrastructure, Chadian villagers did just that. Ottemoeller shows how the same process developed in villages in Uganda dealing with public goods such as local security and dispute resolution. While the LC structure enabled this to occur, essentially local dwellers with social capital held among them worked out the details and managed the institutions to provide these goods that no one else seemed able or willing to provide to them. Other examples of local peoples' provision of public goods using available social capital is well documented throughout the continent (Barkan, McNulty, and Ayeni 1991; Olowu, Ayo, and Akande 1991; Smock 1971; McGaffey 1992; IDS 2001).

Public goods and a local demand for them are important because of the destructive impact that governmental focus on provision of private goods can have on local politics. Since private goods are by definition divisible, their availability through local governments in Africa has frequently stimulated intense, extralegal, and at times violent competition over who gets what share of the goods. This divides local populations into groups of "winners" and "losers." As Chapter 3 suggests, the winners are frequently small elite groups, who then use their control of these goods to consolidate their domination over local politics and governance, and further enrich themselves (Wunsch 1999). This tends to replicate national neopatrimonial dynamics at the local level. Bruce Bueno de Mesquita et al. (2001) provide a parallel analysis of this dynamic at the national level. When elite groups dominate local politics in this way, grassroots support for local governance erodes. Still, when the private sector is weak, as is the case in many local communities across Africa, local governments are called on to stimulate and regulate the production of private services—e.g., credits to women farmers or traders, provide extension facilities to farmers and informal-sector operators, etc. Providing such goods, however, puts local governance at risk, as the opportunities and pressures they offer to return to clientelistic and neopatrimonial patterns are powerful, and the scramble to capture such individualistic goods can erode local social capital.

Also destructive of local governance is a situation where local people are not paying for the provision of local public goods. Exemplified by Nigeria, local governance becomes a game of "pump the commons," and local politics is a game of attempting to capture a share of that commons for oneself or one's constituency. This too becomes an intense and conflictual process, where some win big and others lose. Corruption tends to be high in such situations, and local governance as an accountable process where communities work together to tax themselves, and decide and closely supervise how to provide goods for themselves, never develops. That Botswana has not developed this dynamic in spite of its diamond wealth can be explained only by the consolidation of local contestation and accountability in its democratic context, by its effective administration within its stable rule of law, and by sound leadership at the center that has not flooded the country with diamond wealth.

The frequent cry that decentralization has "failed" Africa, and that local governance is not possible there, is in some measure explained by the weak (or at least weakly expressed) demand for public goods by local populations at the local level, and the disjunction between decentralized legal structures and the levels where social capital exists. This is reinforced by the tendency of national governments to emphasize distribution of divisible goods (rather than enhancing the regulatory capacity of local governments) as part of their strategy to retain power, the incentive structure for local elites created by the public-private mix of local governments (which creates situations of severe moral hazard), and by the occasional availability of "commons" (such as oil money) that a fortunate few can "pump" to enrich themselves and use to manipulate others among the local population, and the tendency to organize local governments along units far too large to be united by existing social capital among either residents or political leaders. All these create incentive structures and opportunities for the clever and ruthless few to exploit the many. In Chad this was avoided by default. In other states, such as Botswana and South Africa, perhaps, favorable national policy and institutional contexts, strong accountability structures, professionalized civil servants, and positive supervisory/regulatory roles played by national (or regional) governments may be able to avoid some of these dynamics. In Ghana and Uganda, the local demand pattern is one where villages and other smaller units of governance or social identity essentially compete for resources that benefit only those subunits. While many of these are "public goods" at that smaller level, the political dynamic they stimulate at the district level is essentially one of competition for divisible and in essence consumable goods, the latter because maintenance of the goods is so consistently poor. This recreates a clientelist, neopatrimonial dynamic at the decisionmaking level. These will always be issues for local governance in Africa, as in fact they are elsewhere.

The fourth and final factor is the challenge of *designing effective local institutions* that simultaneously represent the public in local decisionmaking, hold local executive and administrative personnel accountable, and are themselves accountable to the public. While there may be other frameworks through which these several tasks can be performed, elective bodies, generally called legislative councils of one sort or another, are the most widely used in Africa, as noted in Chapter 3.

Effectiveness of these bodies varies among our cases, with those in Kenya and Nigeria the weakest, Ghana's and Uganda's making progress (though with difficulty), and Botswana's and Chad's seemingly working the most effectively, while South Africa's are in a period of intense transition and therefore faltering. While the severely adverse contextual factors already noted help explain the ineffective councils of Kenya and Nigeria, the other cases reflect more subtle issues.

As discussed in Chapter 1, there are several factors that are obstacles to effective performance by legislatures. These include the concentration of information and resources typically in the hands of the executives in contrast to the few resources legislatures typically control; the unity of action implicit in a single executive in contrast to the fragmentation and competition typical of multimember legislative bodies; and the closer proximity executives have to administrative personnel and discretionary resources than legislatures have. These challenges also include the need to organize legislatures so they can overcome collective-action issues such as achieving agreement on policy and budget matters in the face of their frequently oblique and zero-sum preferences; allocating demanding and tedious information-gathering and analytical tasks necessary to compete with executives and their staffs; and persuading one or more among them to take leadership roles and thereby expose themselves to temptation and/or retaliation when they challenge executive or administrative personnel. Finally, organizing legislatures and performing legislative tasks (analyzing budgets and plans, assessing project proposals, working in committees, squeezing information from reluctant executives or administrative personnel, and the like) are not skills that ordinary citizens normally possess. In summary, establishing and sustaining effective legislative bodies is anything but easy, even when the law makes room for them. Both Kenya and Nigeria suffer from many of these problems. Nigeria's councils, however, may have more potential to resolve these than Kenya's, if

Nigeria can stabilize its structure long enough for the councils to balance their strong executives. Kenya's weak and fragmented councils, lacking any executive power, face serious design problems.

Ghana's and Uganda's councils also reflect these problems. In Ghana, the powerful position held by the local executive combined with his or her appointment by the president meant the legislative bodies were crippled from the start. Ayee's evidence, as well as the work of Crook and Manor (1998), shows how weak they were. In Uganda, the lack of knowledge about legislative roles combined with the strong role played by the locally elected executive meant that the council's role was limited there as well. Furthermore, in Uganda none of the collective-action problems had been resolved, councils were largely untrained in these tasks, and as a result were simply ineffective. However, there a committee system was in place and, in a few councils, was operating. Similarly, a locally controlled and nominally participative budget process was also in place. These are institutional provisions that can be built upon.

Chad's local councils, though without any official status, were effective in raising resources, setting priorities, engaging and supervising personnel, and assessing and revising their programs. While their procedures were not observed, the outcomes of their activities were, and offer rather strong evidence that they had resolved most of the issues raised here. They, of course, avoided the problem of executive domination by not selecting an executive, but acting as a collective one. They developed their internal rules and practices out of their own social capital, including their experience with traditional village councils, thus resolving a set of key collective-action issues. Finally, while they provided goods and services to their villages that the center had patently failed to provide, in reality they kept what they did, its financing, and its supervision relatively simple. In avoiding formal planning processes, budget cycles, etc., they kept their activities within their reach.

Observation of Botswana's councils as well as examination of documentary evidence suggests that they had developed to the point where they could contest policy with the executive, read and analyze budgets, manage committee business, and challenge local administrators. The near quarter century that Botswana's local government system has been in place, as well as the role competing political parties play in organizing many of Botswana's councils, seem likely explanations for these successes. However, the executive power was still effectively accountable to the center, and this impeded true local accountability and probably weakened the councils as a result. These must be treated as hypotheses for further study. Nonetheless, one can infer from these several cases that ineffective local councils will lead to shortfalls in local governance, and that there are many challenges to making them effective.

Some African states have tried to supplement the weakness of their local legislative bodies as institutions for local participation and accountability with institutional devices that enable citizens to control directly the executive branch. These include the use of recall and service delivery surveys, a citizens' charter (South Africa and Uganda), strong local audits, and local judiciaries (Nigeria and Ghana). These local collective-action strategies may help to alter the incentive structures and opportunities available to both legislative and executive personnel. Nonetheless, without resolving the institutional issues discussed here, local governance cannot develop.

Conclusion

There has been, over the past fifteen years, a broad policy shift in favor of local governance in many African states. But there are serious political, contextual, and institutional design issues that undermine these efforts. Hence, as effective local political and managerial institutional mechanisms are still poorly developed, many might conclude overall that decentralization has not produced lively and local governing units in Africa. On the other hand, substantial authority and financial resources have been transferred to local community organs in many countries, and in a few countries local decisionmaking institutions have been established.

In the concluding section of Chapter 1, the authors promised to try to begin to identify and elaborate on the factors that encouraged and discouraged the growth of decentralization reforms into viable and sustained local governance in Africa. Drawing on the political-science and public-administration literature on local governance, the authors developed a working model of the prerequisites of local governance, tested it in fieldwork done at the local level in South Africa and Botswana, and reported in Chapter 4 results that were supportive of the model. Chapter 4 and the remainder of the case studies were analyzed in this chapter to assess their insights regarding their achievement on each of the four elements of the model. Four factors were found important in explaining their successes.

As emphasized in this chapter, the national political context is critical. It makes real or erodes the core legal and constitutional reforms we have argued are necessary to begin "democratic decentralization." It facilitates or obstructs needed further changes in law that become clear as decentralization encounters problems in its implementation. It also provides the context wherein there is, or is not, a clear commitment to democracy and the rule of law. Its actions also strongly affect the economic context in which local governance struggles with fiscal and personnel resource shortfalls, and with local needs. It provides or denies the stable framework in which local rule sets can evolve into working institutions. It can have a fatal or supportive impact on a local political process, and the national government's ability to establish the institutional framework for local governance can resolve or worsen institutional design, principal-agent, and collective-action issues.

Effective mechanisms of intergovernmental relations and intergovernmental mechanisms to help localities manage precious human and fiscal resources also have a powerful impact on local resources. The paucity of resources and the challenge of maintaining effective services in technically demanding areas such as health care, agricultural extension, and fiscal management make these critical. Poor performance in this area can erode the effectiveness of local institutions of collective action, affect the trust of the local community, and if poor or ineffective, erode local government's capacity and eventually its ability to claim autonomy.

Institutional design issues are critical for local governance even when the national context is supportive, and even if intergovernmental relations are effective. This is because the difficulty of transforming any group of individuals into an effective legislative body, one that can represent constituents, set priorities, understand and supervise budgets, balance and check an executive, and hold administrative and service-delivery personnel to account, etc., is rarely understood. It is even more rarely solved. Simple organizational procedures (committee number, size, and structure; legislative role in planning and budgeting; obligations of the executive to the legislature; prerogatives of the legislative leadership) strongly affect a group's ability to resolve the collective-action, principal-agent, and free-rider issues that plague governance everywhere. We can see these issues at play in the chapters on Ghana and Uganda. Similar "design" issues relate to the source of the local executive's mandate, to whom he/she is accountable, and the executive's power regarding local administrative and service personnel. It is a particularly stubborn problem in Africa because of its poverty, its relative inexperience with local governance, and the priority that most scholars and governmental officials still place on national governance. The result of the difficulty of designing local institutions that surmount these and other operational issues is that local institutions of collective action and the open local political process needed to legitimize and hold officials accountable are gravely weakened. As a result, local resources become difficult to raise and manage, and local capacity erodes. The end result is that effective local autonomy, usually under central challenge in any case, shrinks.

The case studies also suggest a final factor—a local demand for public rather than private goods and the congruence between units of governance and levels where social capital may be found—is important in generating a political process that seeks effective leaders and judges them on their performance for the community as a whole, rather than as suppliers of private goods who are then easily corrupted. When public goods are actually being delivered, the community has an incentive to pay attention to governance, rather than to only try to corrupt it. It also seems to vitalize local institutions of collective action, stimulate the flow of local resources into the governance process, and enhance local social capital. The case studies present evidence of high levels of satisfaction, even with impoverished government units, when they provide public goods that are valued by the community they serve, as can be seen in the chapters on Uganda and Chad.

Reinforcing our argument, several patterns can be seen across the cases. For example, there is the limitation of the largely top-down strategies evidenced in Kenya, Ghana, and Nigeria. In contrast to the modest achievements of these largely top-down efforts, those which have grown from locally generated governance initiatives have achieved surprising success. This may be because they were well adapted to the realities of local community life, uniquely understood local priorities, and were therefore able to devise mechanisms to draw crucial resources from their environments. It also seems to be because they were stimulated by locally felt priorities that it seemed no one else was likely to provide, were appropriate in size and scale to local capacity and felt needs, and drew in local leadership. An important consideration in this also seems to be that they built on the existing social capital of a community. While the importance of social capital has recently been given prominence in the social sciences elsewhere, its importance for rebuilding African local governance may not have been as well understood (Putnam 1993; Ostrom, Schroeder, and Wynne 1993; and Dia 1996). Given this, it seems important for African countries to develop local governing structures by building from the bottom-up *and* the top-down, rather than the predominant historical focus only on the latter. At the lowest level, attention should be paid by the center to providing flexible enabling structures that exclude destructive practices at the margins (fraud, violence), rather than detailing and enforcing rigid organizational and operational requirements and/or micromanaging local decisions and activities.

Aside from the many crucial elements already highlighted in this book, decentralization must mobilize one additional "resource" from the center if it is to evolve into local governance: time. This is the *time* required for systems to mature, including the time to learn from their own errors and mistakes. This is a large challenge given the haste with which many central governments have been prone to recentralize recently decentralized functions and powers. This has happened in a number of countries within and outside Africa (Chile in 1990, the Philippines in 1992, Nigeria in the mid-1990s, etc.) (Eaton 2001; Wunsch 2001a). Local governments, as complex institutions with difficult tasks, take many years to mature. Indeed, since local governance is a new experience for many Africans in the postcolonial period, there is a long institutional learning curve that must be traveled. Time must be allowed to learn from error.

All of these issues, ultimately, point toward the need for wise and tenacious leadership at *multiple* levels. Local leaders must help manage local institutions, work with other levels of governance to find and maintain significant elements of local autonomy and resources for local governments, and help make it worthwhile for local dwellers to participate in a local political process. However, in this period of reform, reorganization, and maturation, these reforms must be complemented by sustained, enlightened, and exemplary leadership from the center. Natural "experiments" like Chad's villages exist in many parts of Africa, as discussed in Chapters 3 and 8. These are excellent sources of insight for enhancing local governance. We have argued in this book that such local initiatives reflect substantial social capital and energy that has yet to be tapped in most national programs of decentralization. However, unless the center consciously works to support and protect local initiatives when the scale of problems they encounter transcends those local areas, develops policy and institutional frameworks that build on their learning, encourages them to develop and expand their activities, spreads it to other regions, and helps them gain access to technologies not available at the local level, these occasional flashes of local "genius" will not provide a local governance solution for Africa's many human needs and problems. Nor are they likely to serve as an effective local foundation for a broad and lasting democratic reform in Africa as a whole, unless the center is an active partner with them. The center must lead in a new way, one that respects and nurtures the periphery's capacity to govern itself, so the latter, and indeed all of Africa, can flourish.

Finally, we must note that support from external actors, namely bilateral and multilateral organizations, including northern nongovernmental organizations for local governance, is critical in many cases. Fortunately, it is also currently growing. Many of these organizations have realized the potential of local resources and processes in improving national-level governance. As discussed in Chapter 3, the influence of these institutions has increased in national-level policymaking and this has been a major voice in support of decentralization since the 1990s. These external inputs are crucial in providing much-needed resources to support decentralization and local governance at national and local levels, in building strategic capacities for designing and monitoring decentralization, in providing insights from other comparative experiences, and in enhancing the capacities of civil-society and community-based organizations for local governance.

Throughout this book we have argued that a fundamentally new form of decentralization, what we have called "democratic decentralization," has made significant strides in Africa in the past fifteen years. Under some circumstances it can lead to what we have called effective local governance: governance by Africa's people of their own affairs at the local level. However, there have also been many missed opportunities. While there are many variables that affect the emergence of such governance, we have suggested four that seem critical among these seven cases. If attended to, we believe they can increase the success of democratic decentralization.

Notes

1. In late March 2002, ALGAK and the World Bank held a conference on participation and local governance, one of whose objectives was to help Kenya learn from the positive experiences of other African countries in decentralization.

2. The level of demand for public goods at the locality and the importance of social capital were factors that emerged during our inductive analysis of the cases. Thus our data is uneven and tentative for some of the cases. Key measurement issues need to be explored regarding this topic. Furthermore, there are cause-effect issues that should be explored further. For example, to what extent do higher levels of local social capital and of demand for public goods cause more benign patterns of local governance, and to what extent does causality flow in the other direction, i.e., good governance leading to more local social capital and to higher demand for public goods? In fact, it is probably a reciprical relationship, and broader contextual factors no doubt play a role as well.

In spite of our tentativeness here, it seemed this was an important finding, and needed to be included in this chapter, with these caveats noted.

References

Aborisade, O., ed. 1990. *Traditional Rulers and Local Governments in Nigeria*. Ile-Ife, Nigeria: Obafemi Awolowo University Press.

Acheampong, E. 1995. "Tug of War in Ghana: The Centralizing Features of Decentralization." *Africa Insight* 25, no. 3: 186–194.

Adamolekun, L. 1984. "The Idea of Local Government as Third Tier of Government Revisited: Achievements, Problems and Prospects." *Quarterly Journal of Administration* 18, nos. 3 and 4: 92–112.

———. 1999. "Decentralization, Subnational Governments and Intergovernmental Relations." In L. Adamolekun, ed., *Public Administration in Africa: Main Issues and Country Studies*. Boulder, CO: Westview Press, pp. 49–67.

Adamolekun, L., R. Roberts, and M. Laleye, eds. 1990. *Decentralization Policies and Socio-Economic Development in Sub-Saharan Africa*. Washington, DC: Economic Development Institute.

Adedeji, Adebayo, ed. 1997. *Renewal from the Roots? The Struggle for Democratic Development*. London: Zed Books.

Adu, L. 1964. *The Civil Service in Commonwealth Africa*. London: Allen and Unwin.

African Development Bank. 2001. *African Development Report 2001: Fostering Good Governance in Africa*. Oxford: Oxford University Press.

Africa Today. 1993. "Prospects for Institutionalized Democracy." *Africa Today* 40, no. 1: 7.

Agarwala, A., and J. Ribot. 1999. "Accountability in Decentralization: A Framework with South Asian and West African Cases." *Journal of Developing Areas* 33, no. 4: 473–502.

Ahwoi, K. 1992. "The Constitution of the Fourth Republic and the Local Government System." In S. A. Nkrumah, ed., *Decentralization Under the Fourth Republic*. Legon: School of Administration, University of Ghana, pp. 1–27.

———. 1998. Keynote address delivered on the occasion of the Workshop for the Parliamentary Standing Committee on Local Government and Rural Development on the theme, "Decentralization Policy: A Critical Review," held at the Coconut Grove Hotel, Elmina, Ghana, May 29.

273

Ake, C. 1990. "Sustaining Development of the Indigenous." In World Bank, *Long Term Perspectives Study of Sub-Saharan Africa*, vol. 3. Washington, DC: World Bank, pp. 7–21.

Akivaga, S. K., W. Kulundu-Bitonye, and M. W. Opi. 1984. *Local Authorities in Kenya*. Nairobi, Kenya: Heinemann Educational Books.

Alexander, J. 1997. "The Local State in Post-War Mozambique: Political Practice and Ideas About Authority." *Africa* 67, no. 1: 1–26.

Allen, H. J. B. 1990. "Enhancing Administrative and Management Capacity in Local Government Finance." In *Seminar on Decentralization in African Countries*. New York: United Nations Department of Economic and Social Development.

Anderson, Mary. 1995. *Case Study: Malawi Development Fund*. New York: UNCDF.

Arrow, Kenneth. 1951. *Social Choice and Individual Values*. New York: Wiley.

Asiwaju, A. I. 1985. *Partitioned Africans: Ethnic Relations Across Africa's International Boundaries, 1884–1984*. Lagos, Nigeria: Lagos University Press.

Ayee, J. R. A. 1992a. "Decentralization Under Ghana's Fourth Republic Constitution." *Verfassung Und Recht In Ubersee*. Hamburg: University of Hamburg, vol. 4, pp. 394–406.

———. 1992b. "Decentralization and Effective Government: The Case of Ghana's District Assemblies." *Africa Insight* 22, no. 1: 49–56.

———. 1993. "Decentralization and Local Government Under the PNDC." In E. Gyimah-Boadi, ed., *Ghana Under PNDC Rule*. Dakar, Senegal: Council for the Development of Social Science Research in Africa (CODESRIA), pp. 114–134.

———. 1994. *An Anatomy of Public Policy Implementation: The Case of Decentralization Policies in Ghana*. Avebury, England: Aldershot.

———. 1995. "Financing Subnational Governments in Ghana: The Case of the District Assemblies' Common Fund." *Regional and Federal Studies* 5, no. 3, autumn: 292–306.

———. 1996. "The Measurement of Decentralization: The Ghanaian Experience, 1988–92." *African Affairs* 95, no. 378, January: 31–50.

———. 1997a. "The December 1996 General Elections in Ghana." *Electoral Studies* 16, no. 3: 416–427.

———. 1997b. "The Adjustment of Central Bodies to Decentralization: The Case of the Ghanaian Bureaucracy." *African Studies Review* 40, no. 2, September: 37–57.

———. 1997c. "Local Government Reform and Bureaucratic Accountability in Ghana." *Regional Development Dialogue* (UNCRD, Nagoya, Japan) 18, no. 2, autumn: 86–104.

———. 2002a. "The 2000 General Elections and Presidential Run-off in Ghana: An Overview." *Democratization* 9, no. 2, summer: 148–174.

———. 2002b. "Governance, Institutional Reforms and Policy Outcomes in Ghana." In D. Olowu and S. Sako, eds., *Better Governance and Public Policy: Capacity Building and Democratic Renewal in Africa*. Bloomfield, CT: Kumarian Press, pp. 173–194.

Ayeni, V. 1994. "An Ombudsman for Botswana." *Ombudsman Journal* 12, no. 1: 65–82.

Ayittey, G.B.N. 1991. *Indigenous African Institutions.* New York: Transnational Books.

Bahl, R. 1997. *Fiscal Federalism in Uganda.* Washington, DC: World Bank.

————. 2000. "How to Design a Fiscal Decentralization Program." In S. Yusuf, W. Wu, and S. Evenett, *Local Dynamics in an Era of Globalization.* New York: Oxford University Press, for the World Bank, pp. 94–100.

Bahl, R., and J. Linn. 1992. *Urban Public Finance in Developing Countries.* Oxford: Oxford University Press.

————. 1994. "Fiscal Decentralization and Intergovernmental Transfers in Less Developed Countries." *Publius: The Journal of Federalism* 24, no. 1: 1–20.

Bahl, R. W., and R. O. Mant. 1976. *An Analysis of Local Government Finances in Kenya with Proposals for Reform.* Washington, DC: Fiscal Affairs Department, International Monetary Fund.

Bahl, R., and P. Smoke. Forthcoming. *Restructuring Local Government Finance in Developing Countries: Lessons from South Africa.* Cheltenham, England, and Northampton, MA: Edward Elgar.

Balogun, M. J. 2000. "The Scope for Popular Participation in Decentralization, Community Governance, and Development: Towards a Paradigm of Centre-Periphery Relations." *Regional Development Dialogue* 21, no. 1: 153–173.

Bardill, John E. 2000. "Towards a Culture of Good Governance." *Public Administration and Development* 20, no. 2: 103–118.

Barkan, J. D. 1994. "Resurrecting Modernization Theory and the Emergence of Civil Society in Kenya and Nigeria." In D. E. Apter and C. G. Rosberg, eds., *Political Development and the New Realism in Sub-Saharan Africa.* Charlottesville: University Press of Virginia, pp. 87–116.

————. 1995. "Debate: PR and Southern Africa: Elections in Agrarian Societies." *Journal of Democracy* 6, no. 4: 106–116.

————. 1998. *Decentralization and Democratization in Sub-Saharan Africa.* Occasional Papers 45–49, Iowa City: International Programs, University of Iowa.

————. 2000. "Protracted Transitions Among Africa's New Democracies." *Democratization* 7, no. 3: 227–243.

Barkan, J. D., and Michael Chege. 1989. "Decentralizing the State: District Focus and the Politics of Reallocation in Kenya." *Journal of Modern African Studies* 27, no. 3: 431–453.

Barkan, J. D., M. McNulty, and M. Ayeni. 1991. "Hometown Voluntary Associations and the Emergence of Civil Society in Western Nigeria." *Journal of Modern Africa Studies* 29, no. 3: 457–480.

Barya, J., and J. Oloka-Onyango. 1994. *Popular Justice and Resistance Committee Courts in Uganda.* Kampala, Uganda: Centre for Basic Research.

Bates, Robert. 1981. *Markets and States in Tropical Africa.* Berkeley, CA: University of California Press.

Batkin, A. 2001. *Fiscal Decentralization in Uganda: The Way Forward.* Kampala: Government of Uganda and Donor Sub-Group on Decentralization.

Batley, R., and G. Stoker. 1991. *Local Government in Europe: Trends and Developments.* Houndmills, England: Macmillan.

Bayart, J. F. 1986. "Civil Society in Africa." In P. Chabal, ed., *Political Domination in Africa: Reflections on the Limits of Power.* Cambridge: Cambridge University Press, pp. 109–125.

———. 1993. *The State in Africa: The Politics of the Belly.* New York: Longmans.

Berman, B. 1998. "Ethnicity, Patronage, and the African State: The Politics of Uncivil Nationalism." *African Affairs* 97, no. 388: 305–341.

Beyene, A. 1999. "Ethiopia." In L. Adamolekun, ed., *Public Administration in Africa: Main Issues and Selected Country Studies.* Boulder, CO: Westview Press, pp. 227–249.

Bierschenk, T., and O. de Sardan. 1997. "Local Powers and Distant State in Rural Central African Republic." *Journal of Modern African Studies* 35, no. 3: 441–468.

Bird, R., and F. Vaillancourt. 1998. *Fiscal Decentralization in Developing Countries.* Cambridge: Cambridge University Press.

Blair, H. 1998. *Spreading Power to the Periphery: An Assessment of Democratic Local Governance.* Washington, DC: USAID Program and Operations Assessment Report no. 21.

———. 2000. "Participation and Accountability at the Periphery: Democratic Local Governance in Six Countries." *World Development* 28, no. 1: 21–39.

Boone, C. 1998. "State Building in the African Countryside: Structure and Politics at the Grassroots." *Journal of Development Studies* 34, no. 4: 1–31.

Bratton, M., and D. Rothchild. 1992. "The Institutional Bases of Governance in Africa." In G. Hyden and M. Bratton, eds., *Governance and Politics in Africa.* Boulder: Lynne Rienner Publishers, pp. 263–284.

Bratton, M., and N. van de Walle. 1997. *Democratic Experiments in Africa: Regime Transitions in Comparative Perspective.* Cambridge: Cambridge University Press.

Brett, E. A. 1994. "Rebuilding Organizational Capacity in Uganda Under the National Resistance Movement." *Journal of Modern African Studies* 32, no. 1: 53–80.

Brilliantes, A. 1998. "Capacity Building and Administrative Innovations in the Philippines—The Integrated Capability Program." In G. Bhatta and J. Gonzalez, eds., *Governance Innovations in the Asia-Pacific Region,* Hants, Canada: Ashgate, pp. 245–256.

Briscoe, Andrew, ed. 1995. *Local Government Finance, Planning and Business Promotion.* Gaborone, Botswana: Friedrich Ebert Stiftung.

Britannica Online. 1994. "Book of the Year 1994: World Affairs: Chad," http://www.eb.com:180/cgi-bin/g?DocF=boy/94/H02730.html. Accessed October 3, 1998.

———. 1995. "Book of the Year 1995: World Affairs: Chad," http://www.eb.com:180/cgi-bin/g?DocF=boy/95/I02960.html. Accessed October 3, 1998.

———. 1997. "Book of the Year 1997: World Affairs: Chad," http://www.eb.com:180/cgi-bin/g?DocF=boy/97/K03915.html. Accessed October 3, 1998.

———. 1998a. "Book of the Year 1998: World Affairs: Chad," http://www.eb.com:180/cgi-bin/g?DocF=boy/98/L03915.html. Accessed October 3, 1998.

————. 1998b. "Western Africa: Countries of the Western Sudan: Chad," http://www.eb.com:180/cgi-bin/g?DocF=macro/5006/65/. Accessed October 3, 1998.

Bubba, N., and D. Lamba. 1991. "Urban Management in Kenya." *Environment and Urbanization* 3, no. 1: 37–59.

Bueno de Mesquita, Bruce, James Marrow, Randolph Siverson, and Olastain Smith. 2001. "Political Competition and Economic Growth." *Journal of Democracy* 12, no. 1: 58–72.

Burkey, I. 1991. "People's Power in Theory and Practice: The Resistance Council System in Uganda." Postbaccalaureate paper, New Haven, CT: Yale University Press.

Caiden, Naomi, and Aaron Wildavsky. 1973. *Planning and Budgeting in Poor Countries.* New York: Wiley.

Calvert, H. 1975. *Devolution.* London: Professional Books Ltd.

Cameron, Robert. 1996. "The Reconstruction and Development Programme." *Journal of Theoretical Politics* 8, no. 2: 283–294.

————. n.d. *The History of Devolution of Powers to Local Authorities in South Africa: The Shifting Sands of State Control.* Cape Town, South Africa: Department of Political Studies, University of Cape Town, mimeo.

————. 1997. "South African Final Constitutions: The Elevation of Local Government." Presented at the International Association of Schools and Institutes of Administration Conference, Quebec.

Cameron, Robert, and Chris Tapscott. 2000. "The Challenges of State Transformation in South Africa." *Public Administration and Development* 20, no. 2: 81–86.

Campbell, T. 1997. *Innovations and Risk-Taking: The Engine of Reform in Local Government in Latin America.* World Bank Discussion Paper no. 357, Washington, DC: World Bank.

Carbone, Giovanni. 2001. "Constitutional Alternatives for the Regulation of Ethnic Politics? Institution-Building Principles in Uganda and South Africa's Transitions." *Journal of Contemporary African Studies* 19, no. 2: 229–252.

Chambers, Robert. 1974. *Managing Rural Development: Ideas and Experience from East Africa.* Uppsala, Sweden: Scandinavian Institute of African Studies.

————. 1983. *Rural Development: Putting the Last First.* London: Longmans.

Chanaux-Repond, Maia, and Stan Kanengoni. 1995. *Some Strengths and Weaknesses of Botswana's Development at Local Authority Level.* Gaborone, Botswana: Friedrich Ebert Stiftung.

Chapelle, J. 1986. *Le Peuple Tchadien.* Paris: L'Harmattan.

Cheru, Fantu. 2002. *African Renaissance: Road Maps to the Challenge of Globalization.* London: Zed Books.

Clarke, Vicki Burge. 2001. *In Search of Good Governance.* Unpublished Ph.D. dissertation. DeKalb: University of Northern Illinois.

Cloete, Fanie. 1994. "Local Government Restructuring." *Politikan* 21, no. 1: 42–65.

Cohen, J. M. 1996. "Ethnic Federalism in Ethiopia." Development Discussion Paper no. 519, Cambridge, MA: Harvard Institute for International Development.

Cohen, J. M., and R. M. Hook. 1987. "Decentralized Planning in Kenya." *Public Administration and Development* 7, no. 1: 72–93.

Cohen, J. M., and S. B. Peterson. 1999. *Administrative Decentralization: Strategies for Developing Countries.* West Hartford, CT: Kumarian Press.

Collins, Paul. 2000. *Applying Public Administration in Development.* Chichester: John Wiley and Sons.

Conyers, D. 1983. "Decentralization: The Latest Fashion in Development Administration?" *Public Administration and Development* 3, no. 1: 97–109.

———. 1989. "The Management and Implementation of Decentralized Administration." In Commonwealth Secretariat, *Decentralized Administration in Africa: Policies and Training.* London: Commonwealth Secretariat.

Corkery, J., A. Land, and J. Bossuyt. 1995. *The Process of Policy Formulation: Institutional Path or Institutional Maze?* Maastricht, Netherlands: European Center for Development Policy and Management.

Cornia, G. A., and G. K. Helleinner, eds. 1994. *From Adjustment to Development in Africa.* New York: St. Martin's Press.

Coulibally, C. 1999. "On Subsidiary in Western Africa: A Contribution to Institutional Problem Solving in Africa." A paper presented at the Workshop 2 Conference, Workshop in Political Theory and Policy Analysis, Indiana University, Bloomington, Indiana.

Crane, R. 1997. "Central-Local Transfers in Kenya." A paper prepared for the Kenya Local Government Reform Program, Cambridge, MA: Harvard Institute for International Development.

Crook, R. C. 1994. "Four Years of the Ghana District Assemblies in Operation: Decentralization, Democratization, and Administrative Performance." *Public Administration and Development* 14, no. 4: 339–364.

Crook, Richard, and James Manor. 1998. *Democracy and Decentralization in South Asia and West Africa.* Cambridge: Cambridge University Press.

Crowder, Michael. 1968. *West Africa Under Colonial Rule.* London: Hutchinson.

Dahlgren, Stefan, Tyrrell Duncan, Allan Gustafsson, and Patrick Molutisi. 1993. *SIDA Development Assistance to Botswana: 1966–1993.* Gaborone, Botswana: Swedish International Development Agency (SIDA).

Daily Graphic (Gaborone, Botswana) (January 16–August 29) 1997.

Danevad, Andreas. 1995. "Responsiveness in Botswana Politics: Do Elections Matter?" *Journal of Modern African Studies* 33, no. 3: 381–402.

Davey, K. 1997. "The Local Government Loans Authority: Current Status and Options for Reform." A paper prepared for the Kenya Local Government Reform Program, Cambridge, MA: Harvard Institute for International Development.

Davidson, Basil. 1992. *The Blackman's Burden: Africa and the Curse of the Nation-State.* London: James Currey Publishers.

Davis, D., D. Hulme, and P. Woodhouse. 1994. "Decentralization by Default: Local Governance and the View from the Village in The Gambia." *Public Administration and Development* 14, no. 3: 253–269.

Ddungu, Expedit. 1989. "Popular Forms and the Question of Democracy: The Case of Resistance Councils in Uganda." Working Paper no. 4, Kampala, Uganda: Centre for Basic Research.

————. 1994. "Resistance Councils and the Problem of Autonomization of Power." Paper prepared for the Governance in East Africa Research Program, Jinja, Uganda: East Africa Research Program.

————. 1998. "Decentralization in Uganda: Process, Prospects, and Constraints." In Joel Barkan, ed., *Decentralization and Democratization in Sub-Saharan Africa.* Occasional Paper no. 47, Iowa City: University of Iowa.

Decalo, S. 1980. "Chad: The Roots of Center-Periphery Strife." *African Affairs* 79, no. 17: 491–509.

————. 1992. "The Process, Prospects, and Constraints of Democratization in Africa." *African Affairs* 91, no. 362: 7–35.

Delay, S. 1997. "Training Needs in Local Government Finance: A Preliminary Analysis." A paper prepared for the Kenya Local Government Reform Program, Cambridge, MA: Harvard Institute for International Development.

Devas, N. 1996. "Local Authority Revenue Sources: An Analysis of the Present System and Strategies for Reform." A paper prepared for the Kenya Local Government Reform Program, Cambridge, MA: Harvard Institute for International Development.

Dia, M. 1996. *Africa's Management in the 1990s and Beyond: Reconciling Indigenous and Transplanted Institutions.* Washington, DC: World Bank.

Dillinger, W. 1993. *Decentralization and Its Implications for Urban Service Delivery.* Washington, DC: Urban Management Programme UNDP/UNCHS/WB.

————. 1995. *Better Urban Services: Finding the Right Incentives.* Washington, DC: World Bank.

Doe, L. 1998. "Civil Service Reform in the Countries of the West African Monetary Union." Special Issue on Governance, *Journal of Social Sciences* 155, no. 1: 125–144.

Dovlo, D. 1998. "Health Sector Reform and Deployment, Training, and Motivation of Human Resources Towards Equity in Health Care: Issues and Concerns in Ghana." *Human Resources for Health Development Journal* 2, no. 1: 34–47.

Duke Center for International Development. 2002. "An Assessment of Local Service Delivery and Local Governments in Kenya." Draft study prepared for the World Bank and the Department for International Development, Durham, NC: Duke University.

Eaton, K. 2001. "Political Obstacles to Decentralization: Evidence from Argentina and the Philippines." *Development and Change* 32, no. 1: 101–128.

Economist. 2002. "Oil in Chad: Useful Stuff, Maybe, for Once." September 14, p. 49.

Edge, W., and M. Lekorwe, eds., 1998. *Botswana: Politics and Society.* Pretoria, South Africa: J. L. Zanschak.

Egger, D., D. Lipson, and O. Adams. 2000. "Achieving the Right Balance: The Role of Policy-Making Processes in Managing Human Resources for Health Problems." Discussion paper no. 2. Geneva: World Health Organization. Unpublished document.

Egwurube, J. O. 1988. "Traditional Rulers and Modern Local Government in

Nigeria." In L. Adamolekun, D. Olowu, and M. Laleye, eds., *Local Government in West Africa Since Independence*. Lagos, Nigeria: Lagos University Press, pp. 155–174.

Eigel, U. 1995. "Technical Assistance to Small and Medium-Sized Towns: A Practical Example from Kenya." *The Courier*, no. 194 (January): 89–91.

Ekeh, P. 1975. "Colonialism and the Two Publics in Africa: A Theoretical Statement." *Comparative Studies in History and Society* 19, no. 1: 91–112.

Esman, Milton. 1991. *Management Dimensions of Development*. Bloomfield, CT: Kumarian Press.

Esman, M. J., and N. T. Uphoff. 1984. *Local Organizations: Intermediaries in Rural Development*. Ithaca, NY: Cornell University Press.

Esquieu, P. S., and S. Péano. 1994. *L'enseignement privé et spotané dans le système éducatif tchadien*, Rapport de recherche de l'IIPE no. 103, Paris: UNESCO, Institut international de planification de l'education.

Ethiopia. 1994. *The Constitution of the Federal Republic of Ethiopia*. Unofficial English translation. Addis Ababa: Ministry of Justice.

Evans, H., and B. Lewis. 1996. "Service Assignment in Kenya: Conceptual and Practical Concerns." A paper prepared for the Kenya Local Government Reform Program. Cambridge, MA: Harvard Institute for International Development.

Fass, S. M., and G. M. Desloovere. 1995. "Decentralization et education au Tchad." Document de Travail SAH/D 95 446, Avril, Paris: Club du Sahel–OCDE.

Firmin-Sellers, Kathryn. 1999. "The Concentration of Authority: Constitutional Creation in the Gold Coast, 1950." In M. D. McGinnis, ed., *Polycentric Governance and Development*. Ann Arbor: University of Michigan Press, pp. 186–208.

————. 2000. "Institutions, Context and Outcomes: Explaining French and British Rule in West Africa." *Comparative Politics* 32, no. 3: 253–272.

————. 2001. "The Reconstruction of Society: Understanding the Indigenous Response to French and British Rule in Cameroon." *Comparative Politics* 34, no. 1: 43–62.

Fiszbein, Ariel. 1997. "The Emergence of Local Capacity: Lessons from Colombia." *World Development* 25, no. 7: 1029–1043.

————. 2000. "Public-Private Partnerships as a Strategy for Local Capacity Building: Some Suggestive Evidence from Latin America." In P. Collins, ed., *Applying Public Administration in Development: Guideposts to the Future*. Chichester, England: Wiley and Sons, pp. 163–180.

Fjeldstad, O. 2001. "Taxation, Coercion, and Donors: Local Government Tax Enforcement in Tanzania." *Journal of Modern African Studies* 39, no. 2: 289–306.

Foltz, W. J. 1995. "Reconstructing the State of Chad." In W. Zartman, ed., *Collapsed States*. Boulder, CO: Lynne Rienner Publishers, pp. 15–31.

Fukusaku, K., and R. Hausmann, eds. 1998. *Democracy, Decentralization and Deficits in Latin America*. Paris: OECD.

Furley, O. 2000. "Democratisation in Uganda." *Commonwealth and Comparative Politics* 38, no. 3: 79–102.

Furley, O., and J. Katalikawe. 1997. "Constitutional Reform in Uganda: The New Approach." *African Affairs* 96, no. 383: 243–260.

Gboyega, Alex. 1983. "Local Government Reform in Nigeria." In P. Mawhood, ed., *Local Government in the Third World*. Chichester, England: Wiley and Sons, pp. 235–256.

———. 1991. "Protecting Local Governments from Arbitrary State and Federal Interference; What Prospects for the 1990s?" *Publius: The Journal of Federalism* 21, no. 4: 45–60.

———. 1998. "Decentralization and Local Autonomy in Nigeria's Federal System: Crossing the Stream While Searching for the Pebbles." In J. Barkan, ed., *Decentralization and Democratization in Sub-Sahara Africa*. Occasional paper no. 49. Iowa City: University of Iowa.

Good, Kenneth. 1996. "Towards Popular Participation in Botswana." *Journal of Modern African Studies* 34, no. 1: 53–77.

Gouvernement du Tchad. 1990. "Formation de ressources humaines pour le developpement rural du Tchad a l'horizon 2000 1." N'Djamena, Tchad: Ministere de l'Agriculture.

Government of Kenya. 1967. "Sessional Paper no. 1 of 1967: Proposed Action by the Government of Kenya on the Report of the Local Government Commission of Inquiry." Nairobi: Government of Kenya.

———. 1971. *The Report of the Public Service Structure and Remuneration Commission, 1970–71*. Nairobi: Government of Kenya.

———. 1973. *The Report of the Nyaga Committee*. Nairobi: Government of Kenya.

———. 1978. *Human Settlements in Kenya: A Strategy for Urban and Rural Development*. Nairobi: Ministry of Lands and Settlement, Government of Kenya.

———. 1980. *Report of the Civil Service Review Committee, 1979–80*. Nairobi: Government of Kenya.

———. 1982. *Report and Recommendations of the Working Party on Government Expenditures*. Nairobi: Government of Kenya.

———. 1986. "Sessional Paper no. 1 of 1986: Economic Management for Renewed Growth." Nairobi: Government of Kenya.

———. 1987. *District Focus for Rural Development*. Nairobi: Office of the President, Government of Kenya.

———. 1989. *Sixth National Development Plan, 1989–93*. Nairobi: Government of Kenya.

———. 1994. *Recovery and Sustainable Development to the Year 2010*. Nairobi: Government of Kenya.

———. 1994. *Seventh National Development Plan, 1993–97*. Nairobi: Government of Kenya.

———. 1995. *District Focus for Rural Development*, Revised edition. Nairobi: Office of the President, Government of Kenya.

———. 1997. *Omamo Commission Report on Local Government*. Nairobi: Government of Kenya.

Government of Uganda. 2001. "Fiscal Decentralization in Uganda: Draft Strategy Paper." Fiscal Decentralization Working Group, Kampala: Government of Uganda.

Grosh, B., and R. S. Mukandala, eds. 1994. *State-Owned Parastatals in Africa*. Boulder, CO: Lynne Rienner Publishers.

Guyer, J. 1992. "Representation Without Taxation: An Essay on Democracy in Rural Nigeria, 1952–1990." *African Studies Review* 35, no. 1: 41–80.

Gyimah-Boadi, E. 1998. "The Rebirth of African Liberalism." *Journal of Democracy* 9, no. 2: 18–31.

Harvard Institute for International Development. 1997. "Kenya Intergovernmental Fiscal Relations." A paper prepared for the Kenya Local Government Reform Program, Cambridge, MA: Harvard Institute for International Development.

Haque, S. 1997. "Local Governance in Developing Nations: Re-Examining the Question of Accountability." *Regional Development Dialogue* 18, no. 2: iii–xvi.

Haynes, Jeff. 2001. "'Limited' Democracy in Ghana and Uganda: What Is Most Important to International Actors, Stability or Political Freedom?" *Journal of Contemporary African Studies* 19, no. 2: 183–204.

Helmsing, Bert. 2001. "Decentralization and Emerging Patterns of Local Governance: A Comparative Analysis of Uganda, Zimbabwe, and Zambia." Processed Paper. The Hague: Institute of Social Studies.

Herbst, Jeffrey. 2000. *States and Power in Africa.* Princeton, NJ: Princeton University Press.

Hicks, U. K. 1961. *Development from Below: Local Government and Finance in Developing Countries of the Commonwealth.* Oxford: Clarendon Press.

Holm, John D. 1987. "Botswana: A Paternalistic Democracy." *World Affairs* 150, no. 1: 21–30.

Hope, K. R., and B. C. Chiculo, eds. 2000. *Corruption and Development in Africa: Lessons from Country Case Studies.* London: Macmillan.

Hirata, Koji. 2001. "Democracy in Uganda." *Soshioroji* 45, no. 3: 35–52.

Huntington, S. P. 1968. *Political Order in Changing Societies.* New Haven, CT: Yale University Press.

———. 1991. *The Third Wave: Democratization in the Late Twentieth Century.* Norman: Oklahoma University Press.

Hyden, Goran. 1983. *No Shortcuts to Progress: African Development Management in Perspective.* Berkeley: University of California Press.

———. 1992. "Governance and the Study of Politics." In G. Hyden and M. Bratton, eds., *Governance and Politics in Africa.* Boulder, CO: Lynne Rienner Publishers.

———. 1999. "Governance and the Reconstitution of Political Order." In R. Joseph, ed., *State, Conflict and Democracy in Africa.* Boulder, CO: Lynne Rienner Publishers, pp. 179–196.

Hyden, G., D. Olowu, and W. Okoth-Ogendo. 2000. *African Perspectives on Governance.* Trenton, NJ: Africa World Press.

Idachaba, F. S., C. E. Umegbese, I. O. Akingbade, and A. Adeniyial. 1981. *Rural Infrastructures in Nigeria: Basic Needs of the Rural Majority.* Lagos: Federal Ministry of Rural Development.

IDS (Institute of Development Studies). 2001. *From Consultation to Influence: Bringing Citizen Voice and Client Focus into Service Delivery.* Brighton, England: DFID Consultancy Report, IDS.

Ikhide, S. 1995. "Local Government Finance and Accountability: A Case Study of Selected Local Governments in Nigeria." In D. Olowu, A. Williams, and K. Soremekun, eds., *Governance and Democratization in West Africa.* Dakar, Senegal: CODESRIA, pp. 165– 192.

Ikhide, S., D. Olowu, and J. Wunsch. 1993. *USAID Health and Governance*

Initiatives in Nigeria: A Strategic Assessment. Burlington, VT: Associates in Rural Development.

ILO (International Labour Organization). 2001. *The Impact of Decentralization and Privatization on Municipal Services.* Geneva: ILO.

IMF (International Monetary Fund). 2001. "Nigeria: Selected Issues and Statistical Appendix." *Country Report.* Washington, DC: International Monetary Fund.

Jackson, R., and C. Rosberg. 1986. "Sovereignty and Underdevelopment: Juridical Statehood in the African Crisis." *Journal of Modern African Studies* 24, no. 1: 1–33.

———. 1982. "Why Africa's Weak States Persist: The Empirical and Juridical in Statehood." *World Politics* 35, no. 1: 1–24.

Jeppson, Anders. 2001. "Financial Priorities Under Decentralization in Uganda." *Health Policy and Planning* 16, no. 2: 187–192.

Joseph, R. 1999. *State, Conflict, and Democracy in Africa.* Boulder, CO: Lynne Rienner Publishers.

Karlström, M. 1996. "Imagining Democracy, Political Culture, and Democratization in Buganda." *Africa* 60: 485–505.

Kasfir, N. 1983. "Designs and Dilemmas of African Decentralization." In P. Mawhood, ed., *Local Government in the Third World: The Experience of Decentralization in Tropical Africa.* Chichester, England, and New York: Wiley and Sons, pp. 25–49.

———. 1991. "The Ugandan Elections of 1989: Power, Populism, and Democratization." In Holger Bernt Hansen and Michael Twaddle, eds., *Changing Uganda.* London: James Currey, pp. 247–278.

———. 1998. "Civil Society, the State, and Democracy in Africa." *Commonwealth and Comparative Politics* 36, no. 2: 123–149.

Kelly, R. 1996a. "Property Rates in Kenya: An Analysis of the Present System and Strategy for Reform." A paper prepared for the Kenya Local Government Reform Program, Cambridge, MA: Harvard Institute for International Development.

———. 1996b. "Recommendations for Improving Contributions in Lieu of Rates." A paper prepared for the Kenya Local Government Reform Program, Cambridge, MA: Harvard Institute for International Development.

Kelly, R., and N. Devas. 1996. "Revenue Allocation: Theory and Application to Kenya." A paper prepared for the Kenya Local Government Reform Program, Cambridge, MA: Harvard Institute for International Development.

Kelly, R., and S. Ramakrishnan. 1997. "Intergovernmental Mutual Indebtedness: Analysis, Recommendations and Action Plan for Resolution." A paper prepared for the Kenya Local Government Reform Program, Cambridge, MA: Harvard Institute for International Development.

Khadiagala, G. M. 1995. "State Collapse and Reconstruction in Uganda." In W. Zartman, ed., *Collapsed States.* Boulder, CO: Lynne Rienner Publishers, pp. 33–48.

Khayar, I. 1969. *Le refus de l'ecole.* Paris: Librairie d'Amerique et D'Orient.

Keller, E. 1995. "Remaking of the Ethiopian State." In W. Zartman, ed.,

Collapsed States. Boulder, CO: Lynne Rienner Publishers, pp. 125–142.

Kirschke, Linda. 2000. "Informal Repression, Zero-Sum Politics and Late Third Wave Transitions." *Journal of Modern African Studies* 38, no. 3: 383–405.

Koehn, P. 1989. "Local Government Involvement in National Development Planning Guidelines for Project Selection Based upon Nigeria's Fourth Plan Experience." *Public Administration and Development* 9, no. 4: 417–436.

Kolehmanen-Aitken, Ritta-Lisa. 1998. "Decentralization and Human Resources: Implications and Impact." *Human Resources for Health Development Journal* 2, no. 1: 1–23.

Kooimans, J., ed. 1993. *Modern Governance: New Government-Society Interaction.* London: Sage.

Laleye, M. 1988. "Developments in Francophone West Africa." In L. Adamolekun, D. Olowu, and M. Laleye, eds., *Local Government in West Africa Since Independence.* Lagos, Nigeria: Lagos University Press, pp. 310–341.

Landau, Martin. 1969. "Redundancy, Rationality and the Problems of Duplication and Overlap." *Public Administration Review* 29, no. 1: 346–358.

Langlo, Marilyn, and Patrick Molusti. 1994. *Decentralization and Health Systems Performance: The Botswana Case Study.* Gaborone: Center for Partnership in Development–Norway and University of Botswana.

Langseth, P. 1995. *Civil Service Reform in Uganda.* EDI Working Paper Series no. 95-05. Washington, DC: EDI.

Landell-Mills, P. 1992. "Governance, Cultural Change, and Empowerment." *Journal of Modern African Studies* 30, no. 4: 543–567.

Larbi, G. 1998. "Management Decentralization in Practice: A Comparison of Public Health and Water Services in Ghana." In I. M. Minogue, C. Polidano, and D. Hulme, eds., *Beyond the New Public Management: Changing Ideas and Practices in Governance.* Cheltenham, England: Elgar, pp. 188–206.

Lekorwe, M. 1998. "Local Government and District Planning." In W. Edge and M. Lekorwe, eds., *Botswana: Politics and Society.* Pretoria, South Africa: Schaik Publishers, pp. 173–185.

Leighton, Charlotte. 1996. "Strategies for Achieving Health Financing Reform in Africa." *World Development* 24, no. 6: 1511–1525.

Lemarchand, R. 1986. "The Misadventures of the North-South Dialectic." *African Studies Review* 29, no. 3: 27–41.

———. 1992. "Uncivil States and Civil Societies: How Illusion Became Reality." *Journal of Modern African Studies* 30, no. 2: 177–191.

Levy, N., and C. Tapscott. 2001. *Intergovernmental Relations in South Africa: The Challenges of Cooperative Government.* Cape Town: School of Government, University of Western Cape.

Litvack, J., J. Ahmad, and R. Bird. 1998. *Rethinking Decentralization in Developing Countries.* Washington, DC: Poverty Reduction and Economic Management Series.

Livingstone, Ivan, and Roger Charlton. 1998. "Raising Local Authority District

Revenues Through Direct Taxation in a Low-Income Developing Country: Evaluating Uganda's DPT." *Public Administration and Development* 18, no. 5: 499–517.

―――. 2001. "Financing Decentralized Development in a Low-Income Country: Raising Revenue for Local Government in Uganda." *Development and Change* 31, no. 1: 77–100.

Lodge, Tom. 2002. *Politics in South Africa: From Mandela to Mbeki.* London: James Currey.

Lubanga, F. 1995. "Decentralization in Uganda: A Country Experience in Reforming Local Government." In P. Langseth et al., eds., *Civil Service Reform in Anglophone Africa.* Washington, DC: EDI, pp. 133–144.

Lundin, I. B. 1994. "Cultural Diversity and the Role of Traditional Authority in Mozambique." In D. Rothchild, ed., *Strengthening African Local Initiative: Local Self-Governance, Decentralization and Accountability.* Hamburg: Institut fur Afrika-Kunde, pp. 83–94.

Mabogunje, A. L. 1995a. *A Concept of Development.* Working Paper 95/1, Ibadan, Nigeria: Development Policy Center.

―――. 1995b. "The Capitalization of Money and Credit in the Development Process: The Case of Community Banking in Nigeria." *African Journal of Institutions and Development* 1, no. 1: 1–15.

Mackintosh, M., and R. Roy, eds. 1999. *Economic Decentralization and Public Management Reform.* Cheltenham, England: Elgar.

Makara, S. 1993. "The Role of Resistance Councils and Committees RCs in Promoting Democracy in Uganda." A paper prepared for the Conference on the Dynamics of Political and Administrative Change in Uganda, 1962–1992, Kampala, Uganda: Makerere University.

Makara, Sabiti. 2000. "Decentralization for Good Governance and Development: Uganda's Experience." *Regional Development Dialogue* 21, no. 1: 73–94.

Makhokha, J. 1985. *The District Focus: Conceptual and Management Problems.* Nairobi, Kenya: Africa Press Research Bureau.

Mamdani, M. 1988. "Uganda in Transition: Two Years of the NRA/NRM." *Third World Quarterly* 10, no. 3: 1155–1181.

―――. 1996. *Citizen and Subject: Contemporary Africa and the Legacy of Late Colonialism.* Princeton, NJ: Princeton University Press.

Manor, J. 1995. "Democratic Decentralization in Africa and Asia." *IDS Bulletin* 26, no. 2: 81–88.

Marcus, Richard, Kenneth Mease, and Dan Ottemoeller. 2001. "Popular Definitions of Democracy from Uganda, Madagascar, and Florida, USA." *Journal of Asian and African Studies* 36, no. 1: 113–132.

Mawhood, P. 1983. *Local Government in the Third World: The Experience of Tropical Africa.* Chichester, England, and New York: Wiley and Sons.

Mawhood, P., and K. Davey. 1980. "Anglophone Africa." In D. C. Rowat, ed., *International Handbook of Local Government Reorganization.* Westport, CT: Greenwood Press, pp. 404–414.

Mazrui, Ali A. 1983. "Francophone Nations and English-Speaking States: Imperial Ethnicity and African Political Formations." In D. Rothchild and V. Olorunsola, eds., *State Versus Ethnic Claims: African Policy Dilemmas.* Boulder, CO: Westview Press, pp. 25–43.

Mbeye, Jockley. 1997. "Final Report of Malawi Intergovernmental Fiscal Transfer Study." Blantyre: United Nations Development Programme Secretariat.

McCarney, P. L. 1996. "Reviving Local Government: The Neglected Tier in Development." In P. McCarney, ed., *The Changing Nature of Local Governments in Developing Countries.* Toronto: Centre for Urban and Community Studies, pp. 3–32.

McGaffey, J. 1992. "Initiatives from Below: Zaire's Other Path to Social and Economic Restructuring." In G. Hyden and M. Bratton, eds., *Governance and Politics in Africa.* Boulder, CO: Lynne Rienner Publishers, pp. 243–262.

Mead, T. 1996. "Barriers to Local-Government Capacity in Nigeria." *American Review of Public Administration* 26, no. 2, 159–173.

Meyer, Wayne. 1995. *Phase I Report: Public Works Programs Using Labor-Intensive Methods.* Gaborone, Botswana: Friedrich Ebert Foundation, typescript.

Migdal, J. 1988. *Strong Societies and Weak States: State-Society Relations and State Capabilities in the Third World.* Princeton, NJ: Princeton University Press.

Miles, W. F. S. 1995. "Decolonization as Disintegration: The Disestablishment of the State in Chad." *Journal of Asian and African Studies* 30, nos. 1–2: 40–48.

Ministry of Local Government and Rural Development. 2002. *Decentralization in Ghana: Implementation Status and Proposed Future Direction.* Accra, Ghana: Ministry of Local Government and Rural Development.

Mitra, S. 2001. "Making Local Government Work: Local Elites, Panchayat Raj, and Governance in India." In A. Kohli, ed., *The Success of India's Democracy.* Cambridge: Cambridge University Press, pp. 103–126.

Molutsi, P. P. 1998. "Elections and Electoral Experience in Botswana." In W. A. Edge and M. H. Lekorwe, eds., *Botswana: Politics and Society.* Pretoria, South Africa: Van Schalk Publishers, pp. 363–377.

Mokgoro, Job. 2000. "Provincial Experiences in Managing National Politics on the Transformation of the Public Service." *Public Administration and Development* 20, no. 2: 141–154.

Monga, C. 1998. "Eight Problems of African Politics." In L. Diamond and M. Plattner, eds., *Democratization in Africa.* Baltimore, MD: Johns Hopkins University Press, pp. 48–61.

Moore, Mick. 1998. "Death Without Taxes: Democracy, State Capacity and Aid Dependence in the Fourth World." In M. Robinson and G. White, eds., *The Democratic Developmental State: Politics and Institutional Design.* New York: Oxford University Press, pp. 84–120.

Muitzwa-Mangiza, N. D. 1990. "Decentralization and District Development Planning in Zimbabwe." *Public Administration and Development* 10, no. 4: 355–372.

Mujaju, A. B. 2000. "The Welfare State on Trial: The Triumph of Lockean Politics in Africa." In K. Prah and G. M. Ahmed, eds., *Africa in Transformation.* Addis Ababa, Ethiopia: Organization for Social Science Research in Eastern and Southern Africa (OSSREA), pp. 29–44.

Mutahaba, G. 1989. *Reforming Public Administration for Development: Experiences from Eastern Africa.* West Hartford, CT: Kumarian Press.

Muwanga, N. M. S. 2001. *The Politics of Primary Education in Uganda: Parent Participation and National Reforms*. Dissertation Abstracts International.

Narayan, D., R. Chambers, M. K. Shah, and P. Petesch. 2001. *Voices of the Poor: Crying out for Change*. New York: Oxford University Press.

Nchari, A. 1990. "Cooperatives as Decentralized Socio-Economic Institutions: The Case of Cameroon." In L. Adamolekun, R. Robert, and M. Laleye, eds., *Decentralization Policies and Socio-Economic Development in Sub-Saharan Africa*. Washington, DC: EDI, pp. 60–102.

Ndiyepa, E. 2001. "The Role of Traditional Rulers in Namibia's Decentralization Policy." Master of Public Policy and Administration Research Paper, Windhoek: University of Namibia.

NPP (New Patriotic Party). 2000. *Manifesto of the New Patriotic Party 2000: Agenda for Positive Change*. Accra, Ghana: New Patriotic Party.

N'gethe, N. 1998. "The Politics of Democratization Through Decentralization in Kenya: Policy and Practice with Emphasis on District Focus for Rural Development." Occasional Paper no. 45, Iowa City: Iowa International Program, University of Iowa.

Nicholo, Paseka. 2000. "Reforming the Public Service in South Africa." *Public Administration and Development* 20, no. 2: 87–102.

Nkrumah, S. A. 1998. "Decentralization in Ghana: Central-Local Government Relations." Paper presented at the Workshop for the Parliamentary Standing Committee on Local Government and Rural Development on the theme, "Decentralization Policy: A Critical Review," held at the Coconut Grove Hotel, Elmina, Ghana, May 29, 1998.

Nsibambi, A. 1994. "Facilitators and Inhibitors of Decentralization in Uganda." In D. Rothchild, ed., *Strengthening African Local Initiative: Local Self-Governance, Decentralization, and Accountability*. Hamburg: Institut fur Afrika-Kunde, pp. 109–120.

Ntebeseza, L. 1999. *Land Tenure Reform, Traditional Authorities, and Rural Local Government in Post-Apartheid South Africa*. Research Report no. 3. Bellville, South Africa: School of Government, University of Western Cape.

Nyang'oro, Julius E. 1994. "Reform Politics and the Democratization Process in Africa." *African Studies Review* 37, no. 1: 133–149.

Nyerere, J. 1984. "Interview." *Third World Quarterly* 6, no. 4: 815–838.

Nzokenu, J. M. 1994. "Decentralization and Democracy in Africa." *International Review of Administrative Sciences* 60, no. 2: 213–227.

O'Donovan, I. 1992. "Management and Change in Northern Nigerian Local Government." *Public Administration and Development* 12, no. 4: 355–372.

OECD (Organization for Economic Cooperation and Development). 1997. *Evaluation of Programs of Promoting Participatory Development and Good Governance Synthesis Report*. Paris: OECD.

Okoth-Ogendo, W. 1999. "The Quest for Constitutional Government." In G. Hyden, D. Olowu, and W. Okoth-Ogendo, eds., *African Perspectives on Governance*. Trenton, NJ: Africa World Press, pp. 33–60.

Olagunju, T., and S. Oyovbaire, eds. 1989. *Towards a Better Nigeria: Selected Speeches of IBB*, vol. 1. London: Precision Press.

Olowona, M., et al. 2000. *Fiscal Decentralization and Local Government*

Finance in Relation to Infrastructure and Service Provision in Uganda.
Kampala, Uganda: DANIDA.

Olowu, Dele. 1988a. *African Local Governments as Instruments of Economic and Social Development.* IULA Occasional Paper no. 1415. The Hague, Netherlands: IULA.

———. 1988b. "Developments in Anglophone West Africa." In L. Adamolekun, D. Olowu, and M. Laleye, eds., *Local Government in West Africa Since Independence.* Lagos, Nigeria: Lagos University Press, pp. 277–309.

———. 1989. "Local Institutes and African Development." *Canadian Journal of African Studies* 23, no. 2: 201–231.

———. 1990a. "The Failure of Current Decentralization Programs in Africa." In J. Wunsch and D. Olowu, eds., *The Failure of the Centralized State: Institutions and Self-Governance in Africa.* Boulder, CO: Westview Press. 2nd ed. San Francisco: Institute for Contemporary Studies, 1995, pp. 74–99.

———. 1990b. "Centralization, Self-Governance, and Development in Nigeria." In J. Wunsch and D. Olowu, eds., *The Failure of the Centralized State: Institutions and Self-Governance in Africa.* Boulder, CO: Westview Press, pp. 193–227.

———. 1990c. "African Economic Performance: Current Programs and Future Failures." In J. Wunsch and D. Olowu, eds., *The Failure of the Centralized State: Institutions and Self-Governance in Africa.* Boulder, CO: Westview Press, pp. 100–129.

———. 1990d. "Achievements and Problems of Federal and State Transfers to Local Governments in Nigeria Since Independence." In L. Adamolekun, R. Robert, and M. Laleye, eds., *Decentralization Policies and Socio-Economic Development in Sub-Saharan Africa.* Washington, DC: Economic Development Institute, pp. 116–156.

———. 1993. "Local Institutions and Development: The Nigerian Experience." In E. G. Goetz and S. Clarke, eds., *The New Localism: Comparative Politics in a Global Era.* Newbury Park, CA: Sage, pp. 151–174.

———. 1997. "Comment." *Regional Development Dialogue* 18, no. 2: 107–118.

———. 1999a. "Building Strong Local Government Through Networks Between State and Non-Governmental Religious Institutions in Africa." *Public Administration and Development* 19, no. 4: 409–412.

———. 1999b. "Accountability and Transparency." In L. Adamolekun, *Public Administration in Africa: Main Issues and Selected Country Studies.* Boulder, CO: Westview Press, pp. 139–158.

———. 1999c. "Local Governance, Democracy and Development." In R. Joseph, ed., *State, Conflict, Democracy and Society in Africa.* Boulder, CO: Lynne Rienner Publishers, pp. 285–298.

———. 2000. "Metropolitan Governance in Developing Countries." *Regional Development Dialogue* 6, no. 1: 1–17.

———. 2001a. *African Decentralization Policies and Practices from 1980s and Beyond.* Working Paper no. 334, Institute of Social Studies. The Hague, Netherlands: ISS.

———. 2001b. *African Decentralization Policies and Programs Under*

Structural Adjustment and Democratization. Africa Paper no. 4. Geneva: United Nations Institute of Social Research and Development.

———. 2001c. "Metropolitan Governance in Developing Countries." *Regional Development Studies* 6, no. 1: 1–17.

———. 2003. "Local Political Processes." *Public Administration and Development* 23, no. 1: 1–12.

Olowu, D., D. Ayo, and B. Akande, eds. 1991. *Local Institutions and National Development in Nigeria.* Ile-Ife, Nigeria: Obafemi Awolowo University Press.

Olowu, D., and E. Erero, eds. 1996. *Indigenous Governance Systems in Nigeria Ile-Ife, Local Institutions and Socio-Economic Development Project.* Ile-Ife, Nigeria: Obafemi Awolowo University.

———. 2000. *Governance in Nigeria's Villages and Cities Through Indigenous Institutions.* Ile-Ife, Nigeria: Obafemi Awolowo University.

Olowu, D., and P. Smoke. 1992. "Determinants of Success in African Local Governments: An Overview." *Public Administration and Development* 12, no. 1: 1–17.

Olowu, Dele, and James Wunsch. 1995. "Decentralization, Local Government and Primary Health Care in Nigeria: An Analytical Study." *Journal of African Policy Studies* 1, no. 3: 1–22.

Olowu, D., J. Wunsch, K. Awotokun, J. Erero, O. Okotoni, and F. Soetan. 2000. *Local Governments and Health Sector Decentralization: The Nigerian Experience.* Geneva: World Health Organization.

Olson, Mancur. 1966. *The Logic of Collective Action.* Cambridge, MA: Harvard University Press.

Osaghae, O. 1998. *Crippled Giant: Nigeria Since Independence.* London: Hurst and Company.

Ostrom, Elinor. 1990. *Governing the Commons: The Evolution of Institutions of Collective Action.* Cambridge: Cambridge University Press.

———. 1996. "Crossing the Great Divide: Co-Production, Synergy and Development." *World Development* 24, no. 6: 1073–1087.

Ostrom, E., L. Schroeder, and S. Wynne. 1993. *Institutional Incentives and Sustainable Development: Infrastructure Policies in Perspective.* Boulder, CO: Westview Press.

Ostrom, E., and V. Ostrom. 1977. "Public Goods and Public Choices." In E. S. Savas, ed., *Alternatives for Delivering Public Services: Toward Improved Performance.* Boulder, CO: Westview Press, pp. 7–49.

Ostrom, V. 1980. "Artisanship and Artifact." *Public Administration Review* 40, no. 4: 309–317.

———. 1987. *The Political Theory of a Compound Republic,* 2nd ed. Lincoln: University of Nebraska Press.

———. 1991. *The Meaning of American Federalism: Constituting a Self-Governing Society.* San Francisco: Institute of Contemporary Studies.

———. 1997. *The Meaning of Democracy and the Vulnerability of Democracies.* Ann Arbor: University of Michigan Press.

Ostrom, V., R. Bish, and E. Ostrom. 1988. *Local Government in the United States.* San Francisco: Institute of Contemporary Studies.

Otilhogile, B. 1998. "Constitutional Development in Botswana." In W. A.

Hedge and M. H. Lekorwe, eds., *Botswana: Politics and Society.* Pretoria, South Africa: Van Schalk Publishers, pp. 153–161.

Ottaway, M. 1998. "Africa's New Leaders: African Solutions or African Problem?" *Current History* 97, no. 619: 209–213.

———. 1999. *Africa's New Leaders: Democracy or State Reconstruction?* Washington, DC: Carnegie Endowment for Peace.

Ottemoeller, D. 1996. *Institutionalization and Democratization: The Case of the Ugandan Resistance Councils.* Ph. D. dissertation, University of Florida, Gainesville.

———. 1998. "Popular Perceptions of Democracy: Elections and Attitudes in Uganda." *Comparative Political Studies* 31, no. 1: 98–124.

———. 2000. "Uganda Local Councils—Function and History in Local Government." Typescript.

Owens, Edgar, and Robert Shaw. 1972. *Development Reconsidered: Bridging the Gap Between Government and People.* Lexington, MA: Lexington Books.

Owusu, M. 1992. "Democracy and Africa: A View from the Village." *Journal of Modern African Studies* 30, no. 3: 369–396.

Oyeyipo, E., P. Buisson, J. Egwurube, A. Odoh, and J. P. Daloz. 1989. *Leading Issues in Territorial Decentralisation in Nigeria and France.* Zaria, Nigeria: Ahmadu Bello University Press.

Oyovbaire, Egite. 1985. *Federalism in Nigeria.* London: Macmillan.

Oyugi, W. O. 1983. "Local Government in Kenya: A Case of Institutional Decline." In P. Mawhood, ed., *Local Government in the Third World.* Chichester, England: Wiley and Sons, pp. 107–140.

———. 1990. "Decentralized Development Planning and Management in Kenya: An Assessment." In L. Adamolekun, R. Robert, and M. Laleye, eds. *Decentralization Policies and Socio-Economic Development in Sub-Saharan Africa.* Washington, DC: Economic Development Institute, pp. 157–191.

———. 2000. "Decentralization for Good Governance and Development: The Unending Debate." *Regional Development Dialogue* 21, no. 1: iii–xix.

Paul, S. 1991. *Strengthening Public Service Accountability: Conceptual Framework.* World Bank Discussion Paper no. 136, Washington, DC: World Bank.

———. 1996. "Strengthening Public Accountability Through Participation." In J. Riethbergen-McKracker, ed., *Participation in Practice: The Experience of World Bank and Other Stakeholders.* World Bank Discussion Paper no. 333, Washington, DC: World Bank.

Parson, Jack. 1991. "The Peasantariat, Politics and Democracy in Botswana." In Robin Cohen and Harry Goulbourne, eds., *Democracy and Socialism in Africa.* Boulder, CO: Westview Press.

Peters-Berries, Christian. 1995. *Aspects of Local Government Finance in Botswana.* Gaborone, Botswana: Friedrich Ebert Stiftung.

Picard, Louis A. 1987. *The Politics of Development in Botswana: A Model for Success.* Boulder, CO: Lynne Rienner Publishers.

Potter, David. 2000. "The Power of Colonial States." In Allan Thomas, ed., *Poverty and Development: Into the 21st Century.* New York: Oxford University Press, pp. 271–288.

Price, Robert. 1975. *Society and Bureaucracy in Contemporary Ghana.* Berkeley: University of California Press.

Prudhomme, R. 1995. "The Dangers of Decentralization." *World Bank Research Observer* 10, no. 2, August: 201–210.

———. 2001. "Fiscal Decentralization and Intergovernmental Fiscal Relations." In *United Nations Capital Development Fund, Decentralization for Local Governance in Africa: Conference Proceedings.* New York: UN, pp. 52–58.

Publius. 1991. *Special Issue: Federalism in Nigeria: Toward a Federal Democracy* 21, no. 4.

Putnam, R. 1993. *Making Democracy Work: Civic Traditions in Modern Italy.* Princeton, NJ: Princeton University Press.

Pycroft, C. 1996. "Local Government in the New South Africa." *Public Administration and Development* 16, no. 3: 233–245.

———. 1999. "Restructuring Non-Metropolitan Local Government in South Africa." *Public Administration and Development* 19, no. 2: 179–192.

———. 2000. "Democracy and Delivery: The Rationalization of Local Government in South Africa." *International Review of Administrative Sciences* 66, no. 1: 143–159.

Rakodi, Carole, ed. 1997. *The Urban Challenge in Africa: Growth and Management of Its Large Cities.* Tokyo: United Nations University Press.

Rawlings, J. J. 1991. "New Year Broadcast to the Nation." In *A Year of Bold Actions.* Tema, Ghana: Ghana Publishing Corporation.

Republic of Ghana. 1992. *Constitution of the Republic of Ghana, 1992.* Tema, Ghana: Ghana Publishing Corporation.

———. 1991. *Report of the Committee of Experts to Prepare Draft Proposals for a Constitution of Ghana.* Tema, Ghana: Ghana Publishing Corporation.

———. 1993a. *Local Government Act* (Act 462). Tema, Ghana: Ghana Publishing Corporation.

———. 1993b. *National Development Planning Commission Act Act 479.* Tema, Ghana: Ghana Publishing Corporation.

———. 1993c. *National Development Planning Systems Act Act 480.* Tema, Ghana: Ghana Publishing Corporation.

———. 1995 and 1996. *Report of the Auditor General on Public Accounts of Ghana.* Tema, Ghana: Ghana Publishing Corporation.

Republic of Uganda. 1987. *Report of the Commission of Inquiry into the Local Government System.* Kampala: Republic of Uganda.

———. 1993. *The Local Government Resistance Councils Statute.* Kampala: Republic of Uganda.

———. 1997. *The Local Governments Act, 1997.* Kampala: Republic of Uganda.

Ribot, Jesse. 2000. *Local Actors, Powers and Accountability in African Decentralizations: A Review of Issues.* Geneva: United Nations Research Institute for Social Development.

———. 2002. *Democratic Decentralization of Natural Resources: Institutionalizing Popular Participation.* Washington, DC: World Resources Institute.

Riggs, F. W. 1964. *Administration in Developing Countries: The Theory of Prismatic Society.* Boston: Houghton Mifflin.

Rondinelli, D. 1981. "Government Decentralisation in Comparative Perspective." *International Review of Administrative Sciences* 47, no. 2: 133–145.

Rondinelli, D., J. R. Nellis, and S. Cheema. 1984. *Decentralization in Developing Countries: A Review of Recent Experience*. World Bank Discussion Paper, Washington, DC: World Bank.

Rothchild, D. 1995. "Rawlings and the Engineering of Legitimacy in Ghana." In W. Zartman, ed., *Collapsed States*. Boulder, CO: Lynne Rienner Publishers, pp. 49–68.

Sa'ad, A. 1995. "Law and Justice on Gwoza Hills: An Assessment of the Viability of Informal Justice for Good Governance and Democracy in Nigeria." In D. Olowu et al., *Governance and Democratization in West Africa*. Dakar: CODESRIA, pp. 217–238.

Sandbrook, R., and J. Oelbaum. 1997. "Reforming Dysfunctional Institutions Through Democratisation? Reflections on Ghana." *Journal of Modern African Studies* 35, no. 4: 603–646.

Schiavo-Campo, S. 1998. "Government and Pay: The Global and Regional Evidence." *Public Administration and Development* 18, no. 5: 457–478.

Schroeder, L. 2000. "Social Funds and Local Government: The Case of Malawi." *Public Administration and Development* 20, no. 4: 423–438.

Segal, Lydia. 1997. "The Pitfalls of Political Decentralization and Proposals for Reform: The Case of New York Public Schools." *Public Administration Review* 57, no. 2: 141–149.

Sharma, Keshaw. 2000. "Popular Participation for Good Governance and Development at the Local Level: The Case of Botswana." *Regional Development Dialogue* 21, no. 1: 177–193.

Shezi, S. 1995. "South Africa: State Transition and the Management of Collapse." In W. Zartman, ed., *Collapsed States*. Boulder, CO: Lynne Rienner Publishers, pp. 191–206.

Shivakumar, S. J. 1999. "The Place of Indigenous Institutions in Constitutional Order." Conference Paper, African Principles of Conflict Resolution, Addis Ababa; Ethiopia.

SIDA (Swedish International Development Agency). 1993. *Decentralization in Botswana:Policy Paper and Action Plan*. Gaborone, Botswana: SIDA.

Silverman, J. M. 1992. *Public Sector Decentralization: Economic Policy and Sector Investment Programs*. World Bank Technical Paper no. 186. Washington, DC: World Bank.

Simeon, Richard, and Christina Murry. 2001. "Multi-Sphere Governance in South Africa: An Interim Assessment." *Publius* 31, no. 4: 65–92.

Sklar, R. 1999. "African Politics: The Next Generation." In R. Joseph, ed., *State, Conflict, and Democracy in Africa*. Boulder, CO: Lynne Rienner Publishers, pp. 165–178.

Smith, B. C. 1985. *Decentralization: The Territorial Dimension of the State*. London: Allen and Unwin.

———. 1997. "Decentralization of Health Care in Developing Countries: Organizational Options." *Public Administration and Development* 17, no. 4: 399–412.

Smock, Audrey. 1971. *Ibo Politics: The Role of Ethnic Unions in Eastern Nigeria*. Cambridge, MA: Harvard University Press.

Smoke, Paul. 1987. "Local Government Finance in Kenya." Nairobi, Kenya: Ministry of Local Government, Republic of Kenya, and USAID Regional Office of Housing and Urban Development.

———. 1993. "Local Government Fiscal Reform in Developing Countries: Lessons from Kenya." *World Development* 21, no. 6: 901–924.

———. 1994. *Local Government Finance in Developing Countries: The Case of Kenya.* Oxford: Oxford University Press.

———. 1999a. *Fiscal Decentralization in Developing Countries: A Review of Current Concepts and Practice.* Geneva: United Nations Research Institute for Social Development.

———. 1999b. "Understanding Decentralization in Asia: An Overview of Key Issues and Challenges." *Regional Development Dialogue* 20, no. 2: 1–17.

———. 2000. "Strategic Fiscal Decentralization in Developing Countries: Learning from Recent Innovations." In S. Yusuf, W. Wu, and S. Evenett, eds., *Local Dynamics in an Era of Globalization.* New York: Oxford University Press for the World Bank, pp. 101–109.

———. 2001. *Fiscal Decentralization in Developing Countries: A Review of Current Concepts and Practice.* Geneva: United Nations Research Institute for Social Development.

Smoke, P., and B. Lewis. 1996. "Fiscal Decentralization in Indonesia: A New Approach to an Old Idea." *World Development* 24, no. 8: 1281–1300.

Southall, R., and G. Wood. 1996. "Local Government and the Return of Multipartyism in Kenya." *African Affairs* 95, no. 381: 501–528.

Steffensen, J., and S. Trollegaard. 2000. "Fiscal Decentralization and Sub-National Government Finance in Relation to Infrastructure and Service Provision." In World Bank, *Synthesis Report.* Washington, DC: World Bank.

Steinich, M. 2000. *Monitoring and Evaluating Support to Decentralization: Challenges and Dilemmas.* ECDPM Discussion Paper no. 19. Maastricht, Netherlands: ECDPM.

Stren, R. E. 1989a. "Urban Local Government in Africa." In R. E. Stren and R. R. White, eds., *African Cities in Crisis: Managing Rapid Urban Growth.* Boulder, CO: Westview Press, pp. 20–36.

———. 1989b. "Accountability in Africa." In Economic Development Institute, ed., *Strengthening Local Governments in Africa.* Washington, DC: World Bank, pp. 123–129.

Tangri, R. 1999. *The Politics of Patronage: Parastatals, Privatization and Private Enterprise.* Trenton, NJ: Africa World Press.

Tapscott, Chris. 2000. "Intergovernmental Relations in South Africa: The Challenges of Co-operative Government." *Public Administration and Development* 20, no. 2: 119–128.

Tashakkori, Abbas, and Charles Teddlie. 1998. *Mixed Methodology: Combining Qualitative and Quantitative Approaches.* Thousand Oaks, CA: Sage.

Taylor, H. 1999. "Training of Local Councilors in Tanzania: Learning 'Good Governance.'" *Public Administration and Development* 19, no. 1: 77–91.

Therkildsen, Ole. 2001. "Understanding Taxation in Poor Countries: A Critical Review of Selected Perspectives." *Forum for Development Studies* 28, no. 1: 99–123.

————. 2002. "Uganda's Referendum 2000: The Silent Boycott: A Comment." *African Affairs* 101, no. 403: 231–241.

Tideman, P. 1994. "New Local State Forms and 'Popular Participation' in Buganda, Uganda." In P. Gibbon, ed., *The New Local Level Politics in East Africa*. Uppsala, Sweden: Scandinavian Institute of African Studies, pp. 22–49.

————. 1995. *The Resistance Councils in Uganda: A Study of Rural Politics and Popular Democracy in Africa*. Ph. D. dissertation, University of Copenhagen, Denmark.

Tilly, Charles. 1984. *Big Structures, Large Processes, Huge Comparisons*. New York: Sage.

Tocqueville, Alexis. 1966. Edited by J. P. Mayer. *Democracy in America*. Garden City, NY: Anchor Books.

Tordoff, William. 1988. "Local Administration in Botswana." *Public Administration and Development* 8: 183–202.

————. 1994. "Decentralization: Comparative Experience in Commonwealth Africa." *Journal of Modern African Studies* 32, no. 4: 555–580.

Tripp, Aili Mari. 2001. "Women's Movements and Challenges to Neo-Patrimonial Rule." *Development and Change* 32, no. 1: 33–54.

Turner, S., and H. Ibsen. 2000. *Land Reform and Agrarian Reform in South Africa: A Status Report*. Research Report no. 6, Bellville, South Africa: School of Government, University of Western Cape.

UNCHS (United Nations Center for Human Settlements). 1996. *An Urbanizing World: Global Report on Human Settlements*. Nairobi, Kenya: United Nations.

UNDP (United Nations Development Programme). 1993. *Human Development Report 1993*. New York: Oxford University Press.

————. 1997. *Reconceptualizing Governance*. Discussion Paper no. 2, New York: Management Development and Governance Division, UNDP.

UNICEF (United Nations Children's Fund). 1995. *The Bamako Initiative: Rebuilding Health Systems*. New York: UNICEF.

Uphoff, N. 1986. *Local Institutional Development*. West Hartford, CT: Kumarian Press.

USAID (U.S. Agency for International Development). 2001a. *IPS Decentralization Project: Six Districts*. Research Triangle Park, NC: Research Triangle Institute.

————. 2001b. *Future Directions for USAID Support to Conflict Mitigation in Nigeria*. Burlington, VT: Associates in Rural Development.

————. 2002. *Mali Decentralization Program*. Washington, DC: USAID.

Vengroff, R. 1993. "The Transition to Democracy in Senegal: The Role of Decentralization." *In Depth* 3, no. 1: 23–52.

Vengroff, R., and H. B. Salem. 1992. "Assessing the Impact of Decentralization on Governance: A Comparative Methodological Approach to Tunisia." *Public Administration and Development* 12, no. 5: 473–492.

Wallis, Malcom. 1990. "Development Planning in South Africa: Legacies and Current Trends in Public Health." *Public Administration and Development* 20, no. 2: 129–140.

Wekwette, Kadmiel H. 1997. "Urban Management: The Recent Experience." In Carole Rakodi, ed., *The Urban Challenge in Africa: Growth and*

Management of Its Large Cities. Tokyo: United Nations University Press, pp. 527–552.

WHO (World Health Organization). 1992. *Local Government Focused Acceleration of Primary Health Care: The Nigerian Experience.* Geneva: World Health Organization.

———. 1997. *The Role of Local Government in Health: Comparative Experiences and Major Issues.* Geneva: Division of Strategic Support to Countries in Greatest Need, WHO.

———. 2001. *Local Government Health Systems: Opportunities and Challenges for Developing Countries.* Geneva: Department of Organization for Health Services Delivery, WHO.

Wilson, Rick. 1999. "Transitional Governance in the United States: Lessons from the First Federal Congress." *Legislative Studies Quarterly* 24, no. 4: 543–568.

Woode, S. N. 1989. *Making the District Assembly Work.* Tema, Ghana: Ghana Publishing Corporation.

World Bank. 1981. *Accelerated Development in Sub-Saharan Africa.* Washington, DC: World Bank.

———. 1989a. *Strengthening Local Governments in Sub-Saharan Africa.* Policy Seminar Report no. 21, Washington, DC: Economic Development Institute and the Africa Technical Department, World Bank.

———. 1989b. *From Crisis to Sustainable Development: Africa's Long Term Perspective.* Washington, DC: World Bank.

———. 1989c. *World Bank Annual Report.* Washington, DC: World Bank.

———. 1992a. *Kenya Local Government Finance Study.* Infrastructure Operations Division, Eastern Africa Department, Washington, DC: World Bank.

———. 1992b. *Governance: The World Bank's Experience.* Washington, DC: World Bank.

———. 1993. *Property Tax in Anglophone Africa: A Practical Manual.* Report prepared by S. Keith, Washington, DC: World Bank.

———. 1997. *World Development Report 1997.* New York: Oxford University Press.

———. 1999a. *Entering the 21st Century: 1999–2000 World Development Report.* Washington, DC: World Bank.

———. 1999b. *Regionalization in Ethiopia.* Washington, DC: World Bank.

———. 2000. *Can Africa Claim the 21st Century?* Washington, DC: World Bank.

———. 2002a. "Education Statistics EdStats." Online. http://www1.worldbank.org/education/edstats. Accessed September 24, 2002.

———. 2002b. "Chad: Education Sector Reform Program." Africa Regional Office, Report Number PID9886, September 19. Washington, DC: World Bank.

———. 2002c. *World Development Indicators.* New York: Oxford University Press.

Wraith, R. E. 1972. *Local Administration in West Africa.* London: Allen and Unwin.

Wunsch, James. 1986. "Administering Rural Development Projects: Have

Goals Outreached Organizational Capacity?" *Public Administration and Development* 6, no. 3: 287–308.

———. 1990. "Foundations of Centralization: The Colonial Experience and the African Context." In J. Wunsch and D. Olowu, eds., *The Failure of the Centralized State: Institutions and Self-Governance in Africa.* Boulder, CO: Westview Press, pp. 23–42.

———. 1991a. "Institutional Analysis and Decentralization: Developing An Analytical Framework for Effective Third World Administrative Reform." *Public Administration and Development* 11, no. 5: 431–453.

———. 1991b. "Sustaining Third World Infrastructure Investments— Decentralization and Other Strategies." *Public Administration and Development* 11, no. 1: 5–24.

———. 1999. "Toward a Political-Economy of Decentralization in Africa: Policies, Institutions, Interests and Consequences." Paper presented at the Conference on the Workshop II, Indiana University, Bloomington, Indiana.

———. 2000. "Refounding the African State and Local Self-Governance." *Journal of Modern African Studies* 38, no. 3: 487–509.

———. 2001a. "Decentralization, Local Governance and Recentralization in Africa." *Public Administration and Development* 21, no. 4: 277–288.

———. 2001b. "The District Councils of Uganda, Decentralization and Local Governance: A Progress Report." A paper presented at the African Studies Association Annual Meeting, Houston, Texas, November 2001.

———. 2002. "Decentralization and Local Government Revenues in Africa." A paper presented at the Conference of Taxation and Democracy in Developing Countries, Institute for Development Studies, University of Sussex, England, October.

Wunsch, J., and D. Olowu, eds. 1990a. *The Failure of the Centralized State: Institutions and Self-Governance in Africa.* Boulder, CO: Westview Press, 2nd ed. San Francisco: Institute for Contemporary Studies, 1995.

Wunsch, J., and D. Olowu. 1990b. "The Failure of the Centralized State." In J. S. Wunsch and D. Olowu, eds., *The Failure of the Centralized State: Institutions and Self-Governance in Africa.* Boulder, CO: Westview Press, pp. 1–22.

———. 1996. "Regime Transformation from Below: Decentralization, Local Governance, and Democratic Reform in Nigeria." *Studies in Comparative International Development* 31, no. 4: 66–82.

Wynne, S. 1989. "Institutional Structures for Development Among the Kgalagadi of Botswana." In V. Ostrom, D. Feeny, and H. Picht, eds., *Rethinking Institutional Analysis and Development.* San Francisco: International Center for Economic Growth, pp. 213–246.

Young, Crawford. 1999. *The African Colonial State in Comparative Perspective.* New Haven, CT: Yale University Press.

The Contributors

Joseph Ayee is Dean of the Faculty of Social Studies at the University of Ghana, Legon, and executive director of the Centre for Policy Research and Social Engineering, Ghana. Previously he was Chair in Leadership Studies at the United Nations University Leadership Academy from 2000–2001, and chairman of the Department of Political Science at the University of Ghana from 1995–2000. His current research interests include taxation in the informal sector, coproduction arrangements in the delivery of public toilets in Ghana, and elections and democratization.

Gerrit M. Desloovere holds a joint appointment in the Faculty of Law and Economics and in the graduate program of the Faculty of Ethnology at the State University of Haiti. He is vice consul of Belgium to Haiti. At different times he has acted as executive director of COHAN (a Netherlands aid organization), president of PROTOS (a Belgian aid agency), and president of the Haitian Association of Voluntary Agencies. His work focuses on economic, political, and institutional development, with special emphasis on the role of nongovernmental organizations in the development process.

Simon M. Fass teaches sports economics, research methods, evaluation, and statistics. His work with international organizations spans Africa, Asia, and the Americas. His current research looks at the economics of juvenile justice adjudication and the evolution of pawnbroking in the United States.

Dan Ottemoeller received his Ph.D. in political science at the University of Florida. His research interests include comparative democratization and comparative administration. He has also published on the topic of Ugandan politics in *Comparative Political Studies* and *African Studies Review.*

Paul Smoke is associate professor and director of International Programs at the Robert F. Wagner Graduate School of Public Service at New York University. He previously taught in the Department of Urban Studies and Planning at the Massachusetts Institute of Technology, and worked with the Harvard Institute for International Development. His research and policy interests focus on public sector decentralization and local government, particularly in east/southern African and Southeast Asia.

Index

Abacha, Sani, 43, 107
Accountability of local governments: in Botswana, 97–99; central government efforts, 67–68; conflict-resolving/judicial agencies, 76–77; exit mechanisms, 69–70; in Ghana, 142–146, 242; in Kenya, 221, 224–225; in Nigeria, 116, 119–120; ombsbudsman/complaints bodies, 76; organizations for promotion of, 11–12, 73; participatory budgeting, 74–75; in primary health care, 119–120; service delivery surveys, 75; social capital of community-level government, 77–78; social funds committees, 75; in South Africa, 70, 76, 88–89; taxation, 75–76; voice mechanisms, 69–78
Adamolekun, L., x, 1, 5, 39, 42, 45, 108
Adventist Development and Relief Agency, 146
African states: colonialism's effect on building of, 55–58; decentralization and SAPs, 34–38; economic and political crises in, 48–49; governance of, 14–19; postindependence era, 33–34; weaknesses of, 155–156
Agriculture, 57
Alexander, Jocelyn, 62
Amin, Idi, 183, 193, 249
Anderson, Mary, 38
Anglophone Africa, 31–32

Angola, 50–51
Armed Forces for a Federal Republic (FARF) (Chad), 160
Armed Forces of the North (FAN) (Chad), 160
Arrow, Kenneth, 10
Asia, 52
Association of Local Government Authorities of Kenya (ALGAK), 227, 231, 254, 271$n1$
Association of Parents of Students and Rural Promotion of Djokou Canton (APECD), 170–171, 176–177, 179$n1$
Associations of parents of students (APEs) (Chad), 162, 166, 168–172, 246
Authoritarianism, 42–43, 56–58
Autonomy. *See* Local autonomy and authority
Ayee, Joseph, 25, 43, 125, 192, 241–243, 251

Babangida, Gen. Ibrahim, 43, 107, 110
Baguirmi, 158
Bamako Health Initiative, 76, 260
Banda, Hastings, 16
Bangladesh, 18, 65–66
Bank of Ghana, 151
Bardill, John, 83–84
Barkan, J. D., 183, 234$n13$
Barkin Ladi, Nigeria, 112, 114

About the Book

W hy have some decentralization reforms led to viable systems of local governance in Africa, while others have failed? Exploring this question, the authors outline the key issues involved, provide historical context, and identify the factors that have encouraged and discouraged success.

Detailed studies of African states are grounded in a common analytical framework, one that emphasizes the importance both of national policy and of local problem-solving initiatives. The final chapter of the book revisits the country studies, offering a new approach to explaining the emergence of effective local governance.

Dele Olowu heads the Public Policy and Administration Program at the Institute of Social Studies, The Hague. His most recent publications include *Better Governance and Public Policy: Capacity Building and Democratic Renewal in Africa* and *African Perspectives on Governance*. **James S. Wunsch** is director of the African Studies Program and professor of political science and international studies and department chair at Creighton University. His extensive work on Africa includes *The Failure of the Centralized State: Institutions and Self-Governance in Africa* (coauthored with Dele Olowu) and *Primary Health Care and Local Governance in Nigeria*.